J. C. G. George

Gariock Pud.rt.

London 1980 n.a.

SHAKESPEARE'S HERALDRY

NON SANZ DROICT

The Armorial Bearings of
WILLIAM SHAKESPEARE
of Stratford-upon-Avon.

College of Arms,
London.

*Chester Herald
and Registrar.*

SHAKESPEARE'S HERALDRY

by

C. W. SCOTT-GILES, O.B.E.

Fitzalan Pursuvant of Arms Extraordinary

illustrated by the author

HERALDRY TODAY

10 BEAUCHAMP PLACE, LONDON, S.W.3

<u>CORRIGENDUM</u>

Page 78, line 12: read *martlets* for *molets*

Reprinted with the permission of J. M. Dent & Sons Ltd., London
From the edition of 1950

Heraldry Today edition 1971
Manufactured in the United States of America

International Standard Book Number: 0-900455-12-8

HERALDRY TODAY
10 BEAUCHAMP PLACE, LONDON, S.W.3

TO
MY WIFE

CONTENTS

ILLUSTRATIONS

PLATES IN COLOUR

PLATES IN BLACK AND WHITE

FOREWORD

NONE KNEW better than Shakespeare the limitations of his 'wooden O,' its wardrobe and properties, when he tried to present the splendid and heroical scenes which he saw clearly in his mind's eye. With 'four or five most vile and ragged foils,' some oddments of armour and an assortment of costumes, crowns and insignia, he did his best to recapture the pageantry of the Middle Ages, but in the main he had to rely on his own glowing words working on the imagination of his audiences. 'Eke out our performance with your mind,' he begged them,

> For 'tis your thoughts that now must deck our kings.

Fittingly to deck the kings, nobles and knights who throng the pages of Shakespeare's historical plays, we must know something of the armorial devices on shields, garments and flags, which played so conspicuous and colourful a part in the mediaeval scene. The main purpose of this book is to afford readers of the plays, and producers for stage and screen, heraldic information which will enable them to see more clearly the picture Shakespeare conjures up when he speaks of golden coats, dancing banners, and household badges.

While the book is primarily an heraldic companion to Shakespeare, I hope that conversely it may prove to be a Shakespearean introduction to heraldry. With this in view, I have included a chapter on the rise and growth of mediaeval heraldry, which is well illustrated by the insignia of the characters in the plays. I have avoided unnecessary complexities in heraldic language, and appended a brief glossary, so that the reader with no prior knowledge should, with the aid of the drawings, easily follow the meaning of the verbal 'blazons,' and so acquire a working knowledge of the terms of heraldry.

I had completed the first draft of the book when there came into my possession, through the courtesy of Mr. Percy L. Babington, of Cambridge, a manuscript book entitled, 'The Heraldry of Shakspere, being the Arms, Liveries, Standards, Badges, Banners etc. of the Personages and Towns mentioned in the plays; by Alfred Rodway; Birmingham, MCMXIV.'[1] This is a collection of coloured drawings, with the names

---

[1]There is a copy of this ms. book, dated 1915, in the Birmingham Public Libraries.

of the persons to whom the insignia belonged, but otherwise no written material. The drawings are rather crudely done, and appear to be intended as notes rather than finished work. In so far as they form a record of the known insignia of historical persons, they agree closely with the record I had compiled independently—closely, but not completely, for here and there Mr. Rodway attributes to a character a badge or standard used not by him but by one of his descendants. In the case of semi-historical figures (such as Philip the Bastard in *King John*), fictitious characters (like Sir John Falstaff), and those whose identification with historical persons is doubtful, I find myself sometimes at variance with Mr. Rodway in assigning appropriate coats of arms, but in a few instances I have included and acknowledged suggestions drawn from his work.

Mr. Rodway did not confine himself to the historical plays. Turning his pages, I find the arms of the Duke of Milan in *Two Gentlemen of Verona* and *The Tempest*; of the Montague (Montecchi) and Capulet (Cappelleti) families in *Romeo and Juliet*; of the families of Sly and Carew in connection with *The Taming of the Shrew*; of the Duke of Venice in *The Merchant of Venice* and *Othello*; of the Duke of Luxemburg on the grounds that the Forest of Arden in *As You Like It* is the Ardennes; the Danish *raefen* banner for *Hamlet*; and the arms of the Kingdom of Bohemia for the sea-bordered never-never land of *The Winter's Tale*. There is much here to interest the wanderer in Shakespearean by-ways, but in this book I have thought it best to keep to the high-road of history.

I am grateful to the Chapter of the College of Arms for permission to reproduce documents relating to the grant of arms to John Shakespeare, and to reprint the epitaph of Sir Thomas Stanley attributed to William Shakespeare.

The painting of Shakespeare's arms which forms the frontispiece, signed by Mr. J. D. Heaton-Armstrong, Chester Herald and Registrar of the College of Arms, is the work of Mr. Gerald Cobb. The other colour plates and the line drawings are my own work.

Except where otherwise noted, the text used in this book is that of the New Temple Shakespeare, edited by Mr. M. R. Ridley, M.A.

C.W.S.-G.

Fig. 1.   Richard I, from his Second Great Seal.

CHAPTER I

HERALDRY, MEDIAEVAL AND TUDOR

IN THE armorial devices of the persons in Shakespeare's historical plays, heraldry can be traced from its rise in the twelfth century, to the time of its greatest splendour in the fifteenth, and to the decadence into which it sank at the end of the age of chivalry. In *King John* we have heraldic arms in their simplest and most practical form, consisting of bold signs on shields, lance-pennons, and banners. These signs were adopted by warriors so that they might be recognised in battle and tournament, and were also used on the seals which were their signatures. Leaping nearly two centuries to *Richard II*, we find these devices far more numerous and varied, appearing not only on shields, flags and seals, but also on surcoats, helms and horse-bardings, the liveries of retainers and servants, the costumes of men and women of noble rank, and the furnishings and decorations of court and castle. The battle scenes of *Henry IV* and *Henry V* show the use of armorial bearings in war.   In the

I

plays dealing with the struggle between the houses of Lancaster and York, heraldry illustrates the dynastic questions, and provides emblems for the rival factions. Finally in *Henry VIII* we come to a time when the armorial shield is no longer carried in war, but is displayed in the manor house and the parish church as a monument of genealogy and a demonstration of social standing.

Early heraldry was simple because it served a practical purpose. Leaders in the feudal army needed to be readily recognized by their followers, and distinguished from other fully armed warriors, whether friends or foes. The devices they placed on their shields and flags for this purpose were therefore bold, and were so consistently used that men soon learned to identify a particular design with its bearer, and so to tell lords and knights by their insignia. There was a natural tendency for a son to use the device which his father had borne and perhaps made famous, especially when, through use on a seal, it became identified with an hereditary lordship.

In the eleventh and earlier centuries, warriors were accustomed to decorate their shields and flags: the Bayeux Tapestry shows many examples of this; but only when such decoration became systematic and hereditary did true heraldry emerge, and this development appears to have begun during the second quarter of the twelfth century.

The shield of one of the characters in *King John* provides the earliest known example of an armorial device methodically used and becoming hereditary. William Longespée, or Longsword, Earl of Salisbury, bore six golden lions on a blue shield, and these appear on his effigy at Salisbury (3). He was a bastard son of Henry II by Rosamund Clifford, and thus a grandson of Geoffrey of Anjou, called 'Plantagenet,' the ancestor of the royal house of that name. When Geoffrey married Matilda, daughter of Henry I, in 1129, the King hung round his neck a shield bearing little gold lions;[1] and an enamelled plate formerly on Geoffrey's tomb shows him with a blue shield bearing golden lions—four on the visible part, and presumably two or three more on the hidden part (2). It is a reasonable assumption that William Longespée's shield was inherited from his grandfather, Geoffrey, and as no earlier instance is known of a shield device becoming hereditary, these arms stand as the first monument of true heraldry.

Other descendants of Henry I, in both direct and indirect lines, bore

---

[1] *Clypeus leunculos aureos imaginarios habens collo ejus suspenditur.*—John of Marmoutier.

FIG. 2.   Geoffrey of Anjou.

FIG. 3.   William Longespée, Earl of
Salisbury.

one or more lions in their shields, with such consistency as to suggest that this was not a matter of chance, but that a lion was that king's emblem. There is no evidence that he used it on shield or banner, and it was probably no more than a badge. The earliest evidence we have of the use of true armorial bearings by an English king is the first Great Seal of Richard I, in which he is shown with a single lion in his shield; the lion is rampant and faces towards the sinister, i.e., towards the left of the man bearing the shield. On his second Great Seal (1), made about 1195, Richard's shield displays the three lions passant guardant (termed leopards in early heraldry) which were also borne by King John, and continue to this day as the arms of England (Pl. IV).

John was thus the second English king known to have possessed true armorial bearings. His contemporary, Philip Augustus of France, was probably the first French king to use an heraldic banner sown with fleurs-de-lys, though (like the lion in England) the fleur-de-lys was perhaps a royal emblem in France in earlier reigns. The barons introduced in *King John* were in some cases the first, in others the second of their lines to bear their heraldic arms. The shields of the persons in the play thus make a small group illustrating armorial insignia in their earliest form. They are all bold and simple in design and colour, befitting devices intended to be clearly visible even at a distance. Perhaps the least successful in this respect were the arms of the Earl of Salisbury and the King of France, each consisting of one emblem repeated six or more times; and it is note-worthy that some arms composed of a multiplication of one emblem were later simplified, no doubt for clarity; for example, the many fleurs-de-lys in the French royal arms were reduced to three in the fourteenth century. Probably the reduction in the size of shields contributed to such simplification.

As heraldry was essentially a practical method of securing distinction and recognition, there was not necessarily any symbolic meaning in the devices which warriors assumed. Some primitive symbolism there was in the adoption of creatures characteristic of strength, valour, or fierceness, such as the lion and the eagle; but notwithstanding many legends, there is no evidence that early heraldry recorded particular exploits. From the first, the lion was a popular device, distinction being obtained by differences in number, attitude and colour. Thus the arms of the Marshal, Earl of Pembroke, in *King John*—a red lion rampant on a shield party gold and green—are obviously different from Arundel's gold lion on red, and

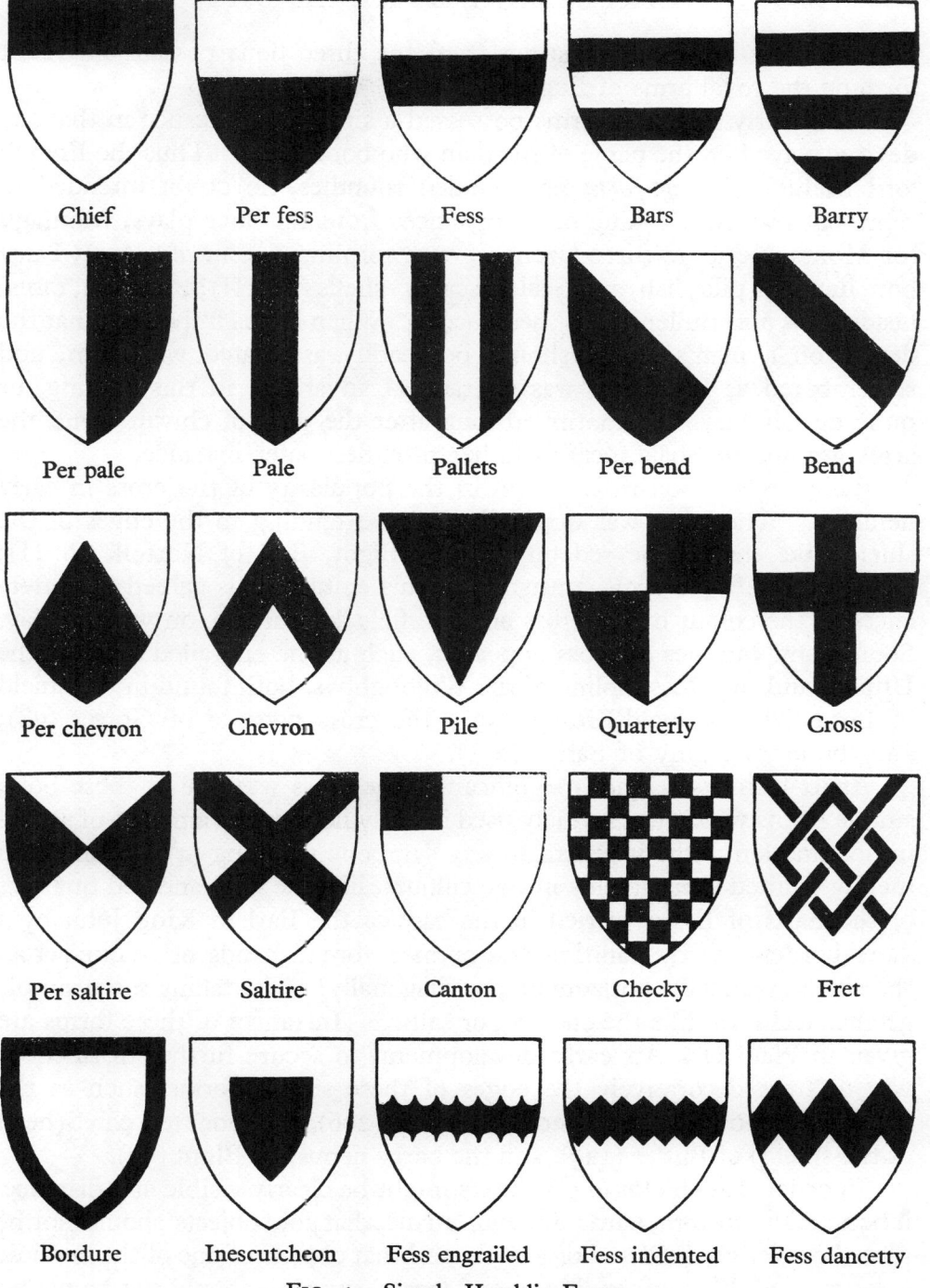

Chief   Per fess   Fess   Bars   Barry

Per pale   Pale   Pallets   Per bend   Bend

Per chevron   Chevron   Pile   Quarterly   Cross

Per saltire   Saltire   Canton   Checky   Fret

Bordure   Inescutcheon   Fess engrailed   Fess indented   Fess dancetty

FIG. 4.   Simple Heraldic Forms.

both of these are clearly distinct from the three lions passant guardant forming the royal arms of England.

Many early shields of arms possessed a simple significance in that the devices played on the name of the man who bore them. Thus the French lord Melun, in *King John*, bore golden roundles, no doubt intended to represent *melons*. Taking other instances from the later plays, Montagu (or Montacute) bore three lozenges, each forming a *mont aigu* (55); Lucy bore luces, or pike-fish, and Scales, scallop-shells (Pl. III); Ramston, rams' heads (69); and Bullen, bulls' heads (234). When it was important that the device on a man's shield should be readily associated with him, and remembered as his, there was a practical advantage in this canting, or punning heraldry. It continued long after the days of chivalry, and the arms granted to Shakespeare's father provide a later instance.

Religious symbolism is shown in the popularity of the cross in early heraldry. The cross was originally plain, extending to the edges of the shield, like that borne red on gold by Bigot, Earl of Norfolk (Pl. II); distinction between arms consisting of this emblem was gained by differences in the colour of the cross and the field, or surface, on which it lay. Soon many varieties of cross appeared, such as the engrailed cross of the Uffords and the cross moline of the Willoughbys, both found in the shield of Lord Willoughby d'Eresby (59); the cross patonce of Gower (98); and the cross raguly of Sands (251).

Apart from its religious significance, the cross was one of those bold, simple forms which were widely used in early heraldry as a means of securing distinction without regard to any symbolic meaning (4). Some men merely painted their shields in two colours, like the gold and red quarters of the Earls of Essex (varied in the case of the Earl in King John by a vaire border); or by painting one or more broad bands of colour across the shield, vertically, horizontally, or diagonally; or by taking some simple geometrical form like the chevron or saltire. (Instances of these forms are given in Plate II.) An early development, to secure further distinction, was to treat decoratively the edges of these simple forms, such as the engrailed bend (diagonal band) of Ratcliff (206), the indented chief (head of the shield) of Butler (123), and the barry nebuly of Blunt (90).

In order that shields and banners might be clearly visible at a distance, it became the custom, hardening into a rule, that gold objects should not be placed on a silver field and *vice versa*, and that objects of one of the heraldic colours—red, blue, green, black, and (rarer) purple—should not be placed on a field of another colour; but that metals and colours should be judiciously mingled to produce a clear, bold design. Metals and colours formed two classes of heraldic 'tinctures'; the third class consisted of furs, originally ermine (23) and vaire (20), each later producing varieties with distinctive forms and names. Perhaps Shakespeare had the effective contrast of heraldic tinctures in mind when he wrote:

> And like bright metal on a sullen ground,
> My reformation, glittering o'er my fault,
> Shall show more goodly, and attract more eyes,
> Than that which hath no foil to set it off.
>
> (1 *Henry IV*, i, 2)

Since distinction was the essence of heraldry, it was obviously undesirable that armorial bearings should be duplicated, at any rate among knights in the same country. When a class of professional heralds sprang up, primarily in connection with the conduct of tournaments, they made it their business to learn the arms of the knights they encountered, and to compile records, in the form of rolls of arms, in which the bearings of lords and knights were depicted, or described in words, i.e. blazoned. These heralds could advise a man as to the choice of arms, having regard to devices already appropriated, so that he should avoid duplicating an existing design. In due course it became the function of the principal heralds—called kings of heralds, or kings of arms—not only to record but actually to grant armorial bearings. But before the development of heraldic records and the officers of arms charged with the regulation of armorial matters, men chose their arms at will; and while the range of devices in current usage was limited, it not infrequently happened that two knights unwittingly assumed the same shield of arms.

As late as the reign of Richard II, it was found that Richard, Lord Scrope of Bolton, and Sir Robert Grosvenor were bearing the same arms: a gold bend on blue (Pl. II), and after a prolonged trial these arms were assigned to Scrope. This Lord Scrope was the father of Sir Stephen Scrope (or Scroop) in *Richard II*, who as a younger son bore the bend with a mark of cadency (61). Grosvenor was required to take other arms. At first he was awarded, *Azure, a gold bend and a gold bordure*; that is, the arms in dispute with the simple addition of a border; but it was later decided that the border did not constitute a sufficient difference between the arms of two persons who were not akin, and finally Grosvenor took as his arms a gold wheatsheaf on blue.

While actual duplication of armorial bearings was inadmissible, because it would lead to confusion, a close resemblance between arms was often sought after. Thus a junior member of a family would normally bear the arms of the head of the house with some minor but sufficient difference, such as a change of tincture or additional charge. Similarly, feudal dependants often assumed arms based on, but clearly different from, those of their overlord. To produce new shields of arms, and to provide distinctive additions to existing shields, many new forms and emblems were introduced into heraldry.

Among the common objects, or 'charges,' of early heraldry found in the arms of Shakespeare's characters are the fleur-de-lys, most famous as the royal emblem of France (22), but also in general heraldic use; the cinque-foil (30); the escallop shell (174); the water budget, or leather bottle (58); the boar's head (99); the Cornish chough (221); the martlet (212); and the garb, or wheatsheaf (31).[1] As heraldry developed, innumerable other objects were introduced, the heralds drawing on the heavenly bodies, living creatures of all kinds—real and imaginary, weapons and equipment of war and the chase, agricultural and household utensils—anything, in fact, which might make a suitable device. Such charges frequently made allusion to the bearer's name, and knights did not disdain to bear humble, everyday things like buckets, trivets and levers, if they best served their purpose.

Arms normally descended from father to son, but sometimes a man took his mother's arms instead of his father's if she were of high rank or if the son inherited some considerable lordship from her. Similarly, a man succeeding to a lordship held by his wife's father might take his arms.

A son added some differencing mark to his father's arms. In the case of the eldest son, this was usually a label (14), and this was removed at his father's death. Younger sons retained and passed on to their descendants the difference they made in their paternal shield. This might take the form of a change in the tincture of the field, or the devices thereon, or both; or the powdering of the field with minor charges, as in the arms of Lucy of Charlecote (100) who added the cross-crosslets to the three luces borne by the senior line of Lucy; or the addition of a bend, border or canton, or of some small object such as a molet (or spur-rowel—61), fleur-de-lys (83), or crescent (159). The shields of members of the Stafford family given in the following chapters provide instances of various

[1] Some of the charges common in early heraldry are shown in Plate III.

differences of the same original coat. The basic arms of Stafford were a red chevron on gold (124); to this, Sir Hugh Stafford added a red border (125); Lord Stafford of Southwick, a black engrailed border (161); Sir Humphrey Stafford, an ermine canton (162); while Sir Humphrey's younger brother, Sir Henry, bore the same arms with a crescent as a secondary difference. The method of differencing for cadency became standardized only in Tudor times, when a crescent became the mark of the second son, a molet of the third son, a martlet of the fourth, and so on.

In the case of the royal arms, the label was commonly used for differencing not only by the eldest son but also by some of the younger sons. The label of the King's eldest son was always plain—originally blue, and later silver—while the younger sons charged their labels with various devices. In some cases, the arms of junior members of the royal house were differenced by a border. The arms of the descendants of Edward III, given in Chapter IV, illustrate the method of marking cadency in the Middle Ages.

When men based their arms on those of some family with which they were connected by feudal ties but not by blood, they generally made some greater difference in the arms than would be made by a cadet branch of the family. Thus Sir Richard Vernon, in *Henry IV*, bore on a gold field a blue fess and thereon three gold wheatsheaves (91), indicating that the Vernons held the barony of Shipbrook from the Earls of Chester, whose arms were three gold wheatsheaves on blue (31).

In the time of *King John*, heraldic arms were displayed only on shields and flags, and this should be observed in productions of the play. Furthermore, the practice of including the arms of two or more families in one shield had not yet arisen. When we come to *Richard II*, we find heraldry more fully developed. Warriors were now wearing surcoats emblazoned with their armorial bearings, and their insignia were also shown on the bardings of their horses. From the heraldic surcoat comes the term 'coat of arms,' or shortly 'coat,' which has come to mean any heraldic composition, whether displayed on surcoat, shield or banner.

In the arms of the characters in *Richard II* and the succeeding plays, we have many instances of two or more separate coats of arms combined to form a single heraldic composition. In its simplest form, such a combination was effected by impalement, i.e. by dividing the shield down the middle, and placing a coat in each half, the principal one on the dexter side. ('Dexter' means the right-hand, 'sinister' the left-hand, from the point of view of the man *behind* the shield.) An example is seen in the arms of Thomas Mowbray, Duke of Norfolk, in *Richard II*, who was granted the arms attributed to Edward the Confessor impaling those of Thomas of Brotherton (52). A Bishop might impale his personal arms with those of his See (151), and a King of Arms his official and personal coats. (This practice now extends to Mayors, but it did not do so in Shakespeare's time, or the historical period of the plays.) The arms of husband and wife were also impaled, the husband's to the dexter; it became the practice that impalement was used for a combination of arms intended to be temporary, while a different method was used for a permanent combination, such as would occur when the children of a marriage inherited the arms of their mother as well as their father. In this case the shield was quartered, i.e. divided vertically and horizontally into four parts, the coats to be combined being arranged in the quarters. Where there were only two coats in the composition, the principal one (usually the paternal coat) was placed in the first quarter and repeated in the fourth, and the other was placed in the second and third quarters of the shield.

This combination of arms by quartering arose from the wish of a man holding more than one lordship to indicate the fact in his heraldry. The possession of two lordships might arise from his inheriting not only from his father but also from his mother, she having no brothers and thus being heir to her father; or a man might add to his patrimony some lordship derived in like circumstances from his wife. Thus the quartered coats of Montagu and Monthermer (55)[1] resulted from the marriage of Sir John de Montagu with the daughter and heir of Sir Thomas de Monthermer; and Henry Percy, first Earl of Northumberland, quartered with his paternal lion the luces of Lucy on his marriage with the sister and co-heir of Anthony, Lord Lucy (57). Other early instances of quartered arms taken from Shakespeare's characters are the shields of Beauchamp, Earl of Warwick (86),[1] and FitzAlan, Earl of Arundel and Surrey (87).

From the reign of Edward III, the royal shield was quartered so as to include the arms of France as well as those of England; but in this case the quartering of the French coat was an indication only of a claim to, not possession of, the throne of France (Pl. IV).

Not only two, but three or four different coats might be included in a shield of four quarters, and a shield might be divided into more than four parts to meet the case of a man holding many lordships, e.g. John

---

[1] Shown in colour in Plate III.

Talbot, Earl of Shrewsbury (158), and Richard Nevill, Earl of Warwick and Salisbury (155); in these cases the manner in which the several quarterings were acquired is shown by the accompanying pedigrees.

A man did not necessarily use on all occasions the various coats he was entitled to quarter. As a general rule, the shield he carried in war would bear only one coat of arms, i.e. his paternal coat, or that associated with his principal lordship, since an elaborate shield would be less easily recognized than a simple one. Probably so bold a combination as that of Montagu and Monthermer would appear on the war-shield, because each coat was so plain that in quartering they would lose little in clarity; but in the case of combined coats, each of some intricacy and detail, like Beauchamp and Neubourg, probably only the coat in the first quarter would be placed on the shield actually carried in war (Pl. III).

The surcoat often bore two coats quarterly but here, too, while heraldry remained practical undue elaboration was avoided. A complicated assembly of coats, such as that of the Kingmaker (155) would appear only on a banner, horse-bardings, seal, or shield displayed for pageantry and decoration. There are often several versions of these multi-quartered shields, due to a selection being made from the quarterings for some purposes, or the order of the quarterings being sometimes varied, or some change of circumstance affecting a man's armorial bearings; but the principal coat (usually the paternal arms) is always placed in the first quarter.

In some cases, arms once combined by quartering were treated as impartible. Thus, from Edward III's reign to the end of Elizabeth's, the royal arms consisted of the quartered coats of France and England, and our sovereigns did not use either of these coats separately. The quartering of the Lucy arms with those of Percy was a condition of the first Earl of Northumberland's inheritance of his second wife's estates, and was therefore obligatory on him and his descendants, and to this day the impartible coat of Percy and Lucy quarterly occupies a quarter of the Duke of Northumberland's shield.

Shields varied in form at different periods. The long shield of the twelfth and early thirteenth century, shown on the effigies of William Longespée, Earl of Salisbury (3), and William the Marshal, Earl of Pembroke (17), gave place to a much shorter shield, and this lasted, with some variation in proportions, until about the time of Agincourt. In the fifteenth century, the use of the shield seems to have declined, no doubt due to the decreasing importance of heavily armed chivalry in warfare. However, it was still used by mounted knights making or meeting a cavalry charge, and also in jousting. With the elaboration of plate armour, the shield took a different form, represented by that on the Garter stall-plates of Richard Nevill, Earl of Salisbury (153), and John Beaufort, Duke of Somerset (5); and these rather fantastic shields, with

FIG. 5.   Armorial Bearings of John Beaufort, Duke of Somerset, from his Garter Stall-plate.

fluted surfaces and sometimes a slot for the lance to rest in, are frequently found in the late fifteenth and early sixteenth century. For the purposes of the heraldic drawings in this book, the earlier and simpler form of shield is generally used; and in productions of *Henry VI* and *Richard III* this conventional and more graceful form may appear rather than the flamboyant type strictly appropriate to the period.

The armorial surcoat, which first appeared in the thirteenth century,

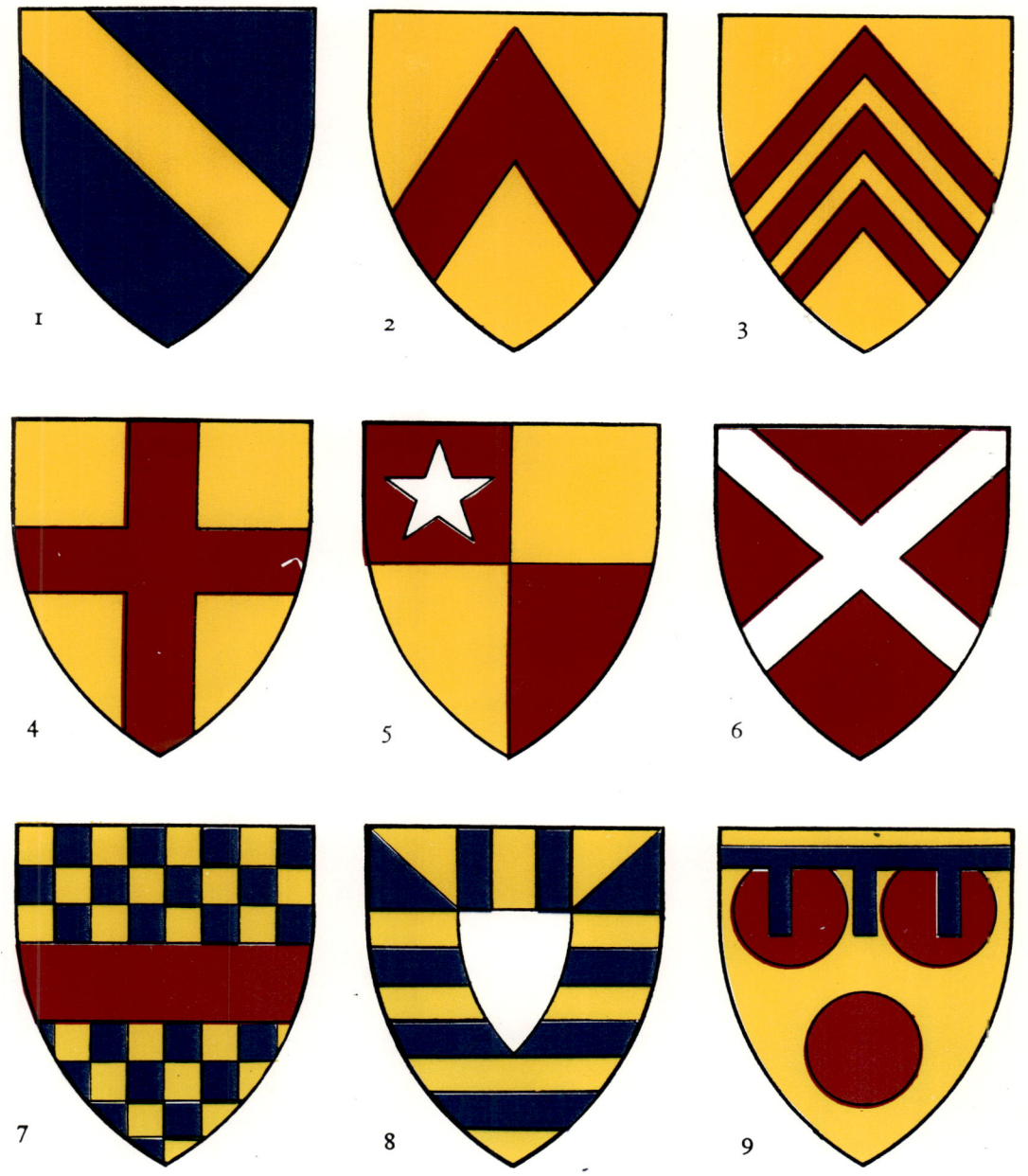

PLATE II. Some ancient shields of arms, illustrating simple heraldic forms.

1. Scrope	2. Stafford	3 Clare
4. Bigot	5. De Vere	6. Nevill
7. Clifford	8. Mortimer	9. Courtenay

took various styles at different periods.   The close-fitting jupon of the late fourteenth and early fifteenth century is shown on the effigy of Sir William Bagot (65).   After Agincourt, the surcoat seems to have been less used, knights being unwilling to hide the rich decoration which armour often assumed at this time, but it may quite properly be worn on the stage. Towards the close of the fifteenth century, the jupon began to be superseded by the tabard, which was open at the sides and could be easily put on and off.   The tabard was probably seldom worn in battle.   It was mainly intended for heraldic display, at a time when heraldry was ceasing to serve a practical purpose, and unlike the simpler surcoat of an earlier period it sometimes bore six or eight quarterings.

Banners of arms were rectangular, and the owner's bearings were displayed over the entire surface, and not placed within a shield form. In the time of King John, banners were of greater depth than width (21-26), and later they were nearly square (42).   In addition to the arms of the king, and of the principal lords and knights, the insignia of national saints were often displayed on banners carried in battle.

Crests on helms, rudimentary in the twelfth century, developed in the thirteenth and became general in the fourteenth century.   They were, however, associated particularly with the great helm, which towards the end of the fourteenth century became mainly a tournament helm, being superseded in warfare by the lighter and more convenient bascinet. Crests were therefore probably worn at tournaments and other occasions for heraldic display rather than in war, since a man going into battle would not be likely to put an unnecessary weight on his head, and something which would give the enemy a handle.   The king and other leaders may have worn crests of moderate size for the purpose of recognition and a rallying point in the *mêlée*, but the towering, top-heavy crests worn by knights when tilting in the lists would certainly not be suited to the battlefield, and in war most knights were probably content with a plume of feathers or a decorative wreath such as is shown in no. 143.   Crests thus have little place in the heraldic production of Shakespeare's plays, and they are not always given in this book.   There is, however, one occasion where the text demands the use of a crest: in 2 *Henry VI, v,* 1, Warwick promises to wear 'the rampant bear chain'd to the ragged staff' on his burgonet, and Clifford vows,

> from thy burgonet I'll rend thy bear
> And tread it under foot with all contempt.

Therefore in the following scene, the battle of St Albans, Warwick must wear the bear on his helm.

Throughout the fifteenth century, badges were widely used. These were different in character and purpose from both arms and crest. They were not as a rule placed on a shield: the Black Prince's use of his badge of three ostrich feathers on his 'shield for peace' is exceptional. A badge was sometimes the same device as a man used as his crest, and it was sometimes a charge taken from his shield, but as often as not it bore no resemblance to either arms or crest. A man might have several badges. Some he reserved for his personal use and adornment; one or more he used as the 'household badge' to be worn by his retainers and servants, who were not entitled to use their master's shield or coat of arms.

Badges were also displayed on standards. These were long, tapering flags, set up on the battlefield and in camp as a rallying point for the men following a particular leader. The standard of an English warrior generally bore the red cross of St George next the staff, the fly being divided into the owner's livery colours, and charged with his badges and *cri*, or motto (104, 105).

Through their appearance on the liveries of retainers and servants, many badges became widely known, and some acquired a popular use far removed from the purposes of chivalry. Richard II's white hart was adopted as an inn sign and is still so employed. The bear and ragged staff of the Earls of Warwick served the same purpose, and has also found its way into the arms of the Warwickshire County Council. Similarly the swan of Bohun, through its association with the Dukes of Buckingham, has become the emblem of Buckinghamshire. In these and other ways many feudal badges have continued in actual use to this day, while their owners' arms often exist only on funeral monuments, or as quarterings in the heraldry of families who have succeeded to their honours. As will be shown later, Shakespeare made dramatic use of the best known royal and feudal badges.

Early in the fifteenth century, supporters came into use for purposes of heraldic display. These consisted of human figures, or creatures of any kind, real or imaginary, represented as flanking and upholding the shield (5). Frequently creatures already in use as badges were made to serve in this way. Supporters had no part in personal adornment or identification, and on the stage they can be introduced only where arms are used decoratively in the royal palace or nobleman's residence.

In *Henry VIII*, heraldry can be used only in stage *décor*. No doubt it played a conspicuous part in the splendours of the Field of the Cloth of Gold, but we do not see them, save in the mind's eye aided by Norfolk's glowing words. Heraldry had become mainly a matter of pageantry. In war, knights no longer displayed their arms for identification; and in peace, heraldic insignia as an adjunct to costume had gone out of fashion, while the use of badges had declined owing to Henry VII's measures against the practices of livery and maintenance. In the play, the armorial bearings of the King, Queen Katharine, Queen Anne, and Cardinal Wolsey may be displayed in the appointments of the appropriate scenes. There is no occasion to show the arms of other characters on the stage, and they are included in this record only for their historic and heraldic interest.

In the Tudor period, heraldry lacked the restraint which practical use had formerly imposed on it. As arms no longer needed to be clearly distinguishable in the field, there was no check on a tendency to undue elaboration. Shields were often overloaded with charges, as may be seen in the arms of Cardinal Wolsey (236) and Thomas Cromwell (238). The addition of quarterings was carried to excess. Already in the latter part of the fifteenth century, some men were beginning to include the arms of distinguished houses from which they were indirectly descended, though they derived no actual lordship therefrom; for instance, Anthony, Lord Rivers, whose mother was a daughter of Peter de Luxemburg, Count of St Pol, quartered the coats of Luxemburg and Baux (164). In the sixteenth century, an accumulation of quarterings came to be regarded as a criterion of noble descent; men searched their pedigrees for any marriage of an ancestor with a technical heiress, and incorporated her arms in his shield (including any quarterings accruing to them), though she had been but the representative of some junior branch of a family of minor gentry, bringing with her no lordship or honour. Thus were built up those complicated shields of eight, twelve, sixteen or more quarterings which are frequently seen in manor houses and on monuments in churches. Shields of arms became pictorial pedigrees, proclaiming pride of race but far removed from their original purpose. Some of them had not even the merit of being truthful in their genealogical claims; for example, the arms devised for Anne Bullen, when Henry VIII intended to marry her, suppressed her paternity and credited her with a far nobler descent than she could claim.

The colourful mosaic of one of these shields of many quarterings was often very pretty, but it lacked the real beauty of many a single coat which was graceful in design, and 'rich, not gaudy.'

In these complex 'achievements of arms,' and not in the plain, practical shields of an earlier day, we find the justification for Gray's words, 'the boast of heraldry.'   In very fact, they pointed the path of glory that 'leads but to the grave,' for in the sixteenth and seventeenth centuries armorial display was a conspicuous feature in the obsequies of the great, and the marshalling of funerals became a principal function of the heralds. Shakespeare refers to this, where the dead Coriolanus is described as

> The most noble corse that ever herald
> Did follow to his urn.

The absence of heraldic pomp at the funeral of Hamlet's father was regarded as suspicious:

> his obscure funeral,
> No trophy, sword, nor hatchment o'er his bones,
> No noble rite, nor formal ostentation,
> Cry to be heard . . . .

A hatchment was a painting of the armorial bearings of the deceased person, which was hung outside his residence as a sign of mourning, and later transferred to the church where he was buried.

The heralds concerned themselves not only with funerals but also with the armories and inscriptions on monuments. Among the records of the College of Arms there is a copy of the epitaph on the monument of Sir Thomas Stanley at Tong, made by Sir William Dugdale and included in his Visitation of Shropshire in 1664. Dugdale, himself a Warwickshire man, attributed this epitaph to Shakespeare.

His note is as follows:

'These following Verses were made by William Shakespeare the late famous Tragedian.

'Written upon the East end of this Tombe.

> Aske who lyes here, but do not weepe
>   He is not dead, he doth but sleepe
> This stony Register is for his bones
>   His fame is more perpetuall than these stones,
> And his own goodnesse wth himself being gone
> Shall live when earthly Monument is none.

'Written upon the West end thereof.

> Not monumentall stone preserves our fame,
>> Nor skye aspiring Piramids our name
> The memory of him for whom this stands
>> Shall out-live marble and defacers hands
> When all to times consumption shall be given
> Stanley, for whom this stands, shall stand in Heaven.'

In the same manuscript is a tinted drawing of the tomb, with its effigies and 'skye aspiring Piramids,' by the hand of Francis Sandford, Lancaster Herald.

Sir Thomas Stanley, who died in 1576, was the second son of Edward, third Earl of Derby, and a descendant of the 'Lord Stanley' of *Richard III*. He was uncle to William, sixth Earl of Derby, a patron of players in Shakespeare's time. Although Shakespeare was only thirteen years of age at the time of Sir Thomas's death, this does not make his authorship of the epitaph unlikely, as the monument for which it was written was apparently not erected until early in the seventeenth century.[1]

The decadent period of heraldry lasted until the latter part of the nineteenth century. Its renaissance in modern times is not within the scope of this outline.

How much did Shakespeare know of heraldry? That he was interested in it is certain. Perhaps his interest was first aroused when he was a child, and his father obtained the draft of a coat of arms. It was clearly shown when William, in the days of his prosperity, secured the long-delayed grant of arms for his family. But an interest, however strong, does not necessarily imply any deep knowledge; and while the arms of the characters, and the occasional heraldic references in the plays, can be used to illustrate a brief survey of mediaeval heraldry, it by no means follows that Shakespeare himself was well versed in the subject.

At least he knew enough of the language of heraldry to use it at need with reasonable accuracy, though not so meticulously as a herald would have done. Sometimes he misused a term, but he generally had a literary reason for doing so, as where he made the Duke of York (in 2 *Henry VI*) speak of the white rose badge as the *arms* of York, because he needed the word 'arms' for the imagery of the following line, 'to *grapple* with the

[1] The whole question was discussed by Mrs. Arundell Esdaile in "The Times," 22nd April and 23rd May, 1929.

house of Lancaster.' Heraldic language had for him nothing of the sanctity with which the armorists of his day sought to endue it. He could make fun of it, as in the opening scene of *The Merry Wives of Windsor*, with the reference to the 'dozen white louses' in an old coat, and Evans's blundering idea that to quarter a coat meant cutting off the skirt of an actual garment.

Heraldic terms came readily to his mind in passages concerned with warfare, as where Timon bids Alcibiades 'with man's blood paint the ground gules, gules.' Gules (heraldic red) and sable (black) occur again in a passage in *Hamlet*:

> The rugged Pyrrhus, he whose sable arms,
> Black as his purpose, did the night resemble,
> When he lay couched in the ominous horse,
> Hath now this dread and black complexion smear'd,
> With heraldry more dismal head to foot;
> Now is he total gules, horridly trick'd
> With blood of fathers, mothers, daughters, sons . . .
>> (*Hamlet, ii, 2*)

'Total gules,' or *gules plein*, is a description of a shield, surcoat or banner of red throughout with no charge thereon, like the French oriflamme. 'Tricked' is an heraldic word applied to a shield of arms which is roughly sketched and uncoloured, the tinctures being indicated by letters or signs. Shakespeare here uses 'trick'd' to imply 'emblazoned in colour,' which is contrary to its true heraldic meaning; but he needed a monosyllable, and presumably relied on his audience not being so well versed in heraldic terms as to cavil at the liberty.

Occasionally heraldic imagery came to Shakespeare's mind in connection with very different matters, as in Helena's reference to her friendship with Hermia as 'an union in partition,'

> like coats in heraldry,
> Due but to one, and crowned with one crest.
>> (*Midsummer Night's Dream*)

In *The Rape of Lucrece*, he wrote, not very happily, of the 'heraldry in Lucrece' face,' and of

> Their silent war of lilies and of roses,
> Which Tarquin view'd in her fair face's field.

Again, in *Othello* we find,

> the hearts of old gave hands,
> But our new heraldry is hands not hearts.

Here it may be noted that Shakespeare used the word 'heraldry' with two meanings.   Generally he employed it as a synonym of 'armory,' that branch of the herald's lore which has to do with insignia centering on the shield; but occasionally he used it with the wider meaning of the general customs and usages of chivalry, with which the herald was concerned. Thus in *Hamlet* we find a reference to

> a seal'd compact,
> Well ratified by law and heraldry,

under which Fortinbras of Norway forfeited his lands to his conqueror, King Hamlet.

But the use of heraldic terms does not necessarily imply any real knowledge of heraldry.   What evidence have we that Shakespeare knew anything of the subject itself?

He knew enough of the arms of the English kings who appear in his plays to make frequent use of the symbol of the lion in referring to them, and to allude to the fleurs-de-lys in their arms as signs of their pretensions to the throne of France:

> Awake, awake, English nobility!
> Let not sloth dim your honours, new-begot:
> Cropp'd are the flower-de-luces in your arms;
> Of England's coat one half is cut away.
>
> (1 Henry VI, i, 1)

In Shakespeare's day the royal arms were still *Quarterly France and England,* and the significance of the lions and the fleurs-de-lys must have been a matter of common information.

Shakespeare knew the principal badges of the various sovereigns.   In *Richard II,* sun imagery is used with such method and consistency that Shakespeare must have been well aware that the sun was that King's particular badge.   A passage in this play suggests that he had noted the angels supporting the King's arms in Westminster Hall.   In *Henry VI,* the sun appears again as the emblem of the house of York, and in *Richard III,* the King is several times referred to by his badge of the boar; these two badges are mentioned in the chronicles which were the source of the plays.   Shakespeare was familiar with the roses of York and Lancaster, and knew that they were united to form the Tudor rose, but this must have been common knowledge in his time.   Certain passages in the plays may contain indirect references to other royal badges—the *planta genista,* the tree-stock of Woodstock, and Edward III's sword encircled by crowns.

B

On the whole it seems that, apart from the casual references he found in Hall and Holinshed, and the general knowledge he shared with most well-informed men, Shakespeare had access to some record of royal heraldry, and that he marked and remembered devices which might be aptly used in dramatic imagery.

He also knew something of the armorial devices assigned by the heraldic writers of his day to the heroes of the pre-heraldic era. In *Love's Labour's Lost*, Sir Nathaniel, representing Alexander in the pageant of the Nine Worthies, says,

> My scutcheon plain declares that I am Alisander,

and Costard refers to the device as

> Your lion, that holds his pole-axe sitting on a close-stool.

Shakespeare may well have derived this from Gerard Leigh's *Accedence of Armorie* (1591) where Alexander's arms are blazoned as, *Geules, a Lion or, seiante in a chayer, holding a battle-axe argent.*

In the tournaments of the sixteenth century—occasions rather for pageantry than for military exercise—knights sometimes displayed not their true heraldic arms, but devices adopted for the event. We have a reflection of this in the 'triumph' in *Pericles* (ii, 2), where six knights appear, Thaisa declaring their devices and mottoes. Of the devices described, two were actually used by historical persons. The fourth knight bore,

> A burning torch that's turned upside down;
> The word, 'Quod me alit, me extinguit.'

This was an emblem of Jean de Poitiers, Seignieur de Saint-Valier, borne on his ensigns at the battle of Marignano.

> The fifth, an hand environed with clouds,
> Holding out gold that's by the touchstone tried;
> The motto thus, 'Sic spectanda fides.'

This was a device of King Francis II of France.[1]

Shakespeare himself designed such devices, or impresses, on occasion, as appears from an entry in the accounts of the steward to the Earl of Rutland in connection with the celebrations on the King's accession day, 1613.

'To Mr. Shakespeare in gold about my Lord's impresa 44s.; to Richard Burbage for painting and making it, in gold 44s.'

----

[1] Mrs. Bury Palliser, *Historic Devices.*

Coming to the nobles and knights who people Shakespeare's historical plays, we read of warriors in gay or glittering coats, and of plumes, colours and flags, presenting a general picture of heraldic splendour; but references to particular devices are few. The only badge of a nobleman (other than royal persons) which Shakespeare specifically mentions is the bear and ragged staff of the Earls of Warwick, which a Warwickshire man had good reason to know; but here his knowledge was faulty, for he made the Kingmaker speak of the badge as coming from his father, the Earl of Salisbury, whereas in fact he had it, through his wife, from the former Earls of Warwick.

It is also significant that Shakespeare sometimes missed opportunities of making dramatic use of heraldry, presumably because he had not the knowledge to recognize them. For example, had he known that the dragon, the lion and the wolf of Merlin's prophecy were in fact the heraldic emblems of Glendower, Percy and Mortimer, he would surely have brought this out in the scene at Bangor (1 *Henry IV, iii,* 1.)

In examining the plays from the heraldic viewpoint, there is a danger of reading an armorial allusion where none was intended. I have perhaps done this myself—for example, where I suggest that the groom of the stable in *Richard II* was wearing the King's badge of a white hart (Chapter IV). An instance occurs in the Rodway manuscript: in Othello's gift to Desdemona of a handkerchief 'spotted with strawberries,' Rodway discerns an allusion to the mulberries in the arms of Cristofero Moro, the Venetian Governor in 1570, the year of Selim II's attack on Cyprus. Had Shakespeare known that the historical Moro bore the mulberry (or *morus*, allusive to his name), and intended the strawberry to be its counterpart as Othello's device, he would surely have brought out the fact that Desdemona had parted with something of special value to Othello since it bore his armorial insignia; but while a detailed account of the handkerchief's history is given, nothing is said to indicate that the strawberries were anything more than decoration.

Again, in *Hamlet* we have Ophelia's remark, 'Oh, you must wear your rue with a difference.' An attempt to link this with the crown of rue in the arms of Saxony is ingenious but unconvincing. If Ophelia's words are addressed to the King, they may be meant to imply that he had borne the difference of a younger son, and only ceased to do so through the murder of his brother and the usurpation of the throne. However, this is rather involved, and the more probable explanation is that the words 'with a difference' have no heraldic intent, but, addressed to the Queen, mean that while Ophelia wears her rue for sorrow, Gertrude must wear hers for repentance—the other significance of the herb.

Shakespeare's outlook on heraldry was, naturally enough, Tudor rather than mediaeval, especially in his association of arms with gentility. In the age of chivalry, only persons holding land by military tenure, and leading their own unit in the feudal army, had occasion to use heraldic shields and banners. This led to the conception that only those who belonged to the class of gentry had a right to heraldic arms. Shakespeare refers to this in *The Taming of the Shrew*:

> *Petruchio.* Good Kate, I am a gentleman.
> *Katharina.*　　　　That I'll try. *She strikes him.*
> *Pet.* I swear I'll cuff you, if you strike again.
> *Kat.* So may you lose your arms:
> 　　　If you strike me, you are no gentleman;
> 　　　And if no gentleman, why then no arms.
> *Pet.* A herald, Kate? O put me in thy books!
> *Kat.* What is your crest? a coxcomb?
> *Pet.* A combless cock, so Kate will be my hen.

Similarly, in *Twelfth Night*, Olivia comments on Viola's claim to be a gentleman:

> 　　I'll be sworn thou art;
> Thy tongue, thy face, thy limbs, actions, and spirit,
> Do give thee five-fold blazon.

And again, in *Hamlet*:

> *First Clown.* Come, my spade; there is no ancient gentlemen but
> 　　　　　gardeners, ditchers, and grave-makers: they hold up Adam's
> 　　　　　profession.
> *Second Clown.* Was he a gentleman?
> *First Clown.* A' was the first that ever bore arms. . . . The Scripture
> 　　　　　says Adam digg'd: could he dig without arms?

This association of heraldry with gentility was carried a stage further by the heralds of the Tudor period. Not content with holding that only a gentleman could possess arms, they asserted that only a person possessing arms could rank as a gentleman.

In *Richard II* Shakespeare suggests the value a man placed on his arms as tokens of his gentility. Bolingbroke, returned from banishment, addresses Bushy and Green:

. . . you have fed upon my signories,
Dispark'd my parks and fell'd my forest woods,
From my own windows torn my household coat,
Raz'd out my impress, leaving me no sign,
Save men's opinions, and my living blood,
To show the world I am a gentleman.

This is Tudor rather than Plantagenet in sentiment.   Bolingbroke would
no doubt be annoyed at having his windows broken, and would probably
take the defacement of his arms as a personal affront, but he would hardly
feel himself any the less Edward III's grandson and a nobleman.   But in
Shakespeare's time, to tear the arms from the windows of a manor house
would be to assert that the owner was not a gentleman.   In fact, such a
thing might actually be done with that very intention, for at their periodic
visitations the heralds were empowered to enter into churches, castles and
houses, and to 'revise, put down, or otherwise deface' coats of arms
unlawfully borne on 'plate, jewels, paper, parchment, windows, gravestones
and monuments,' and to proclaim as infamous any person who had
unlawfully usurped the title of esquire or gentleman.   In practice, matters
were seldom if ever carried to such lengths.   A person calling himself
esquire or gentleman, and being unable to justify it to the heralds, had
either to petition for a grant of arms, or sign a statement acknowledging
that he was 'no gentleman.'   Only if he refused to adopt either alternative
would action be taken against him.

In *All's Well That Ends Well*, Shakespeare gives an example of the
snub that a man might court if he made too free with those of a higher
station.   The old Lord Lafeu says to Parolles, 'You are more saucy with
lords and honourable personages than the commission of your birth and
virtue gives you heraldry.   You are not worth another word, else I'ld
call you knave.'

Shakespeare's information about heraldry appears to have been
derived from various sources, some sound, others of doubtful value.   On
the one hand he may have heard of Henry V's proclamation exempting
those who fought at Agincourt from the prohibition against assuming
arms without authority:

For he to-day that sheds his blood with me
Shall be my brother; be he ne'er so base,
This day shall gentle his condition.

On the other hand, he picked up from some heraldic writer of his time the fallacy that a man guilty of some disgraceful action might have a mark of dishonour added to his shield, which must be passed down to his descendants:

> Yea, though I die, the scandal will survive,
> And be an eyesore in my golden coat;
> Some loathsome dash the herald will contrive,
> To cipher me how fondly I did dote;
> That my posterity, shamed with the note,
>   Shall curse my bones, and hold it for no sin
>   To wish that I their father had not been.
>
> (*Lucrece*, 204-210)

This quite accurately reflects sixteenth century heraldic theory. De-flowering a maid was one of the dishonourable actions specified as deserving an armorial 'abatement.' Such a blemish was supposed to be literally a 'dash,' i.e. a *tache*, or stain, neither one of the metals nor true colours of heraldry being used for it, but one of the 'stainand colours,' such as tawny or murrey. Nevertheless Shakespeare was misled, because heraldry has in practice never known such a thing as an abatement of honour, or 'a blot on the scutcheon.' Even if the 'loathsome dash' had existed, there would be no obligation on the man so disgraced, or his descendants, to use the arms containing it.

From Leigh's *Accedence of Arms*, already mentioned as the probable source of Alexander's shield, Shakespeare may also have derived the words, 'glittering in golden coats', in his description of the Prince of Wales and his followers in 1 *Henry IV*, *iv*, 1. Leigh, classifying heraldic tinctures in combination as 'most rich, most faire, and most glittering', wrote, 'when golde is the fielde, and verte occupieth the same, then is it most glittering.'

Another book to which Shakespeare seems to have had access is Richard Crompton's *Mansion of Magnanimitie* (1599), from which the passage in 1 *Henry VI*, iv, 7, setting forth Talbot's titles appears to have been derived.

On the whole, the evidence suggests that Shakespeare had an interest in heraldry (as in so much else), and an appreciation of its dramatic possibilities in historical plays; that he had dipped into heraldic records and books, and perhaps discussed the subject with the officers of arms; but that he had no deep knowledge—little more, in fact, than the average studious man of his time might pick up from casual observation and inquiry.

In view of the ingenious use which has been made of heraldic material
to support one or other of the theories as to the authorship of the plays,
it may be added that the sentiment towards heraldry which they reveal
appears to be not that of a man of high station, born to symbols of honour
and taking them for granted, but rather that of a man of middle class,
valuing these tokens the more because he has known the lack of them; and
that man had a bias towards Warwickshire.

Limited though it may be, the heraldic evidence is consistent with the
traditional view that the plays were the work of William Shakespeare of
Stratford-upon-Avon.

In this book, I have used a modified form of blazoning, i.e. the description of insignia in heraldic terms, and the reader with no prior knowledge
of the language of heraldry should be able to follow it with the aid of the
glossary and by reference to the illustrations.   In blazoning, the field (or
surface of the shield) is first described, whether it be of one tincture,
divided into two tinctures, or *semé* (scattered with small charges).   Then
comes the principal charge or charges, and finally any secondary charges.
I use 'gold' and 'silver' rather than 'or' and 'argent,' but I have retained
the heraldic names of the other tinctures.   I have eschewed unnecessary
refinements of blazon, such as cumbersome phrases to avoid repetition of
tincture or number.

In the following pages, the two parts of *Henry IV* have been treated
as one play and are dealt with in the same chapter; and similarly the three
parts of *Henry VI* are the subject of one chapter.

The periods covered by the historical plays are:

King John		1199—1216
Richard II		April 1398—March 1400
Henry IV	Part 1	June 1402—July 1403
	Part 2	July 1403—1413
Henry V		1414—1420
Henry VI	Part 1	1422—1444
	Part 2	1445—1455
	Part 3	1455—1471
Richard III		1471—1485
Henry VIII		1520—1533.

To assist the identification of characters, and to show the relationships between them, the following tables are included in the chapters on the historical plays:

CHAPTER II

SHAKESPEARE'S ARMS

B U T O N E halfpenny worth of fact to an intolerable deal of supposition—such is the matter for a note on Shakespeare's arms; as, indeed, on anything to do with him personally. The facts are:

(1) Two rough drafts, both dated 20th October 1596, of a grant of arms to John Shakespeare of Stratford-upon-Avon, preserved at the College of Arms. Extracts are given below, and a composite copy is printed in full at the end of the chapter. The first draft is illustrated in fig. 6.

(2) A note at the end of one of these drafts that John Shakespeare showed a pattern, or design for the proposed arms, prepared by Cook, Clarenceux King of Arms, twenty years earlier.

(3) A rough draft of an assignment of arms for Arden, to be impaled with those of John Shakespeare and quartered by his descendants, dated 1599, also preserved at the College of Arms.

(4) Records, at the College, of a controversy between Brooke, York Herald, and Sir William Dethick, Garter King of Arms, as to the heraldic propriety of the arms granted to Shakespeare.

(5) The arms on the monuments of William Shakespeare and some of his descendants.

Let us begin with (2), which takes us back to the earliest recorded move by the Shakespeares to obtain armorial bearings.

The note on the 1596 draft of a grant of arms to John Shakespeare states that 'this John showeth a pattern thereof under Clarent. Cook's hand in paper xx years past'—that is, a suggested design on paper (and not a finished and approved drawing on parchment) by Robert Cook, Clarenceux King of Arms. The note adds that John Shakespeare had been a Justice of the Peace and Bailiff of Stratford-upon-Avon. Cook became Clarenceux in 1567, and had a commission to visit his province the following year. John Shakespeare became Bailiff in 1568, and Chief Alderman in 1571. 'Twenty years past' may be taken as an approximation, and it is probable that the proposal to obtain arms was first mooted, and a tentative design prepared, either in the year of Cook's visitation and Shakespeare's service as Bailiff, or soon afterwards.

Apart from the note on the 1596 draft, there is no record of this preliminary approach at the College of Arms, and Sir Sidney Lee[1] suggested that it may have been 'a formal fiction designed by John Shakespeare and his son to recommend their claim to the notice of the heralds.' But the absence of other record is hardly sufficient reason to discredit the note, and we may believe that John Shakespeare took the first step to obtain arms while William was still a child.

This is to some extent borne out by the document of 1599, which states that John Shakespeare produced 'his ancient coat of arms heretofore assigned to him whilst he was Her Majesty's officer and Bailiff of that Town.' Probably this refers to Cook's original 'pattern', prepared in 1568 but not actually granted until 1596.

That John Shakespeare might reasonably expect to obtain such tokens of honour cannot be doubted. 'Bailiffs of cities and ancient boroughs or incorporated towns' are included by Sir John Ferne[2] among holders of 'offices of dignity and worship' meriting a grant of arms. Moreover, John Shakespeare's wife was the daughter and one of the heirs of Robert Arden of Wilmcote, a cadet of a family reputed to possess arms (though, as we shall see, there appeared later to be some doubt as to the actual arms he was entitled to).

No doubt John's wife wished to see the arms of her family descend to their children, but this could only be arranged if John himself obtained a coat of arms with which the Arden coat could be combined and handed down.

For some reason John Shakespeare did not proceed with his early application for a grant. We may hazard a guess that in view of the considerable fees to be paid he put the matter off until ready money should be available, and before he was in a position to resume it he became involved in the financial difficulties which continued for some twenty years. The eventual improvement in his affairs coincided with his son's rise to pros-

[1] *Life of William Shakespeare*, 1898.
[2] *The Glorie of Generositie*, 1586.

perity, and it is a reasonable deduction that William Shakespeare helped to restore his father's fortunes.

The approach to the heralds for a grant of arms in 1596 was therefore a renewal of John Shakespeare's earlier application, but it is generally believed that it was William, acting in his father's name, who now took the initiative in the matter. It is hardly likely that John, then in his sixties, would come to London for the purpose when he had on the spot a son with some knowledge of heraldry, a public figure, and probably personally known to some of the officers of arms. An interesting feature of the two drafts of 1596 is that the terms, and particularly the alterations and additions, probably represent information given and suggestions made by William Shakespeare sitting in conference with the heralds.

After the usual preamble in the extravagant style of the time, the first draft states that the parents and late antecessors of John Shakespeare 'were for their valiant and faithful service advanced and rewarded by the most prudent prince King Henry the Seventh of famous memory, sithence which time they have continued in those parts in good reputation and credit, and that the said John hath married Mary, daughter and one of the heirs of Robert Arden of Wilmcote in the said county, esquire'—for the last word, 'gent.' was written, and altered to 'esquire' in the second draft. The document then proceeds to assign and blazon the arms, to which we will come later.

It will be noted that the matters singled out for mention are the services of John's forebears, and his own marriage. There is no reference in the draft to the fact that he had been Bailiff of Stratford; but this is stated in the note at the foot of the second draft, probably made at the prompting of William, and it may be that the fact was included in the final document, as it was in the assignment of 1599.

The reference to John Shakespeare's ancestry is tantalizingly vague. Above the word 'antecessors' in the second draft is written 'grandfather,' suggesting a specific person whose 'valiant and faithful services' were referred to. But the draft of the assignment of 1599 speaks of John's 'parent, great-grandfather and late antecessor' having been advanced and rewarded with lands and tenements in Warwickshire. The confusion may have arisen from the heralds momentarily forgetting that they were dealing with the grantee's son, so that when William spoke of 'my great-grandfather' they took it to mean John's great-grandfather. Had they stated the name of the ancestor referred to, and the nature of his services, the draft grant would have thrown welcome light on Shakespeare's ancestry. As it is, the vagueness of the passage leaves us wondering whether it was anything more than a complimentary way of saying that the earlier Shakespeares were respectable but undistinguished.

William Harrison, writing in 1577,[1] noted that in their grants the heralds 'do of custom pretend antiquity and service, and many gay things,' and it appears that the grant to Shakespeare followed the usual form. However, it has been noted by G. R. French[2] that there were 'four soldiers of the same surname [Shakespere] holding the rank of archers, only half a century later than the Battle of Bosworth, and doubtless some of their forefathers had also been archers, either on horse or foot, serving in some of the great wars abroad, or in the unhappy strife of the Two Roses. . . . There would be nothing remarkable in an ancestor of John Shakespeare, if he had fought on Richmond's side at Bosworth, even in no higher rank than that of an archer, being rewarded in some manner by the conqueror.'

We may see William Shakespeare's prompting again in the alteration of the style of his grandfather, Robert Arden of Wilmcote, from 'gent.' to 'esquire.' *Armiger*, or esquire, was a degree above *generosus*, or gentlemen, and since the Arden marriage was to be mentioned in the Shakespeare grant, William would naturally be anxious to see that his mother's family had their due. Have we in *The Merry Wives of Windsor* his amused recollection of his own insistence on his ancestor's dignity?

> . . . a gentleman born . . . who writes himself
> 'Armigero' in any bill, warrant, quittance or
> obligation, 'Armigero.'

We come to the part of the first draft grant dealing with the armorial bearings:

'In consideration whereof, and for the encouragement of his posterity, to whom such blazon or achievement may descend by the ancient custom of the laws of arms, I have therefore assigned, granted, and by these presents confirmed this shield or coat of arms, viz. *Gold, on a bend sable a spear of the first, the point steeled proper*; and for his crest or cognizance *a falcon, his wings displayed, argent, standing on a wreath of his colours, supporting a spear gold, steeled as aforesaid,* set upon a helmet with mantles and tassels as hath been accustomed and more plainly appeareth depicted on this margin. Signifying hereby that it shall be lawful for the said John Shakespeare gent. and for his children, issue and posterity . . .

[1] *Description of England.*
[2] *Shakespeareana Genealogica,* 1869.

to bear and make demonstration of the said blazon or achievement . . . .'
In the margin of both drafts is a rough sketch of the shield and crest (figs.
6 and 7a).

No special significance can be read into the design except for the spear's
obvious play on the surname. I have toyed with the idea that the original
thought was to make the bird a shag, so that the crest should be completely
allusive to the name Shagspere (its form in William's marriage bond), but
that the shag ('insatiate cormorant') had unpleasant associations and was
replaced by the nobler falcon; but this is mere speculation.

French notes that the falcon was 'one of the badges of Edward the
Fourth, father of Henry the Seventh's Consort; no person therefore would
venture to adopt such a cognizance except by special favour.' (He might
have added that it was a badge of Queen Elizabeth.) It by no means
follows that because a common heraldic device (such as the falcon) is or
has been a royal badge, it can only become part of the crest or arms of a
private family by special favour, and there is no reason to suppose that
the Shakespeare crest has such significance.

It is worth noting that the falcon was a bearing in the arms of Shakespeare's patron, Henry Wriothesley, Earl of Southampton: *Azure, a gold
cross between four silver falcons, their wings closed and their bells of gold*; but
if the arms as finally granted followed a pattern drawn in William Shakespeare's boyhood, the falcon cannot have been adopted out of compliment
to Southampton.

Above the sketch of the arms on the drafts is written the motto. In
the earlier draft, two attempts were made before this took a satisfactory
form. It was first written as *Non, sanz droict*.

'Play with your fancies!' William Shakespeare, master of punctuation,
saw that unwanted comma reversing the sense of his motto, denying the
title it was intended to assert. 'No, not right!' he exclaimed; 'not *No!
without right*, but *Not without right*'. This did nothing to clarify the
matter. The clerk struck the words out, and supposing from Shakespeare's tone that what he wanted was greater emphasis, tried the same
thing with initial capitals: *Non, Sanz Droict*. At that point someone
seized a pen and firmly printed at the head of the document, *NON SANZ
DROICT* (fig. 6).

'What history lies behind this self-conscious challenge is not known,'
writes G. B. Harrison,[1] 'though much can be guessed'—which perhaps

[1] *Introducing Shakespeare.*

condones the bit of guess-work above.   Maybe it was an assertion of the
merits and standing of the grantee's family, notwithstanding his son's
association with 'these harlotry players.'   If it was a challenge, it seems to
have been taken up by Ben Jonson. In *Every man out of his humour* (1599)
he introduced a wealthy rustic named Sogliardo who obtained a grant of
arms which included a boar's head, whereupon Puntarvolo suggested the
motto should be *Not without mustard*.   (The arms attributed to Sogliardo
bore no resemblance to those of Shakespeare.)

It has been said that the draft of 1596 was not fully executed[1] and that
the arms were not actually granted until 1599.   The failure to trace a fair
copy of the draft of 1596 is no evidence that none was made, and there
seems to be no good reason to think that the draft was not executed.   We
may take 1596 as the year in which John Shakespeare received his grant
of arms, and he and his son might write themselves 'gentlemen.'

The application of 1599 was for an exemplification of the arms with
the inclusion of the coat of Arden, for John Shakespeare's wife.   (I
assume it was granted though Sir E. K. Chambers thinks the document
may never have been issued.) This authorized John to bear the Shakespeare arms either alone, or impaling those of Arden—that is, the shield
was divided vertically into two halves, the Shakespeare coat being placed
in the dexter and the Arden coat in the sinister half—

> . . . an union in partition . . .
> > like coats in heraldry,
> Due but to one, and crowned with one crest.
> > > > *Midsummer Night's Dream, iii, 2.*

The children and descendants of the marriage were empowered to quarter
the arms—that is, the shield might be divided into four quarters, the
Shakespeare coat being placed in the first and fourth and that of Arden
in the second and third quarters.

It appears that some doubt arose as to the arms proper to the Ardens
of Wilmcote. In the sketch on the draft (7b), the Shakespeare arms were
first shown impaled with [*Ermine*], *a fess checky* [*gold and azure*], the coat of
the Ardens of Park Hall, Warwickshire; but this Arden coat was scribbled
out and another drawn beside it, namely, *Gules, three cross-crosslets fitchy
gold, and on a gold chief a martlet gules*.   This is a differenced form of
another Arden coat.   At the Dunstable tournament of 1308 an Arderne
bore *Gules semé of gold crosslets and a gold chief*; at the siege of Calais,

---

[1] Sir Sidney Lee, *Life of Shakespeare*.

1345–8, he or another Arderne bore the same arms with the crosslets fitchy, i.e. pointed at the foot. This coat, later simplified by the reduction of the crosslets to three, seems to have been regarded as the ancient arms of Arderne or Arden, and with some difference was assigned to persons of the name not connected with those who bore the chequered fess. Consequently the heralds, finding that Robert Arden of Wilmcote could not be shown to be descended from the Park Hall Ardens, assigned him the old coat with a difference.

'This question of assigning what is called the "old coat" of Arden in impalement has often been discussed, viz. by Mr. Halliwell, Mr. Gough Nichols, Mr. G. R. French and others; but I am inclined to think that Dethick and Camden were perfectly justified in allowing it as they did, charging the chief with a martlet. The claim to the fess coat was soon negatived, and if the mother of Shakespeare was entitled to any arms (for although there is the strongest circumstantial evidence of her descent, it has not, as far as I know, ever been satisfactorily established), it could only have been to the so called " old coat " ; and this was eventually assigned, with the saving clause of differencing the chief—an addition which modern representations of the impaled arms omit in error'.[1]

There is no evidence that William Shakespeare ever used the quartered coats of Shakespeare and Arden; the arms on his tomb consist of the coat of Shakespeare alone. It has been suggested that some lingering doubt as to his grandfather's title to the arms deterred him from using them; but this is unlikely in view of the formal assignment of the arms by the heralds. Perhaps he was disappointed at not having established his mother's connection with the Park Hall Ardens and his right to quarter their arms, and declined to use a second-best coat; but I prefer to think that he had sufficient artistic and heraldic taste to realize that the simple beauty and dignity of the Shakespeare arms would be impaired rather than enhanced by quartering.

In fact, it is rather remarkable that so simple a coat should have been granted at a time when heraldry was becoming increasingly elaborate, and many shields were overloaded with emblems and fussy in detail. Happily, in what was generally a bad period there were good interludes, and to one of these Shakespeare's arms belong. Since they are 'not of an age but for all time,' it is fortunate that they form one of the finest coats in English heraldry.

---

[1] Stephen Tucker, Somerset Herald, in *Miscellanea Genealogica et Heraldica*, 1886, I, 109.

In the hands of another herald than Clarenceux Cook (assuming that the arms as finally granted followed his original 'pattern'), the Shakespeares might easily have fared worse, for some of the officers of arms made new coats unduly elaborate to avoid any possibility of infringement of older arms. Indeed, the Shakespeare arms were the subject of some controversy among the heralds. Ralph Brooke, York Herald, who delighted to find fault with other people's work, accused Sir William Dethick, Garter (who had approved and granted Cook's design), of having granted John Shakespeare arms too closely resembling those of Lord Mauley, *Gold, a bend sable*. Cadet branches of the Mauley family bore these arms with the addition of secondary emblems placed on the bend for distinction; thus one bore on the bend three dolphins, another three eagles, and a third three wyverns. Brooke's contention appears to have been that the arms granted to Shakespeare might be taken for a differenced coat of Mauley instead of the arms of an entirely separate family. His objection was in fact trivial, and as Garter pointed out—his note[1] is still preserved at the College of Arms—it might equally be made to the coats of Harley, Ferrers, and others bearing a black bend on gold with other devices. 'As for the spear on the bend,' wrote Dethick, 'it is a patible difference'— that is, too prominent a feature of the arms to be regarded merely as a minor addition for cadency.

Ralph Brooke seems to have been sufficiently familiar with Shakespeare's work to quote it, though perhaps unconsciously. In his *Catalogue and Succession of the Kings, Princes, Dukes, Marquesses, Earles, and Viscounts of this Realme of England* (1619), he refers to the Kingmaker in the words, 'This famous and great Earle of Warwicke, did set up and pull downe Kings at his pleasure'—surely an echo of Shakespeare's line about Warwick,

> Proud setter up and puller down of kings.

On the other hand, Brooke may have derived his sentence from Shakespeare at second-hand through Michael Drayton, who wrote in *Poly-Olbion* (published in 1613),

> This puissant setter up, and plucker down of kings.

So William Shakespeare, in his prosperity, helped his father out of his financial difficulties, and gratified the old man's ambition (and no doubt his own) by obtaining the long-desired coat of arms. The gold spear steeled with silver, in shield and crest, is thus associated with the son's

[1] Printed at the end of this chapter and reproduced in fig. 7c.

efforts to restore the father's position—'to furbish new the name of John . . .' It may be no more than coincidence, but it is worth noting that a lance or tilting spear has just that significance in *Richard II*, written in 1595 or 1596 when Shakespeare must have been dealing with the heralds about the arms. In the lists at Coventry (*i*, 3) Bolingbroke addresses Lancaster:

> O thou, the earthly author of my blood,
> Whose youthful spirit, in me regenerate,
> Doth with a two-fold vigour lift me up
> To reach at victory above my head,
> Add proof unto mine armour with thy prayers,
> And with thy blessings steel my lance's point,
> That it may enter Mowbray's waxen coat,
> And furbish new the name of John a Gaunt,
> Even in the lusty haviour of his son.

In the same speech, Bolingbroke declares,

> As confident as is the falcon's flight
> Against a bird, do I with Mowbray fight.

It would be pressing the point too far to suggest that Shakespeare intended a parallel between himself and Bolingbroke; but at least it seems to be rather more than chance that, at a time when the grant of arms to his father was much in his mind, he should allude to both the falcon and lance in a speech of filial sentiment.

The spear is used as a symbol of honour in 1 *Henry IV*, *i*, 3, written in 1597. Worcester opens to Hotspur a matter

> deep and dangerous,
> As full of peril and adventurous spirit
> As to o'er-walk a current roaring loud,
> On the unsteadfast footing of a spear.

And Hotspur, carrying on the metaphor of the bridging spear, declares,

> Send danger from the east unto the west,
> So honour cross it, from the north to south,
> And let them grapple.

It was as a symbol of honour that Shakespeare must have valued his arms. He could have made little actual use of them, for though the grant authorized him to place them on 'shields, targets, escutcheons, coats of arms, pennons, guidons, rings, edifices, buildings, utensils, liveries, tombs or monuments, or otherwise,' in fact a man of his station and period had little occasion for heraldic display. Maybe he bought himself a seal-ring (not 'some eight-penny matter,' but 'worth forty mark'), and he perhaps set up his arms in stained glass or woodwork at New Place, and had them engraved on some of his plate. Their importance lay not in how he used them, but rather in what they meant to him, as a sign

> To show the world I am a gentleman.

To-day, a man who can claim to be a gentleman on the strength of 'men's opinions and my living blood' has the essentials, and though he may esteem heraldry he need not feel himself the less a gentleman for having none. By our standards, William Shakespeare was intrinsically a gentleman, but by the assay of his own time he was not one until he obtained the hall-mark. Having the instincts, breeding and education of a gentleman, he must have felt a sense of incompleteness until the heralds' grant gave him the tokens and style. The grant of arms satisfied an inward need rather than a desire for outward show. Certainly there was no question of snobbism in a man who wrote

> we are gentlemen,
> That neither in our hearts nor outward eyes
> Envy the great nor do the low despise.
> (*Pericles, ii, 3*)

One deep cause for regret he must have had when he received his patent of arms: his only son, Hamnet, had died a few weeks earlier.

The following is a composite copy of the two drafts of the grant of arms to John Shakespeare, the second draft being taken as the basis and gaps due to mutilation being supplied from the first. (Fig. 6 shows a reproduction, reduced in size, of the first draft, and Fig. 7a a portion of the second.)

Shakespere
Non sanz droict
(*Trick of crest
and shield of
arms*)

To all and singuler Noble and Gentilmen: of what Estate [or] Degree bearing Arms to whom these presentes shall come, William Dethick Garter principall King of Arms sendeth greetinges. Knowe yee that whereas by the authorite and auncyent pryveleges perteyning to my office from the Quenes most excellent Majeste and by her highnesse most noble and victorious progenitors, I am to take generall notice and record and to make declaration and testemonie for all causes of Arms and matters of Gentrie thoroughe all her Majestes Kingdoms, Dominions, Principalites, Isles and Provinces, To the'nd that as manie gentlimen by theyre auncyent names of families, kyndredes and descentes, have and enjoye

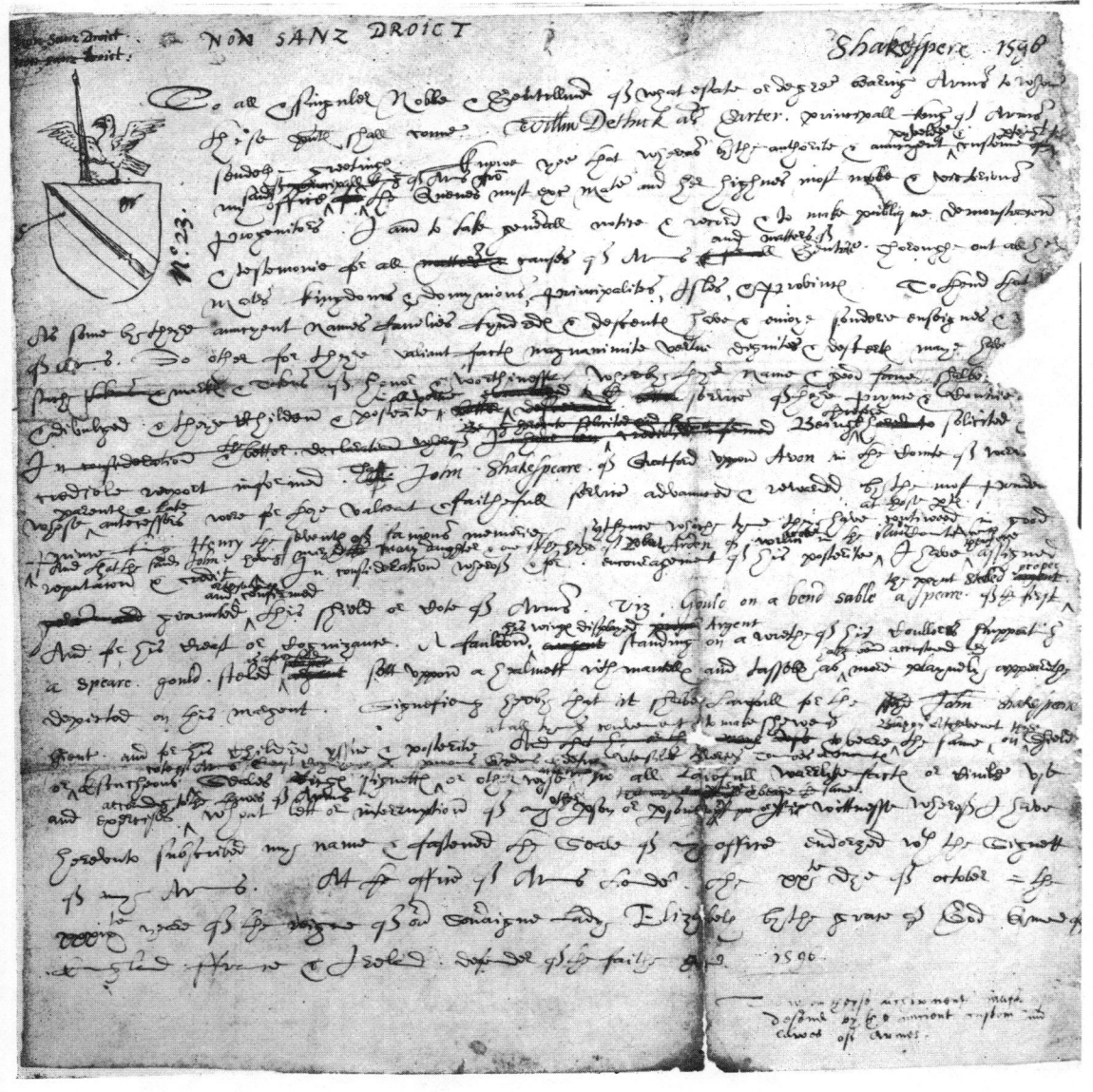

FIG. 6.   First draft of the grant of arms to John Shakespeare, 1596.

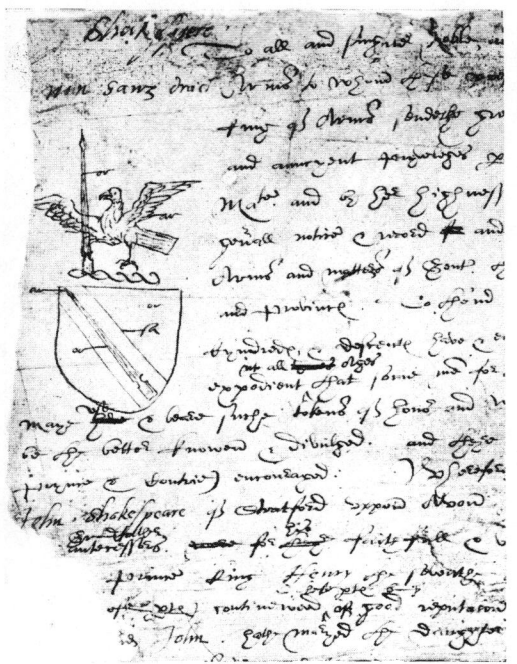

FIG. 7 (a). Portion of second draft of the grant of arms to John Shakespeare, 1596.

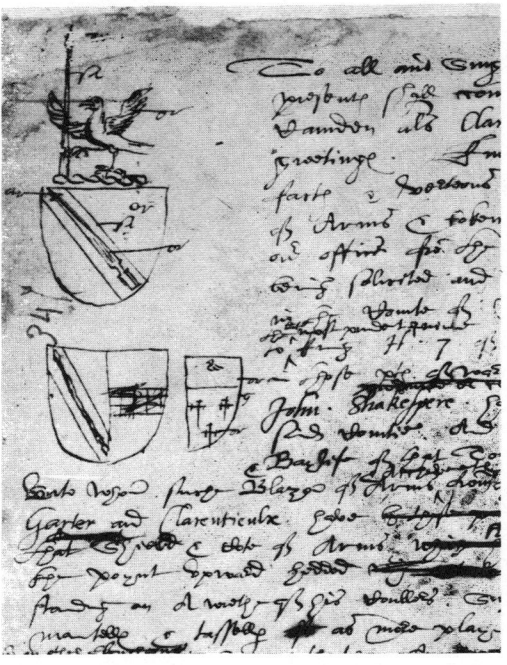

FIG. 7 (b). Portion of exemplification of arms of John Shakespeare with assignment of arms for Arden, 1599.

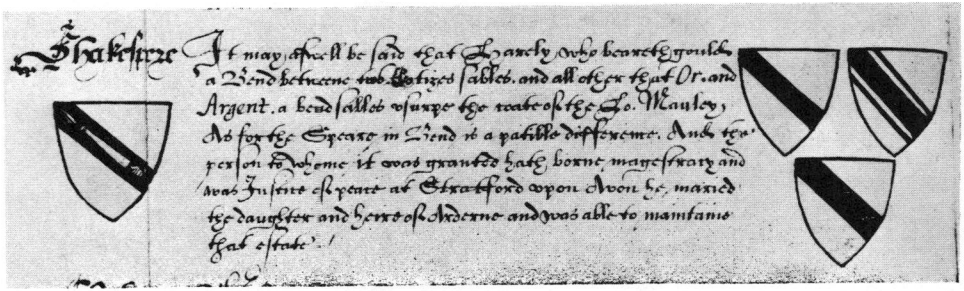

FIG. 7 (c). Answer by Garter and Clarenceux to York Herald's criticism of the arms granted to John Shakespeare.

certeyne enseignes and cottes of Arms, So it is verie expedient in all ages that some men for theyre valeant factes, magnanimite, vertu, dignites and desertes may use and beare suche tokens of honor and worthinesse, whereby theyre name and good fame may be the better knowen and divulged, and theyre children and posterite (in all vertu to the service of theyre Prynce and Contrie) encouraged. Wherefore being solicited and by credible report informed that John Shakespeare of Stratford uppon Avon in the counte of Warwik, whose parentes and late grandfather for his faithfull and valeant service was advaunced and rewarded by the most prudent Prince King Henry the Seventh of famous memorie, sythence which tyme they have continewed in those partes, being of good reputacion and credit, and that the said John hath maryed the daughter and one of the heyrs of Robert Arden of Wilmcote in the said counte esquire, and for the encouragement of his posterite to whom such Blazon or Atchevement by the auncyent Custome of the Lawes of Arms maye descend, I the said Garter King of Arms have assigned, graunted and by these presentes confirmed this shield or cote of Arms, viz. Gould on a Bend sables a Speare of the first steeled argent, And for his creast or cognizance a falcon his winges displayed argent, standing on a wrethe of his coullors, supporting a speare gould steeled as aforesaid, sett uppon a helmett with mantelles and tasselles as hath ben accustomed and dothe more playnely appeare depicted on this margent. Signefieing hereby and by the authorite of my office aforesaid ratefieing that it shalbe lawfull for the said John Shakespeare gent. and for his children, yssue and posterite (at all tymes and places convenient) to beare and make demonstracion of the said Blazon or Atchevement uppon theyre Shieldes, Targets, Escucheons, Cotes of Arms, Pennons, Guydons, Seales, Ringes, Edefices, Buyldinges, Utensiles, Lyveries, Tombes or Monumentes or otherwise for all lawfull warrlyke factes or civile use or exercises according to the Lawes of Arms, and customes that to gentillmen belongeth, without let or interruption of any other person or persons for use or bearing the same. In witnesse and perpetuall remembrance hereof I have hereunto subscribed my name and fastened the seale of my office endorzed with the signett of my Arms. At the Office of Arms London, the xx daye of October the xxxviij yeare of the reigne of our Soveraigne Lady Elizabeth, by the grace of God Quene of England, France and Ireland, Defender of the Fayth etc. 1596.

The following notes are written at the foot of the draft:

This John shoeth a patierne thereof under Clarent. Cookes hand in paper
xx years past.

A Justice of Peace and was Baylife the Q. officer and cheffe of the towne
of Stratford uppo Avon xv or xvi years past.

That he hath lands and tenements of good wealth and substance 500 li.

That he married [a daughter and heyre of Arden, a gent. of worship].

The draft exemplification of 1599 is as follows:

Trick of Shakespeare arms, and impaled arms of Shakespeare and Arden (see fig. 7B)
To all and singuller Noble and Gentelmen of all estates and degrees bearing arms to whom these presentes shall come. William Dethick, Garter principall King of Arms of England and William Camden alias Clarentieulx King of Arms for the Sowthe, East andWeste partes of this Realme sendeth greetinges. Knowe yee that in all nations and kingdoms the record and remembrances of the valeant factes and verteous dispositions of worthie men have ben made knowen and divulged by certeyne shieldes of Arms and tokens of chevalrie, the grant and testemonie wherof apperteynethe unto us by vertu of our offices from the Quenes most excellent majestie and her highness most noble and victorious progenitors. Wherefore being solicited and by credible report informed, That John Shakespere, now of Stratford uppon Avon in the Counte of Warwik, Gent., whose parent, great grandfather and late antecessor for his faithefull and approved service to the late most prudent prince King H 7 of famous memorie, was advaunced and rewarded with landes and tenementes geven to him in those partes of Warwikshere where they have continewed bie some descentes in good reputacion and credit. And for that the said John Shakespere, having maryed the daughter and one of the heyrs of Robert Arden, of Wellingcote[1] in the said Countie, and also produced this his auncient cote of arms heretofore assigned to him whilest he was her Majesties officer and Baylife of that Towne. In consideration of the premisses, and for the encouragement of his posterite unto whom suche Blazon of Arms and Atchevements of inheritance from theyre said mother by the auncyent custome and Lawes of Arms may lawfullie descend, We the said Garter and Clarentieulx have assigned, graunted and confirmed and by these presentes exemplefied unto the said John Shakespere and to his posterite that shield and cote of arms viz. In a field of Gould uppon a Bend Sables a Speare of the first the poynt upward hedded

---

[1] An error, Wilmcote was intended.

Argent, and for his creast or cognizance a Falcon with his wynges displayed standing on a wrethe of his coullers supporting a Speare armed hedded or steeled sylvor fixed uppon a helmet with mantelles and tasselles as more playnely maye appeare depicted on this margent.   And we have lykewise uppon an other escucheone impaled the same with the auncyent arms of the said Arden of Wellingcote,[1] signefeing thereby that it maye and shalbe lawefull for the said John Shakespere gent. to beare and use the same shieldes of arms single or impaled as aforesaid during his natural lyffe, and that it shalbe lawfull for his children, yssue and posterite (lawfully begotten) to beare use and quarter and shewe forthe the same with theyre dewe differences in all lawfull warlyke factes and civile use or exercises, according to the Lawes of Arms and Custome that to Gentelmen belongethe without let or interruption of any person or persons for use or persons bearing the same.   In wytnesse and testemonye wherof we have subscribed our names and fastened the seales of our offices.   Geven at the Office of Arms London the   in the xlij yeare of the reigne of our most gratious Soveraigne Elizabeth by the grace of God [Quene of England] France and Ireland, Defender of the Fayth etc. 1599.

The following[1] is the relevant extract from 'the answeres of Garter and Clarenceux Kings of Arms to the Scrowle of Arms exhibited by Raffe Brokesmouth (or Brooke) called York Herald':

Shakespere.   It may aswell be said that Harely who beareth gould a Bend betweene two Cotizes sable, and all other that [bear] Or and Argent a bend Sables usurpe the coate of the Lo. Mauley.   As for the Speare in Bend [it] is a patible difference. And the person to whome it was granted hath borne magestracy and was Justice of peace at Stratford upon Avon, he maried the daughter and heire of Arderne and was able to maintaine that estate.

In the margins are tricked the arms of Shakespeare, Mauley (*Gold, a bend sable*), and Harley (as above blazoned). Another copy shows the fourth shield as that of Ferrers (*Gold, on a bend sable three silver horseshoes*).

The arms of Shakespeare (without the Arden quartering), with the crest but no motto, appear on William Shakespeare's monument at Stratford-upon-Avon.   The Shakespeare coat is impaled (to the sinister) with that of Hall, *Sable, three gold talbot's heads erased*, on the tombs of John Hall and his wife Susanna, daughter of William Shakespeare. Their daughter, Elizabeth Hall, bore *Quarterly Hall and Shakespeare*,

---

[1] Illustrated in fig. 7C.

and these arms are impaled to the sinister with *Quarterly Nash and Bulstrode* on a shield on the tomb of Thomas Nash who married Elizabeth Hall.   The last two coats are: Nash, *Azure, on a silver chevron between three silver ravens' heads erased, a roundle between four cross-crosslets all sable*; Bulstrode, *Sable, a silver buck's head caboshed with gold antlers, between the antlers a gold cross paty and in the mouth a gold arrow fesswise, point to the dexter.*   (The tinctures of the above coats are not shown on the monuments, and here taken from French, *Shakespeareana Genealogica.*)

Descendants of John Shakespeare, showing their arms.

Thomas Quiney, who married William Shakespeare's daughter Judith, bore for arms, *Gold, on a bend sable three silver trefoils slipped*, and may have impaled the arms of Shakespeare therewith.

During the last hundred years, armorial bearings have been granted to three families of the name of Shakespeare, and in each case a spear or spears on a bend, sometimes with other charges, have formed the arms, while a bird and spear have appeared in the crest.

In 1858, Charles Bowles, who took the name of Shakespeare on inheriting the estate of his uncle John Shakespeare (1774–1858), was granted as arms, *Gold, on a bend indented gules, two gold tilting-spears counterturned* (8) and for crest, *on a mount vert, in front of a falcon with wings elevated per fess azure and gules, a gold tilting-spear erect.* The considerable differences between these armorial bearings and those granted to William Shakespeare's father suggest that the heralds who granted them had little reason to believe that the Shakespeares represented by the grantee were connected with those of Stratford.

FIG. 8. Shakespeare, alias Bowles, granted 1858.　　FIG. 9. Shakespeare, granted 1918.　　FIG. 10. Shakespeare, Bt., granted 1946.

In 1918 a gentleman named Shakespeare was granted, *Gold, on a bend sable a gold tilting-spear headed silver; in chief a grenade sable fired proper, and in base an elephant also proper* (9); Crest: *a falcon, wings endorsed and inverted, proper, supporting with the dexter claw a gold tilting spear in bend, the head silver.*

In 1946, arms were granted to the widow of the late Rev. John Howard Shakespeare, and are now borne by his son, Sir Geoffrey Shakespeare, Bt. These are, *Gold, on a bend sable a gold spear; in chief a portcullis and in base an anchor, both sable* (10). Crest: on a wreath gold and sable, *in front of a portcullis sable, an eagle rising, grasping with the dexter claw a gold spear, barbed silver.* Motto: NON SANZ DROICT. The basic similarity between these arms and those granted to John Shakespeare in 1596 is justified by the strong presumption that the ancestor of Shakespeare Bt., Humphrey Shakespeare of Feckenham, was of the same stock as the Shakespeares of Stratford-upon-Avon.

NON SANZ DROICT has been adopted as the motto of the Warwickshire County Council.

FIG. II. King John in arms, from his Great Seal.

CHAPTER III

KING JOHN

WHEN KING JOHN came to the throne in 1199, the use of heraldic insignia, which had begun some seventy years earlier, was becoming general, at least among the great barons. Nevertheless, few nobles possessed arms going back more than a generation, and many were the first of their line to use them. Even the royal arms of England were of recent adoption, for although Henry II, and possibly Henry I, had used a lion as an emblem, the first definite appearance of the three leopards (later termed lions passant guardant) in the shield of an English king was on the second Great Seal of Richard I, c. 1195 (1).

At this period, heraldic devices were primarily a method of identifying the armoured warrior in the field. For this, the distinctive shield and banner or pennon were sufficient, and in staging *King John* it would be incorrect to show heraldry on anything else. The practice of emblazoning arms on surcoats had not yet begun. Crests were not generally used (the rudimentary crest on Richard I's helm, presently to be dealt with, being exceptional), and Shakespeare was slightly out of period when, in *King John*, he made Salisbury say,

> This is the very top,
> The height, the crest, or crest unto the crest,
> Of murder's arms.

The same applies to the words of the English herald:

> There stuck no plume in any English crest
> That is removed by a staff of France.

FIG. 12. Arms, crown and badges of King John.

The monuments of William Longespée, Earl of Salisbury (3) and William the Marshal, Earl of Pembroke (17), show the shape of the shield, and also the armour and accoutrements of a warrior in the early part of the thirteenth century. The shield was longer than it later became. Banners at this time were oblong, and of considerably greater depth than width.

King John's arms were, *Gules, three gold lions passant guardant* (12 and Pl. IV). These arms are briefly referred to as *England*. On John's Great Seal, from which no. 11 is drawn, the arms appear on his shield alone. However, Richard I's second Great Seal (1), made not more than four years before John's accession, shows the King wearing a helm with a fan-shaped top with a lion passant guardant painted on the side—clearly a forerunner of the heraldic crest. While this does not appear on John's seal, for stage purposes it would be permissible to give him such a crest

FIG. 13.   King John enthroned, from his Great Seal.

when he is in full armour. Alternatively, he might wear round his mail cap a gold circlet heightened with trefoils, such as appears on Richard I's first seal. This would give visual force to his words addressed to the citizens of Angiers:

> Doth not the crown of England prove the king?

It would not be the state crown that the King would wear when in armour, but a circlet of lighter make. The royal crown used on state occasions is shown in no. 12, which is based on the damaged crown on John's effigy at Worcester.

No. 13, based on the obverse of John's Great Seal, shows him enthroned and crowned, and bearing the sword of state and sceptre. When he appears thus in the play, his arms may be displayed behind the throne, and his badges may be worked into the decorations. These were the *planta genista*, derived from Geoffrey 'Plantagenet'[1] of Anjou, and a star above a crescent, probably representing the sun and moon (12).

Prince Henry probably bore the same arms as his father. The practice of differencing the arms of the King's eldest son with a label began with the next generation; but if it is thought desirable for dramatic purposes, a blue label might be added to the shield of England in the case of Prince Henry (14).

It is significant that in a play in which the symbol of the lion figures prominently, its only application to King John suggests a cowed beast in need of rousing:

> What, shall they seek the lion in his den,
> And fright him there? and make him tremble there?
> O, let it not be said: forage, and run
> To meet displeasure farther from the doors,
> And grapple with him ere he come so nigh.
>
> (*v*, 1)

Indeed, the regal and heroic figure in the play, particularly associated with the lion emblem, is not the King, not one of the historical persons, but a symbolic character representing the spirit and valour of the Plantagenets. John is uneasy in his 'borrow'd majesty' held by 'strong possession' and propped up by a double coronation. His nephew and rival, Arthur, is but a 'little prince having so great a title to be more prince.' Only at the end of the play does Prince Henry put on 'the lineal state and glory of the land.' Royalty lies rather in him who came 'one way of the Plantagenets,' Philip, the bastard son of Coeur-de-Lion. Dubbed knight in his father's name, 'Sir Richard, and Plantagenet,' avenger of Richard's death, exhorter of Richard's successor to 'show boldness and aspiring confidence' in the face of invasion and rebellion, Philip appears to be something more than the late King's bastard: he is a projection of Coeur-de-Lion not only in the 'large composition' of his body, but also in heart and spirit. In very truth he could say to the Dauphin,

> Now hear our English king,
> For thus his royalty doth speak in me.

Shakespeare derived the Bastard from his source-play, *The Trouble-*

---

[1] Geoffrey was so called from his practice of wearing a sprig of broom in his cap. While his descendants were collectively known as the house of Plantagenet, the name was not applied to individuals until the latter part of the fifteenth century, and Shakespeare used licence when he employed it as a surname in the earlier plays.

some Raigne of King John, and ultimately from a reference in Holinshed:

> The same year [1199] Philip, bastard son to King Richard, to whome his
> father had given the castell and honor of Coinacke,[1] killed the viscount
> of Limoges in revenge of his father's death, who was slaine (as yee have
> heard) in besieging the castell of Chaluns Cheverell.

For the association of this Philip with the Faulconbridges, Shakespeare
had no grounds. He seems to have picked on the name of Faulconbridge
through a recollection of the historical Bastard of Fauconberg, a natural
son of Sir William Neville, Baron of Fauconberg and Earl of Kent, in the
fifteenth century.

FIG. 14. England with a   FIG. 15. Philip the Bastard,   FIG. 16. William Longespée,
label, for Prince Henry.   'Sir Richard Plantagenet.'   Earl of Salisbury.

Clearly, no true armorial bearings can be assigned to a character who
is at best pseudo-historical, but he may be credited with the arms Richard I
used when the Bastard was born, with a suitable brizure to denote
illegitimacy.

Philip must have been born before Richard came to the English throne.
Richard's early arms, as shown on his first Great Seal, consisted of a single
lion rampant to the sinister. (The shield is rounded, and it has been
conjectured that the hidden half bore a second lion rampant to the dexter,
making the arms two lions combatant; but while arguments may be advanced in support of this theory, the only known fact is that Richard's
seal shows a single lion on his shield.) The early arms of Richard I are
therefore held to have been *Gules, a gold lion rampant to the sinister*; to

---

[1] Cognac, in Guienne; Speed says it was Sumac, in Poictou, and that Philip's descendants bore the
name of Sumac.

which his bastard son may have added (as the most likely difference for illegitimacy at that time) *a baston azure* (15).

Associated with Richard I's use of a lion as a device—and probably arising from it—is the nick-name Coeur-de-Lion, and the legend that during his captivity in Austria, Richard was pitted against a lion and tore out the beast's heart, afterwards stripping it of the hide. To quote the ancient romance:

> The lyon was hongry and megre,
> And bette his tayle to be egre;
> He loked aboute as he were madde;
> Abrode he all his pawes spradde.
> He cryde lowde, and yaned wyde.
> Kynge Richarde bethought hym that tyde
> What hym was beste, and to hym sterte,
> In at the throte his honde he gerte,
> And rente out the herte with his honde,
> Lounges and all that he there fonde.
> The lyon fell deed to the grounde:
> Rycharde felte no wem, ne wounde.
> He fell on his knees on that place,
> And thanked Jesu of his grace.
> (Romance of *Richard Ceur-de-Lyon*.)

To this Shakespeare refers in *King John*, when Philip the Bastard says to his mother:

> Needs must you lay your heart at his dispose,
> Subjected tribute to commanding love,
> Against whose fury and unmatched force
> The aweless lion could not wage the fight,
> Nor keep his princely heart from Richard's hand.
> He that perforce robs lions of their hearts
> May easily win a woman's.
> (*i*, 1)

It is the skin of the very lion Richard killed that the Duke of Austria wears in *King John*. Shakespeare leaves this to be inferred, but it is clearly stated in the source-play, *The Troublesome Raigne*. As the name indicates, 'Lymoges, Duke of Austria' is a composite character blended of Leopold, Duke of Austria, who held Richard captive on his return from the Holy Land, and the Viscount of Limoges against whom Richard was warring when he met his death. Austria is thus Richard's comprehensive

enemy, flaunting the skin of the dead lion in triumph at Coeur-de-Lion's
overthrow—a challenge which Richard's son takes up:

The Troublesome Raigne—

> *Bastard:* My father's foe clad in my father's spoil!
> A thousand furies kindle with revenge
> This heart . . .
> Delay not, Philip, kill the villain straight,
> Disrobe him of the matchless monument,
> Thy father's triumph o'er the savages.

King John—

> *Bastard:* You are the hare of whom the proverb goes,
> Whose valour plucks dead lions by the beard:
> I'll smoke your skin-coat, an I catch you right;
> Sirrah, look to't; i' faith I will, i' faith.
> *Blanche:* O, well did he become that lion's robe
> That did disrobe the lion of that robe!
> *Bastard:* It lies as sightly on the back of him
> As great Alcides' shoes upon an ass:
> But, ass, I'll take that burthen from your back,
> Or lay on that shall make your shoulders crack.   (*ii*, 1)

Constance, Arthur's mother, when Austria favours the truce between
England and France to her son's detriment, rounds on him with a sneer
at his lion's skin in the words 'ramping fool,' and—

> Thou wear a lion's hide? doff it for shame,
> And hang a calf's skin on those recreant limbs;

whereupon the Bastard seizes on the last line and harps on it provocatively.

In *The Troublesome Raigne*, the Bastard pounces on the lion's skin, and
is wearing it himself when he slays Austria. In *King John* he merely
comes on with Austria's head, and we hear no more of the skin, but a leaf
might be taken from the old play to make the Bastard wear the skin after
Austria's death.

Among other characters in the play, heraldic pride of place must be
given to the King's bastard brother, William Longespée, or Longsword,
Earl of Salisbury. He bore an armorial shield derived from as far back
as his grandfather, Geoffrey of Anjou. This shield is blazoned, *Azure,
six gold lions rampant* (16). Its significance as marking the emergence of
true heraldry from the unmethodical decoration of earlier times, and also
pointing to the lion as an emblem of royalty in England as early as Henry
I's reign, has been dealt with in Chapter I. William Longespée also used
as a device his long sword, and this appeared on his seal.

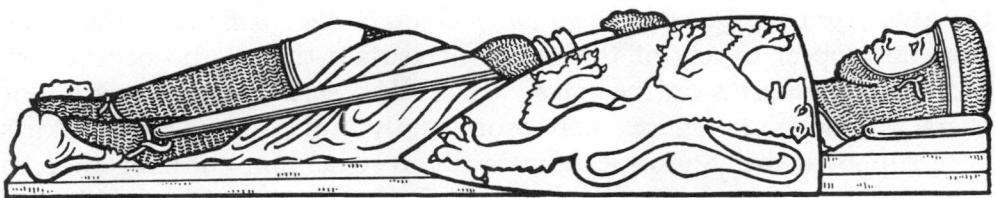

FIG. 17. William the Marshal, Earl of Pembroke : effigy on his tomb.

William the Marshal, Earl of Pembroke, son of John, Marshal of England in the reign of Richard I, succeeded his father in that office and bore the arms appropriate to it: *Per pale gold and vert, a lion rampant gules* (18). He became Earl of Pembroke in 1199, having married the daughter and heir of the last Earl, Richard de Clare. He died in 1219, and was buried in the Temple Church, London, where his effigy (17) remained until the bombing of the church in the Second World War.

His five sons, successively Marshals of England and Earls of Pembroke, died childless, and his eldest daughter carried the office of Marshal to her husband, Hugh Bigot, Earl of Norfolk, son of the next named.

The Lord Bigot in *King John* is Roger le Bigot, Earl of Norfolk and Suffolk, who was sometimes styled Earl Bigot. He bore *Gold, a cross gules* (19). About 1300 his successors ceased to use these arms and took those of the office of Marshal.

The Earl of Essex in *King John*, since he appears only in the early part of the play, is presumed to be Geoffrey FitzPiers, who was Earl from 1199

FIG. 18. William the Marshal.
Earl of Pembroke.

FIG. 19. Roger le Bigot,
Earl of Norfolk.

FIG. 20. Geoffrey FitzPiers,
Earl of Essex.

to 1213. He bore *Quarterly gold and gules, a bordure vaire* (20), but as he does not appear in any of the scenes of warfare there is no occasion to represent these arms on the stage. In Shakespeare's play he is a minor character, though he figures more prominently in the source-play. It has been supposed that Shakespeare intended to strike him out altogether, to avoid any risk of implied reference to the Earl of Essex of Elizabeth's day, and that the Earl's brief appearance in *King John* is an oversight. It is certainly significant that no other Earl of Essex figures in one of Shakespeare's plays.

FIG. 21. Banner of Austria.   FIG. 22. Royal Arms of   FIG. 23. Banner of Bretagne.
France.

It is unlikely that Shakespeare intended the Hubert de Burgh of the play to represent the historical person of that name whom Henry III created Earl of Kent. The real Hubert was descended from Robert of Mortain, the Conqueror's half-brother, and connected with some of the great ruling families. Bigot would scarcely address such a man as, 'Out, dunghill! darest thou brave a nobleman?' nor would King John describe him as

> A fellow by the hand of nature mark'd,
> Quoted and sign'd to do a deed of shame.

The historical Hubert de Burgh bore for arms *Lozengy gules and vaire.* The Hubert of the play is not of a station to which heraldic arms appertained, and it would be out of character to give him an armorial shield.

For stage purposes, Philip, King of France, may be given a shield and banner, *Azure, semé of gold fleurs-de-lys* (i.e. *France Ancient*—22) though this may be slightly to antedate the use of a shield of arms by a King of France.   His son, Lewis, may bear these arms with a label.   The eldest son of the French King was not yet called the Dauphin, and did not bear the dolphin in his arms, the Dauphiné being held at this date by the Count of the Viennois.

As the Duke of Austria is a composite and unhistorical character, it would be misleading to credit him with genuine arms, and in any case the

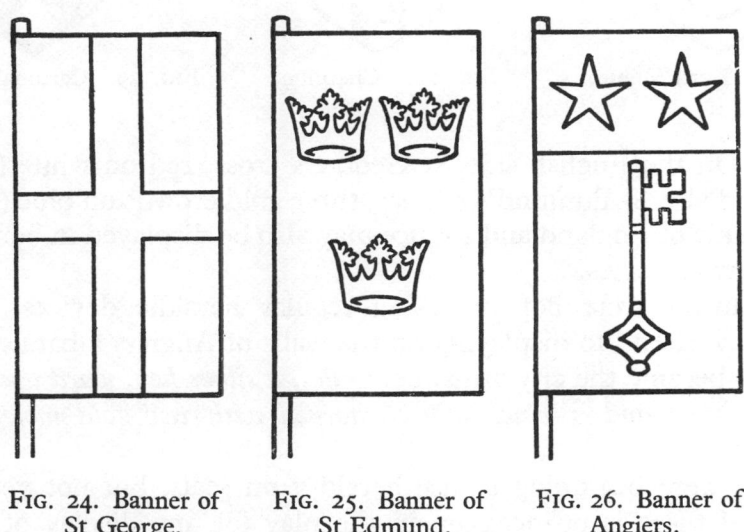

FIG. 24. Banner of
St George.

FIG. 25. Banner of
St Edmund.

FIG. 26. Banner of
Angiers.

lion's skin sufficiently distinguishes him.   However, in the scene before Angiers, where his colours are mentioned, the banner of the duchy of Austria, *Gules, a silver fess* (21), may be displayed.

Arthur of Bretagne, posthumous son of John's elder brother, Geoffrey, is represented by Shakespeare as too young a boy to use heraldic arms. No arms are attributed to him, nor are any needed for stage purposes, but the ermine banner of Bretagne (23) may be borne among the 'flags of France' advanced before Angiers.

'The dancing banners of the French' may also include the oriflamme, a scarlet streamer, its fly cut into three tongues, each ending in a green tassel. Rodway illustrates the banner of St Denis, a white cross on blue; that of St Martin, a gold cross on blue; and that of Bretagne, a black cross

C

FIG. 27. Lord Melun.   FIG. 28. Chatillon.   FIG. 29. Cardinal Pandulph.

on gold. On the English side St George's cross, red on white (24), may appear, and also St Edmund's banner, three gold crowns on blue (25). The royal insignia of England and France may also be displayed in banner form in the martial scenes.

While towns were not yet using regular heraldic devices, dramatic licence may extend to displaying on the walls of Angiers a banner bearing what later became the city arms, i.e. *Gules, a silver key, ward upwards and to the sinister, and a chief azure charged with two gold molets of five points* (26).

Women were beginning to use heraldry on seals, but not yet on garments, and there is no occasion in the play for any display of armorial devices by Queen Elinor, Constance of Bretagne, or Blanch of Spain.

The French lord Melun may be assumed to have borne what were later the arms of the family of that name, *Azure, six gold roundles and a gold chief* (27). The roundles probably represent melons, allusive to the name. Chatillon does not appear in any scene in which the use of heraldry would be appropriate; he may be regarded as a member of the family of Chatillon, Counts of St Pol, who bore, *Gules, three pallets vaire and a gold chief* (28). Cardinal Pandulph is credited with arms: *Sable, a cross of gold lozenges, and in the first and second quarters a gold escallop shell* (29).

As the coat of arms had not yet been introduced, the English and French heralds should appear in the costume of the period without any heraldic garment, though to identify them on the stage they might wear as a badge one lion or one fleur-de-lys respectively. The stage directions in act ii, sc.1., *Enter Herald of France with trumpets*, and *Enter English*

Fig. 30. Falkes de Bréauté.   Fig. 31. The Earl of Chester.   Fig. 32. The Earl of Clare.

Herald with trumpet, have contributed to the misconception that the instrument was part of a herald's equipment. For 'trumpet' we must understand 'trumpeter'. Heralds did not carry trumpets, or blow their own fanfares; they left this duty to their attendants.

In King John's reign, *Dieu et mon Droit* had not yet become the English royal motto; nevertheless Shakespeare seems to refer to it indirectly in the play. To the French King, championing the cause of Arthur, he gives the words, 'God and our right', while he makes John assert his title to the throne in the declaration,

> Our strong possession and our right for us,

as though substituting his own might for the divine will.

In scenes where a display of shields and banners is needed to indicate the presence of barons and knights, additional to those named by Shakespeare, the following arms may be shown. They are mostly taken from the marginal shields painted in manuscripts of Matthew Paris's *Chronica Majora,* which forms one of our earliest heraldic records.

Gules, a gold lion rampant.—William, Earl of Arundel.

Gules, a silver cinquefoil.—Falkes de Bréauté; he is thought to have contributed to the character of Philip the Bastard, but we should not be justified in assigning to Philip the arms of de Bréauté (30).

Gules, three gold fleurs-de-lys.—William de Cantelupe.

Azure, three gold wheatsheaves.—Ranulph, Earl of Chester (31).

Gold, three chevrons gules.—Richard, Earl of Clare and Hertford (32).[1]

Gold, a fess between two chevrons, all gules.—Robert FitzWalter; being

[1] Illustrated in colour in Plate II.

akin to the family of Clare, he differenced their arms by changing the middle chevron to a fess (60).

Gold, three chevrons gules, a label azure.—Richard de Muntfichet; he was also kin to the family de Clare.

Azure, a silver bend between six gold lions rampant.—Henry de Bohun, Earl of Hereford; this is an early form of the de Bohun arms; later the bend was placed between gold bendlets, or cotices.

Gold, three bars azure, over all a bend gules.—Gilbert de Gant, Earl of Lincoln.

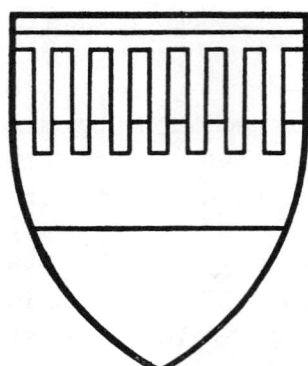  

FIG. 33. DeQuincey, Earl of Winchester.   FIG. 34. De Percy.   FIG. 35. De Vesci.

Quarterly gules and gold, in the first quarter a silver molet.—Aubrey de Vere, Earl of Oxford (169).[1]

Gold, a fess gules, a label of seven points azure.—Saer de Quincey, Earl of Winchester (33).

Azure, five silver lozenges cojoined fesswise.—Richard de Percy (34); these were the ancient arms of Percy, which were later superseded by *Gold, a lion rampant azure.*

Gules, three silver water-budgets.—Robert de Ros (58).[2]

Gules, a silver cross paty.—Eustace de Vesci (35).

Checky gold and azure.—Hamelin, Earl of Warren.

Barruly silver and azure.—Hugh le Brun, Count of Marche, who was taken prisoner by King John at the same time as Arthur.

[1] Illustrated in colour in Plate II.
[2] Illustrated in colour in Plate III.

TABLE I

CHARACTERS IN *KING JOHN*

The following table shows the relationship between the principal persons in the play (whose names are in capitals), dates being omitted as inapplicable since Shakespeare compressed the events of sixteen years into a stage time of four months.

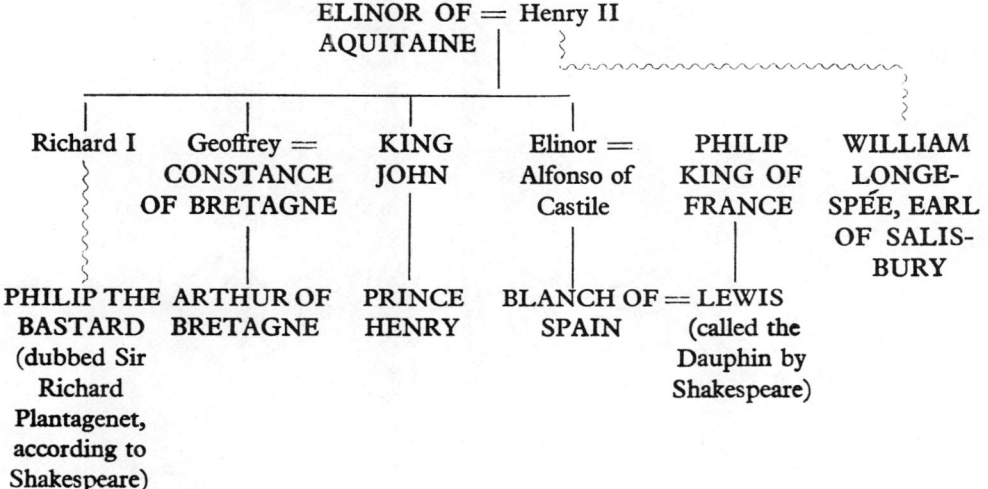

FIG. 36. Richard II, from his Great Seal.

CHAPTER IV

KING RICHARD II

COMPARE THE armoured figure on Richard II's Great Seal (36) with that on John's, and the advance made by heraldry in the course of two hundred years is at once apparent. The royal arms now consisted of two quartered coats, and appeared on the surcoat and horse-bardings as well as on the shield. The helm was topped by a crest. Another important development (not illustrated by this seal) was the extensive use of badges. By the reign of Richard II, heraldry was fully developed except for supporters of arms, and these (as will be seen) were beginning to make their appearance.

Before dealing in particular with the arms of the characters in *Richard II*, the development of royal heraldry since the reign of King John must be briefly surveyed. The methods of differencing the royal arms employed by the sons of Edward III will then be noted, and the characters connected with the royal house will be dealt with in order of their descent from Edward III.

The Royal Arms

The three lions passant guardant, gold upon red, forming the arms of England, remained the royal arms until the reign of Edward III. To these arms, cadets of the royal house added some differencing mark. In the case of the King's eldest son, this was a blue label of three or five points (14), which was removed from his shield when he succeeded to the throne. The differences of junior lines became permanent in the arms. Thus Edmund, second son Henry III, added to the arms of England a label of France, i.e. *azure, semé of gold fleurs-de-lys* (derived from his wife), and this became the characteristic difference of his successors, the Earls and Dukes of Lancaster (48). Edward I's second surviving son, Thomas of Brotherton, bore *England with a silver label*, and these arms were quartered by his descendants, the Dukes of Norfolk. Edmund of Woodstock, youngest son of Edward I, bore *England with a silver bordure*, and these became the arms of a branch of the family of Holland which descended from him (53). We shall encounter instances of these arms in the heraldry of Shakespeare's characters.

In the early part of his reign, Edward III bore the arms of England alone, but in 1340 he made a significant change: as an heraldic indication of his claim to the French throne, he incorporated in his shield the arms of France (i.e. France Ancient: *Azure, semé of gold fleurs-de-lys*), placing them in the first and fourth quarters of his shield, and the arms of England in the second and third quarters. *France Ancient and England quarterly* (41) remained the English royal arms until about 1405.

Edward III is the first English king after Richard I who is known to have used a crest upon his helm. This was a gold lion, crowned with an open crown, standing on a red chapeau guarded with ermine. On seals and paintings the lion is shown guardant, i.e. with his head turned so as to face the spectator, but when actually worn on the helm it would no doubt look straight before it, as it does on the Black Prince's helm preserved at Canterbury. This point should be observed in stage productions. The crested helm was used in tournaments and other occasions of pageantry rather than in war, and it would be unrealistic to make any general use of crests in battle scenes; nevertheless, for dramatic purposes it is permissible to give the king a crest of moderate size.

In 1348, Edward III founded the Order of the Garter, and within a few years some members of the Order, in representations of their arms, began to encircle their shields with the blue Garter with its motto, in gold letters, HONY SOIT QY MAL Y PENSE. Richard II's shield may be shown encircled by the Garter, as in no. 41, though this practice did not become usual with the royal arms until later. While possessing a high prestige, the Garter at this date had not the pre-eminence it later enjoyed. It rarely appears on effigies of the fourteenth or early fifteenth century; there are a number of effigies of Knights of the Order wearing collars of York or Lancaster, but not their Garters. An example of an armoured knight wearing the Garter is provided by the monument of Sir Simon de Felbrigge (66).

A badge of Edward III, adopted in reference to the manor of Woodstock, was a gold stock of a tree, uprooted and cut short (37). This may have been in Shakespeare's mind when he referred to Edward's sons as

> seven fair branches springing from one root.

The badge was used by Edward's son, Thomas of Woodstock, so named because he was born there. Thomas, who became Duke of Gloucester, was murdered at Calais in 1397. It was believed that Thomas Mowbray, Duke of Norfolk, was chiefly concerned in his death, with the connivance of Richard II. The Duchess of Gloucester, appealing to John of Gaunt to avenge her husband's death, uses a metaphor which may again have been suggested by the Woodstock badge:

> . . . Thomas, my dear lord, my life, my Gloucester,
> One vial full of Edward's sacred blood,
> One flourishing branch of his most royal root,
> Is crack'd, and all the precious liquor spilt,
> Is hack'd down, and his summer leaves all faded,
> By envy's hand, and murder's bloody axe.
>
> (i, 2)

Fig. 37.
The Badge of Woodstock

This is a piece of the imagery which (as Dr Caroline Spurgeon points out) runs through the historical plays, namely 'growth as seen in garden and orchard, with deterioration, decay and destruction brought about by the ignorance and carelessness on the part of the gardener . . . or on the other hand by the rash and untimely cutting or lopping of fine trees.'[1] The

[1] *Shakespeare's Imagery.*

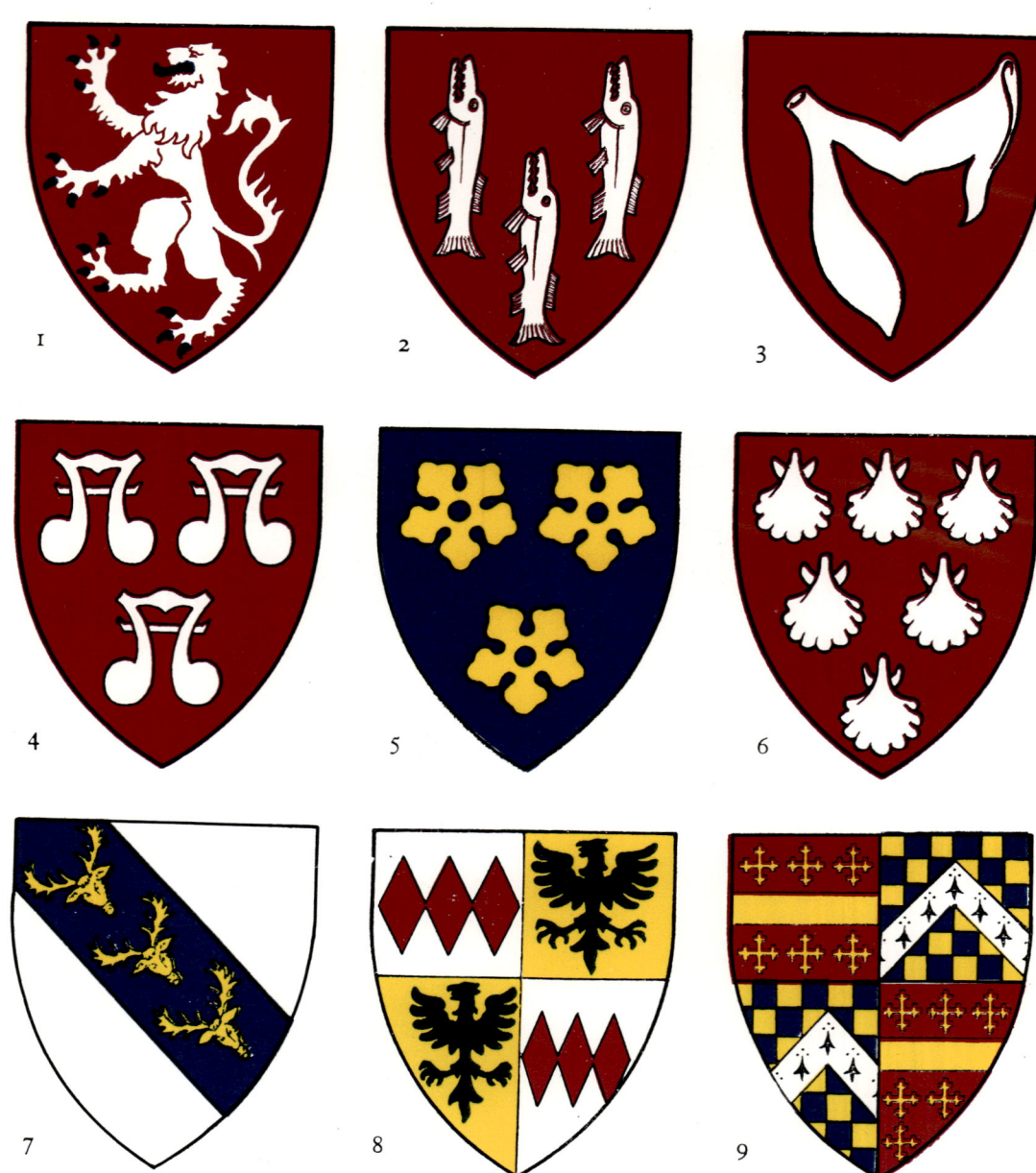

PLATE III. Some ancient shields of arms, illustrating common heraldic charges.

1. Mowbray	2. Lucy	3. Hastings
4. De Ros	5. Bardolph	6. Scales
7. Stanley	8. Montagu and Monthermer quarterly	9. Beauchamp and Neubourg quarterly

metaphor was probably suggested to Shakespeare by the royal badges of plants, flowers and trees: *planta genista*,[1] the roses of York and Lancaster, and the Woodstock badge. The allusions to such heraldic emblems must therefore be viewed against the general background of imagery representing the royal house as a tree, and its members as branches, sprays, flowers and thorns.

The sons of Edward III, were:

1. Edward, Prince of Wales: he had two shields of arms, one for war and the other for peace:

FIG. 38.   Shield for War.   FIG. 39.   Shield for Peace.
Edward, the ' Black Prince.'

In war was never lion rag'd more fierce,
In peace was never gentle lamb more mild,
Than was that young and princely gentleman.
(*Richard II, ii,* 1)

His shield for war bore his father's arms, *France Ancient and England quarterly*, with a silver label of three points (38). (The colour of the heir's label was changed from blue to silver when the introduction of the French arms, with their azure field, made a blue label insufficiently distinctive. The silver label has ever since remained the appropriate difference of the heir apparent to the throne.) The Prince's shield for peace, probably derived from the heraldry of his mother, Philippa of Hainault, was *Sable, three silver ostrich feathers, their quills passing through scrolls, on each scroll*

---

[1] See 3 Henry VI: 'Plant Plantagenet, root him up who dares.'

the words ICH DIENE (39). The predominant sable of these arms, repeated on his surcoat and horse-bardings, gave rise to his nick-name, 'the Black Prince,' to which Shakespeare refers in *Henry V*, when the French King recalls

> our too much memorable shame
> When Cressy battle fatally was struck,
> And all our princes captiv'd, by the hand
> Of that black name, Edward, Black Prince of Wales;
> Whiles that his mountain sire, on mountain standing,
> Up in the air, crown'd with the golden sun,
> Saw his heroical seed, and smil'd to see him . . . .
>
> (*ii*, 4)

(Incidentally, though Shakespeare did not necessarily have it in mind when he wrote these lines, a burst of sunrays was a badge of Edward III—45.)

Though by later usage the ostrich feathers became associated with the heir to the throne, they were not at this time peculiar to the Prince of Wales. Variously tinctured and differenced, they were used as badges by other descendants of Edward III.

The Black Prince married Joan, daughter of Edmund of Woodstock, Earl of Kent, youngest son of Edward I; she was the widow of Sir Thomas Holland. The heraldry of the Black Prince's son, Richard II, is dealt with later. Joan's son by her first marriage was the father of the Duke of Surrey in *Richard II*.

2. William of Hatfield, died young.

3. Lionel of Antwerp became Earl of Ulster *iure uxoris*, having married Elizabeth, daughter and heir of William de Burgh, the former Earl. He accordingly differenced the royal arms with a gold label of five points, each charged with a red cross (40a), derived from the arms of Ulster, *Gold, a cross gules*. On being created Duke of Clarence (i.e. the honour of Clare, his wife's grandmother having been the heiress of Gilbert de Clare, Earl of Hertford and Gloucester), he assumed the appropriate difference, a silver label of three points, each charged with a canton gules (40b). His only child, Philippa, married Edmund Mortimer, third Earl of March, who accordingly bore, *Quarterly Mortimer and Ulster* (82), the Mortimer coat being, *Gold, three bars azure, on a gold chief two pallets azure between two gyrons azure and over all a silver inescutcheon.*[1]

---

[1] The arms of Mortimer are shown in colour in Plate II.

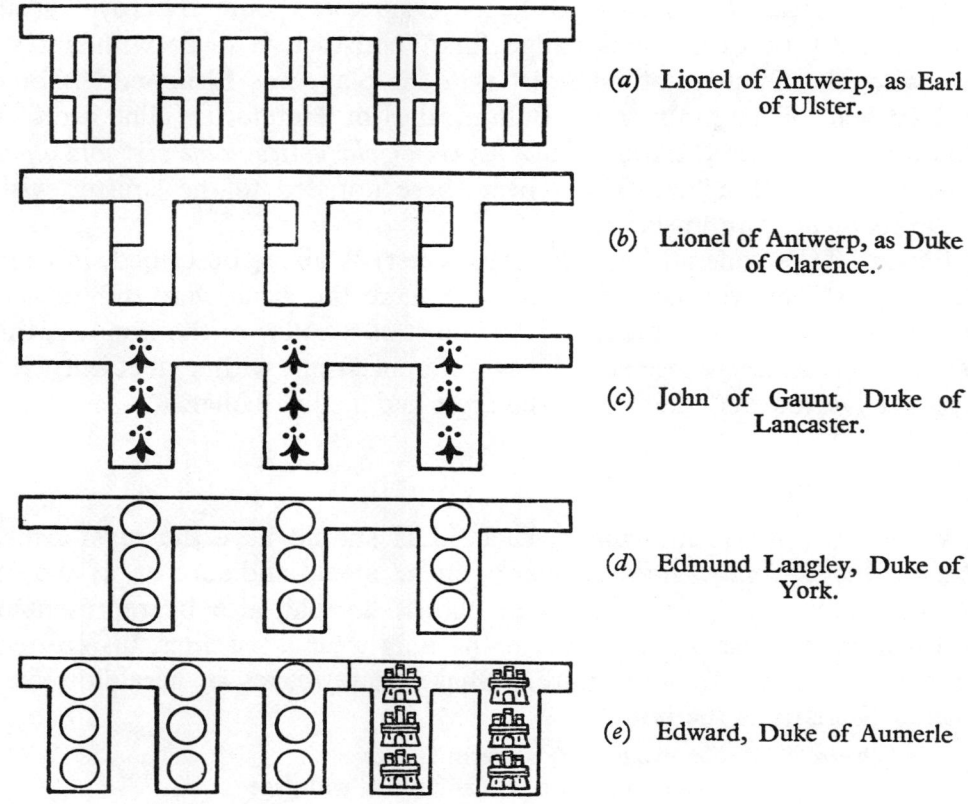

(a) Lionel of Antwerp, as Earl of Ulster.

(b) Lionel of Antwerp, as Duke of Clarence.

(c) John of Gaunt, Duke of Lancaster.

(d) Edmund Langley, Duke of York.

(e) Edward, Duke of Aumerle

FIG. 40. Labels of the Plantagenets.

Earl Edmund and Philippa had three children:

(i) Roger, who became the fourth Earl, and had a son, Edmund, the Earl of March in *Henry IV*.

(ii) Sir Edmund Mortimer.

(iii) Elizabeth (called 'Kate' by Shakespeare) who married Sir Henry Percy ('Hotspur').

Shakespeare confuses Sir Edmund Mortimer with his nephew Edmund, son of Earl Roger. It was Sir Edmund who fought Glendower and married his daughter, but it was Edmund, the fifth Earl, who was recognised by Richard II as heir to the throne. (See Table III, page 92.)

4. John of Gaunt, Duke of Lancaster—see *Lancaster and Bolingbroke*.

5. Edmund Langley, Duke of York—see *York and Aumerle*.

6. William of Windsor, died young.

7. Thomas of Woodstock, Duke of Gloucester, bore the royal arms with a silver bordure. His badge for Woodstock is dealt with above. His wife, the Duchess of Gloucester in the play, was Eleanor, daughter and co-heir of Humphrey de Bohun, Earl of Hereford. The arms of Bohun were, *Azure, a silver bend between gold cotices and six gold lions rampant.* The Duchess would bear these impaled to the sinister with the arms of her late husband.

Edward III's sons all bore the royal crest, as above described, in each case with the appropriate difference. Where the arms were differenced with a label, this was repeated on the crest as a collar to the lion. In the case of Gloucester, whose shield was differenced not with a label but with a plain silver border, the lion in the crest had a silver collar.

King Richard II

Where he appears in armour, Richard II should have the royal arms, *France Ancient and England quarterly,* on his shield and surcoat, as shown on his Great Seal (36). As stated above, he may also be represented with the royal crest on his helm; or he may wear a bascinet, his crested helm being carried by an esquire. Shakespeare makes an heraldic reference to Richard as the lion:

> *Queen:* The lion dying thrusteth forth his paw,
> And wounds the earth, if nothing else, with rage
> To be o'erpower'd; and wilt thou pupil-like
> Take the correction, mildly kiss the rod,
> And fawn on rage with base humility,
> Which art a lion and the king of beasts?
>
> *K. Richard:* A king of beasts, indeed; if aught but beasts,
> I had been still a happy king of men.
>
> (*v*, 1)

In Richard's banner, and in emblazonments of his arms about his court, he made an innovation of some significance: he impaled the royal arms with those attributed to Edward the Confessor, *Azure, a gold cross flory and five gold doves;* placing the Confessor's arms in the dexter half, and the quartered arms of France Ancient and England in the sinister (42). Holinshed attributes this to self-glorification, speaking of Richard as

> esteeming himselfe higher in degree than anie prince living, and so pre-
> sumed further even than his grandfather did, and tooke upon him to beare
> the armes of saint Edward, ioining them unto his owne armes.

FIG. 41. Arms and crest of Richard II.   FIG. 42. Banner of Richard II.

Against this view must be set the fact that Richard was not alone in impaling the Confessor's arms. His kinsmen Bolingbroke and Surrey both did so, presumably with the King's consent and perhaps at his recommendation. Mowbray, Duke of Norfolk, also did so by grant from Richard II. The banners of the national Saints George, Edmund, and Edward the Confessor were commonly displayed in military array beside the banner of the royal arms, and it was only a step from this to combining the arms of saint and king in one banner. Richard's motive may have been piety rather than vainglory. However, Holinshed's view of the matter may have contributed to Shakespeare's portrayal of Richard as presumptuous in his claim to divine sanction and support: witness the parallel he draws between himself and Christ in the deposition scene, and such lines as:—

> . . . we thought ourself thy lawful king;
> And if we be, how dare thy joints forget
> To pay their awful duty to our presence?
> If we be not, show us the hand of God
> That hath dismiss'd us from our stewardship . . .
> . . . my master, God omnipotent,
> Is mustering in his clouds on our behalf
> Armies of pestilence.   (*iii*, 3)

Here another feature of Richard II's heraldry may be noted. Consistent with his claim to divine appointment, and his association of St Edward's arms with his own, is his adoption of angels to support his shield. In the roof of Westminster Hall, which he rebuilt,[1] Richard placed a line of angels, each holding a shield of his arms. Alone, these might be regarded merely as an architectural feature of no more heraldic significance than the angel roofs in many churches; but he carried the theme further, flanking the entrance to the hall with shields of the Confessor's arms and his own, each supported by three angels, one on each side and one behind the shield with his hart badge below it. Boutell, in his *Manual of Heraldry*, regarded Richard's use of angels as heraldic, and saw in them the precursors of the supporters of the royal arms which developed in the fifteenth century. It may well be that Shakespeare had seen the double rank of angels in Westminster Hall, each bearing a shield of Richard's arms, and the angels grouped about his shield at the entrance to the Hall, and that the impression they made on his mind came out in the lines:

> For every man that Bolingbroke hath press'd
> To lift shrewd steel against our golden crown,
> God for his Richard hath in heavenly pay
> A glorious angel: then, if angels fight,
> Weak men must fall, for heaven still guards the right.
>
>   (*iii*, 2)

It may also be noted that in the Wilton Diptych the angels grouped about

---

[1] It is said that the first meeting of Parliament in the Hall which Richard had so nobly restored was for the purpose of his deposition. 'Had Shakespeare been aware of these facts,' writes Professor Dover Wilson, ' he would assuredly have made dramatic capital out of them.'

the Madonna all wear Richard's badge of a white hart and collars of broom-cods, as though his partisans.

In the setting of the play for stage or film, it would certainly be appropriate in the court scenes, and particularly in the deposition scene in Westminster Hall, to show the arms of the Confessor and Richard II upheld by angels; and in the scenes in the field, to display the arms impaled on a square banner (42). Such a banner appears on the monumental brass (at Felbrigg, Norfolk) to Sir Simon de Felbrigge, Richard's banner-bearer (66).

  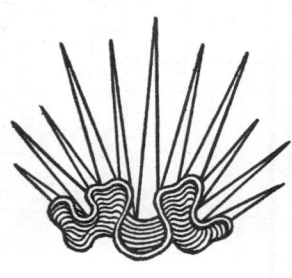

FIG. 43. Planta genista.   FIG. 44. The white hart.   FIG. 45. The sunburst.
                            Badges of Richard II.

There is another piece of Richard II's heraldry which is freely used in the imagery of the play, namely his badge of the sun; or rather, his two badges, for he used both the 'sun-burst' (45) derived from Edward III, and the 'sun-in-splendour'—the full orb surrounded by rays (46). The sun is, of course, a natural and common emblem of sovereignty, used by several English kings, but particularly by Richard II. If it occurred only casually in the play, we might regard it as no more than a happy chance that in using this symbol of majesty Shakespeare picked on one of the King's badges. But in fact Shakespeare employs the sun image in Richard II with such frequency and dramatic effect as to suggest that he knew full well that the sun was the special emblem of this King, and that he was using it with conscious regard to its heraldic aptness. Shakespeare could have seen the sun-burst, with the *planta genista* (43) and the white hart (44), on the robes of Richard II's effigy in Westminster Abbey. In dramatic presentation it would add point to some of the passages quoted below if the King were to appear with the sun worked into his garments. However, it should *not* be placed on the surcoat worn over his armour (as has been done), the heraldic surcoat being the place for a man's arms, not his badges. The sun appeared on Richard's standard, and on the sail of the ship which carried him on his Irish expedition; and no doubt so favourite a device would be extensively used in the decoration of the court. Professor Dover Wilson, noting the heraldic associations of the sun-image, suggests that 'a representation of the rising sun

FIG. 46. Standard of Richard II.

behind the royal seat in the lists at Coventry might assist the imagination of moderns unaccustomed to the suggestions of mediaeval heraldry.' This would certainly add point to the words of Bolingbroke and Mowbray in their farewell to the King when he banishes them:

> *Bolingbroke:* . . . this must my comfort be,
> That sun that warms you here shall shine on me,
> And those his golden beams to you here lent
> Shall point on me, and gild my banishment.
>
> (*i*, 3)

Let it be manifest that the sun is an emblem of Richard's majesty, and this passage holds the symbolic meaning that Bolingbroke, though exiled for a time, is not wholly cut off from his Sovereign's radiance. But Mowbray, banished never to return, has no hope of seeing England's majesty again:

> *Mowbray:* Then thus I turn me from my country's light,
> To dwell in solemn shades of endless night.
>
> (*i*, 3)

The sun imagery that permeates the latter part of *Richard II* begins with Salisbury's foreboding reference to the King:

> Thy sun sets weeping in the lowly west,
> Witnessing storms to come, woe and unrest.
>
> (*ii*, 4)

In the next act, Richard himself, in the passage which has far more point when we remember that the sun was his heraldic badge, likens his return from Ireland to a new sunrise:

> Knowst thou not
> That when the searching eye of heaven is hid,
> Behind the globe, that lights the lower world,
> Then thieves and robbers range abroad unseen
> In murders and in outrage bloody here,
> But when from under this terrestial ball
> He fires the proud tops of the eastern pines
> And darts his light through every guilty hole,
> Then murders, treasons and detested sins,
> The cloak of night being plucked from off their backs,
> Stand bare and naked, trembling at themselves?
> So when this thief, this traitor, Bolingbroke,
> Who all this while hath revell'd in the night,
> Whilst we were wandering with the antipodes,
> Shall see us rising in our throne, the east,
> His treasons will sit blushing in his face,
> Not able to endure the sight of day,
> But self-affrighted, tremble at his sin.   (*iii*, 2)

In the remainder of the scene, Richard alternates between resolution and despair, as ill tidings pass like clouds across the sun's face, and he closes it with the words:

> Discharge my followers, let them hence away,
> From Richard's night to Bolingbroke's fair day.

The sun theme is continued in the scenes between Richard and Bolingbroke. At Flint Castle:

> . . . King Richard doth himself appear,
> As doth the blushing discontented sun
> From out the fiery portal of the east,
> When he perceives the envious clouds are bent
> To dim his glory, and to stain the track
> Of his bright passage to the occident.   (*iii*, 3)

And Richard, called down from the walls to confer with Bolingbroke in the base court, cries:

> Down, down, I come, like glistering Phaeton,
> Wanting the manage of unruly jades.

Here the allusion is classical rather than heraldic. Phaeton, the son of Apollo, tried to drive the horses of the sun but was unable to control them and was thrown from the chariot and killed.

Again, in the abdication scene Richard metaphorically parts with the sun-badge to Bolingbroke (who in fact sometimes used it when he became king), wishing him 'many years of sunshine days,' and referring to himself as:

> king of snow
> Standing before the sun of Bolingbroke.
>
> (*iv*, 1)

The sun badge appears to have been reserved to the King himself, only to be borne on his person, his standard, and the appurtenances of his royal state. Richard also used as badges the *planta genista* (43), common to all the Plantagenets, and the white hart lodged with a gold coronet about its neck and therefrom a gold chain (44). The white hart was the badge worn by his servants and adherents, and may be so employed on the stage. Shakespeare does not directly mention it, but Holinshed tells of one:

> Jenico d'Artois, a Gascoigne, that still ware the cognisance or devise of his maister King Richard (after the King's fall), that is to saie, a white hart, and would not put it from him, neither for persuasions nor threats, by reason whereof, when the duke of Hereford understood it, he caused him to be committed to prison within the castell of Chester. This man was the last . . . which ware that devise and shewed well thereby his constant hart toward his maister, for the which it was thought he should have lost his life, but yet he was pardoned, and at length reconciled to the dukes favour, after he was king.

Holinshed's spelling emphasizes the play on words whereby the white hart is symbolic of the man's own constant heart. Have we not here the source of Shakespeare's 'groom of the stable', who visits Richard in captivity at Pomfret, and leaves him with the words, 'What my tongue dares not, that my heart shall say'? Whether or not Shakespeare intended it, it would be an effective piece of stage business for the man, uttering these words, to draw aside his cloak so as to give Richard a glimpse of the white hart badge on the breast of his tunic.

Richard's badges appeared on his standard (46). This was a tapering flag, with the red cross of St George on white next to the staff, the fly parted white and green, the hart white with a gold collar and chain, the suns gold, and the motto DIEV ET MON DROYT across it. This might be suitably displayed on the wall of Flint Castle to show that it 'royally is mann'd,' and would illustrate the sun references in the scene there.

The queen in the play is Richard II's second wife, Isabel, daughter of Charles VI of France. The Kings of France had made a change in their

FIG. 47. Impaled arms of The Confessor, Richard II, and Queen Isabel.

arms, reducing the number of fleurs-de-lys to three, and these arms, *Azure, three gold fleurs-de-lys*, are known as France Modern. A shield representing both Richard and his Queen was divided vertically into three, the arms of Edward the Confessor being placed in the first division, France Ancient and England quarterly in the second, and France Modern in the third. The illustration (47) also shows the royal crown in the form it took in Richard II's reign.

Lancaster and Bolingbroke

John of Gaunt, Duke of Lancaster, K.G., differenced the royal arms (*France Ancient and England quarterly*) with an ermine label (40c). He had been created Earl of Richmond in infancy; his predecessors in the earldom had also been Dukes of Brittany, and the ermine of Brittany was thus associated with the title of Richmond, and became the characteristic of John of Gaunt's label. Gaunt's badges included an ostrich feather, which he bore sometimes ermine (76) and sometimes argent; a fetterlock; an eagle standing on a fetterlock; a falcon with a padlock in its beak; and a red rose. His colours were white and blue—the livery colours of Lancaster.

The most important of these badges, in view of Shakespearean allusions, is the rose. Gaunt derived this, with the dukedom of Lancaster, from his first wife, Blanche, daughter and co-heir of Henry, Duke of Lancaster, great-grandson of Henry III. The rose is thought to have been introduced into English royal heraldry by Henry III's queen, Eleanor of Provence. A golden rose was a badge of their son, Edward I; and his younger brother, Edmund, Earl of Lancaster, bore it red for difference. The red rose thus became a badge of Lancaster, and was borne by the later earls and dukes. In Gaunt's time, the red rose of Lancaster was not yet at variance with the white rose of York, and there are no allusions to it in *Richard II*. In 1 *Henry IV*, i, 3, Richard II is described as 'that sweet lovely rose' in antithesis to 'this thorn, this canker, Bolingbroke'—'canker' being here the dog-rose. Probably Shakespeare did not intend this as an heraldic allusion, but it is worth noting that the golden rose of Edward I had descended to his successors as a royal emblem, and while Richard II does not appear to have used it as a regular badge it occurred decoratively on some of his possessions. Froissart tells us that a book of 'amours and moralities' that he had engrossed for presentation to Richard II was 'covered with crimson velvet, with ten buttons of silver and gilt, and roses of gold in the midst;' and Richard inherited from his father, the Black Prince, a blue vestment embroidered with ostrich feathers and golden roses.

During John of Gaunt's lifetime, his son, Henry of Bolingbroke, Duke of Hereford, K.G., bore the arms derived from the earlier Earls and Dukes of Lancaster through his mother, Blanche. He must therefore be shown in the lists at Coventry with *England with a label of France* (48) on his shield and surcoat. On such an occasion he may well have worn a crested tilting helm, and the crest would be the royal lion on a chapeau (looking straight before it) with the label of France round its neck. Holinshed tells us that, at Coventry, Bolingbroke was 'mounted on a white courser, barded with greene and blew velvet imbrodered sumptuouslie with swans and antelops of goldsmiths woorke.' A white swan with a gold coronet about its neck, and therefrom a gold chain passing over its back, was a badge of Bohun which Bolingbroke derived, with the honour of Hereford, from his first wife, Mary, daughter and co-heir of Humphrey de Bohun, Earl of Hereford. The golden antelope was another of his badges, probably also from the Bohuns; it was not the natural but the heraldic antelope —a deer-like creature with a horn on the nose and serrated antlers. It may be seen on one of Henry V's standards (105) and among the badges

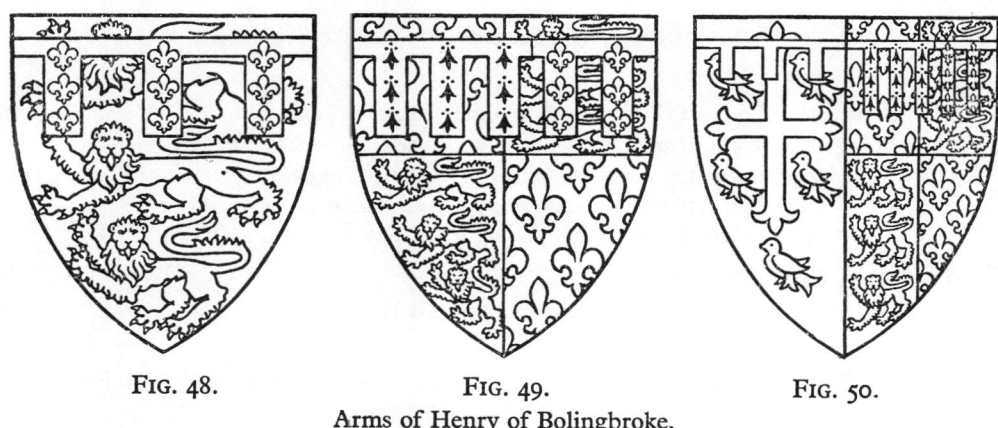

FIG. 48.   FIG. 49.   FIG. 50.
Arms of Henry of Bolingbroke.

on his tomb (140). Bolingbroke's badges also included the red rose of Lancaster, the tree-stock of Woodstock, and a fox's tail. These, together with the swan, appeared on his standard (51). This consisted of the cross of St George next to the staff, and a forked fly divided down its length into white and blue and bearing one large and six small roses, the white swan with gold collar and cords, five fox-tails, and six gold tree-stocks; the border was compony of white and blue. Other badges of Bolingbroke are dealt with in the chapter on *Henry IV*.

After John of Gaunt's death, Bolingbroke ceased to use his early arms and bore the royal shield (*France Ancient and England quarterly*) with a label of five points combining his father's label of Brittany and his own of France—that is, three points ermine, and two azure each charged with three gold fleurs-de-lys (49). He may appear with these arms on his shield, surcoat and banner on his return from banishment. This would be in keeping with, and give heraldic emphasis to, his insistence on the title of Lancaster:

FIG. 51.   Standard of Bolingbroke.

> Berkeley: My lord of Hereford, my message is to you.
> Boling.:   My lord, my answer is—to Lancaster;
>   And I am come to seek that name in England;
>   And I must find that title on your tongue,
>   Before I make reply to aught you say.   (ii, 3)

And later in the same scene:

> As I was banish'd I was banish'd Hereford;
> But as I come, I come for Lancaster.

In 1399 Bolingbroke, for some occasions, impaled the arms of Edward the Confessor with his own, as Richard II did. The Confessor's arms, differenced by a label, were placed in the dexter half of the shield; and the royal arms with Bolingbroke's own label, half Brittany and half France, in the sinister (50). (In some instances he also impaled in the sinister the arms of Bohun: *Azure, a silver bend with gold cotises between six gold lions rampant*, for his wife.) The inclusion of the Confessor's arms, in imitation of Richard II, suggests an aspiration to regal state, and a banner bearing the arms thus marshalled might be displayed in the scene in Westminster Hall (iv, 1) when Bolingbroke receives Richard's resignation of the crown.

In act v of *Richard II*, Bolingbroke has been crowned and is addressed as king, and his heraldic achievement should be that of the Sovereign (see *Henry IV*).

York and Aumerle

Edmund Langley, Duke of York, K.G., bore the royal arms with a white label of three points, each point charged with three red roundles (40d).

This label became the particular difference of the house of York.   It formed a collar to the lion in the royal crest as used by the Duke.   His badges included a silver ostrich feather, a silver falcon, a silver falcon standing within a gold fetterlock, and a falcon holding a scroll inscribed BON ESPOIR.   He derived the falcon from his father, Edward III, and it is said that in placing it within the fetter-lock he indicated that as a younger son he was locked away from any hope of succeeding to the crown. He should wear a surcoat of his arms in the scene when, as lord governor of England, he appears 'with signs of war about his aged neck' (ii, 2). His heraldry may be used decoratively in the scene in his palace (v, 2).

Edward, Duke of Aumerle (Albemarle), K.G., son of York by his first wife, Isabella of Castile, during his father's lifetime bore the royal arms with a label of five points, three white and each charged with three red roundels (for his father) and two red and each charged with three gold castles (for his mother, the castles being from the arms of Castile) (40e). He differenced the royal crest with a similar label.   His badge consisted of a silver ostrich feather with a gold chain along the quill, and the motto ICH DIEN (79).   In act v he appears as Earl of Rutland, having been deprived of his dukedom by Bolingbroke.   He succeeded his father as Duke of York, and so appears in *Henry V*.

The Duchess of York in *Richard II* is historically Langley's second wife (his first having died before the period of the play), namely Joan, daughter of Thomas Holland, second Earl of Kent.   She bore her husband's arms impaled with her paternal coat of Holland (*England with a silver bordure*). However, in act v, scene 2, Shakespeare clearly intends the Duchess to be Aumerle's mother, and therefore Langley's first wife, Isabella of Castile and Leon.   In view of this discrepancy it would be better not to identify the Duchess by any display of heraldry.   York had no children by his second marriage.

Other Characters

Thomas Mowbray, Duke of Norfolk, K.G., Marshal of England and first to be styled Earl Marshal, was descended from Thomas of Brotherton, Earl of Norfolk, second son of Edward I (see Table IX).   Brotherton had also held the office of Marshal and his arms had become associated with that office.   By grant of Richard II, Norfolk bore the arms of Brotherton (*England with a silver label of three points*) impaled to the sinister with the arms attributed to Edward the Confessor.   The king also granted Norfolk as a crest a golden lion with a silver coronet, its tail extended, standing on a chapeau; and authorised him to place an ostrich feather on each side of the shield. These were flanked by two escutcheons, that to the dexter being *Gules, a silver lion rampant,* for Mowbray, and that to the sinister *Sable, a silver lion rampant with a gold crown,* for Segrave (his mother's family).

FIG. 52.   Thomas Mowbray, Duke of Norfolk.

Since the Brotherton arms related to the office of Marshal, which Surrey filled at Norfolk's contest with Bolingbroke, it is unlikely that Norfolk used them in the lists at Coventry. Holinshed says that on that occasion Norfolk's horse was 'barded with crimosen velvet imbrodered richlie with lions of silver and mulberie trees'—that is, the lion of Mowbray and the mulberry badge allusive to the name. It is therefore probable that at Coventry his shield and surcoat bore the white lion rampant on red of Mowbray.

PLATE IV.   The royal arms of England.

The arms from King Henry IV to Queen Elizabeth.

The arms of King John.

In the scene in the lists, the king bids Norfolk give up Bolingbroke's gage, adding, 'lions make leopards tame.' It has been suggested that this is an heraldic reference, implying that the royal lion could command the beast in Norfolk's arms. In heraldic language, the lion rampant of Mowbray could not be called a leopard, but this term might be applied to the lion statant forming his crest, the lion in any attitude but rampant having been termed a leopard, or *lion leopardé*, in ancient heraldry. If, to point the king's words, it is decided to give Norfolk a crested helm for this scene, the beast forming the crest should be the stylized heraldic lion, not spotted or otherwise made to resemble the natural leopard. In the illustration (52), the lion on Norfolk's crest is shown guardant, but when actually used on a helm it should look straight before it.

Thomas Holland, Duke of Surrey, third Earl of Kent, K.G., was a grandson of Joan of Kent (by her first marriage) and was thus descended from Edmund of Woodstock, Earl of Kent, third son of Edward I. He bore the arms of Earl Edmund, *England with a silver bordure* (53). These were sometimes impaled to the sinister with the arms attributed to Edward the Confessor differenced with an ermine bordure, and might be so represented on his surcoat and banner (54).[1] Surrey used the royal crest, the lion looking straight before it and differenced by a silver collar about its neck. Holinshed states that at the contest between Bolingbroke and Mowbray at Coventry, Surrey was 'for that turne Marshal of England,' the Earl Marshal himself being one of the disputants. Shakespeare introduces a separate character as the Lord Marshal, but there is no reason why Surrey should not fill the office on the stage. His appointment might be indicated by the King handing him a baton at the end of act i, sc. 1, at the words:

> Lord marshal, command our officers of arms
> Be ready to direct these home alarms.

Surrey could then appear in the lists in a surcoat of his own arms, and bearing the baton as a sign of the office he is performing. As an adherent of Richard II, Surrey was degraded to the title of Earl of Kent by Henry IV, and joined the conspiracy to kill that king at Oxford. He was seized and beheaded, and is referred to by Northumberland in act v, sc. 6:

> I have to London sent
> The heads of Oxford, Salisbury, Blunt and Kent.

Sir John de Montagu (or Montacute), third Earl of Salisbury, was the

---

[1] From the drawing, no. 54, it will be observed that where a coat with a bordure is impaled, the portion of the bordure on the side formed by the impalement line is omitted.

FIGS. 53, 54. Thomas Holland, Duke of Surrey. FIG. 55. John de Montagu, Earl of Salisbury.

son of another Sir John (second son of the first Earl; see Table VI) who had married the heiress of Monthermer. Accordingly he bore: *Quarterly Montagu and Monthermer,* i.e. *Argent, three lozenges cojoined in fess gules,* for Montagu, and *Gold, an eagle displayed vert,* for Monthermer (55).[1] (The lozenges, each forming a *mont aigu,* are a play on the name, characteristic of early heraldry.) Salisbury would bear his quartered arms on both shield and surcoat. His crest was a gold griffin's head between two wings.

Thomas, Lord Berkeley, bore *Gules, semé of silver crosslets formy, and a silver chevron.* His crest consisted of a mitre charged with these arms. His badge was a mermaid, and on his monumental brass at Wotton-under-Edge he is shown with a collar decorated with mermaids. This possibly denoted adherence to the Black Prince, whose badges included 'mermaids of the sea.'

Henry Percy, Earl of Northumberland, bore, *Gold, a lion rampant azure.* These arms were assumed by his great-grandfather, the first Lord Percy, on his marriage with the daughter of John FitzAlan, Earl of Arundel, and appear to have been derived from the coat of the Earls of Arundel, *Gules, a gold lion rampant.* The ancient arms of Percy, which the lion superseded, were *Azure, five gold lozenges cojoined fesswise* (34). The Earl of Northumberland married, as his second wife, Maud, sister and co-heir of Anthony, Lord Lucy, and quartered the arms of Lucy with the lion-coat of Percy as a condition of the inheritance to certain lordships. Accordingly at the period of the play he bore: *Quarterly,* 1 *and* 4, *Gold, a lion rampant*

[1] Shown in colour in Plate III.

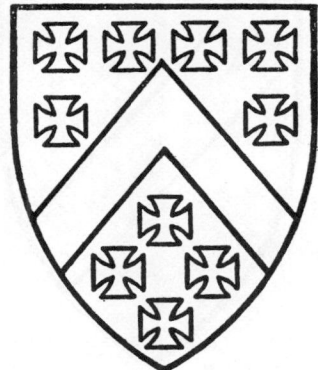

FIG. 56. Berkeley.   FIG. 57. Percy,   FIG. 58. De Ros.
Earl of Northumberland.

azure; 2 and 3, Gules, three silver luces (or pike-fish) hauriant (57). His
badge was a crescent, which was used both on flags and on the liveries of
his followers.

Sir Henry Percy, called 'Hotspur', was the son of the Earl of Northumberland by his first marriage. He first bore the Percy arms with a
difference, *Gold, a lion rampant azure with a label of three points gules.* On
the death of his step-mother, he quartered her arms, as his father did,
with a label over all. Shakespeare makes Hotspur's step-mother survive
him, and introduces her in 2 *Henry IV.* Hotspur is further dealt with in
the chapter on *Henry IV.*

William, Lord Ross (de Ros): *Gules, three silver water-budgets* (58).[1] He
used one water-budget as a badge.

William, Lord Willoughby de Eresby, K.G.: *Quarterly, 1 and 4, Sable,
a gold cross engrailed; 2 and 3, Gules, a silver cross moline* (59). These are
the arms of Ufford and Willoughby quarterly, Sir William's grandfather,
John, Lord Willoughby, having married Cecily, co-heir of the last Ufford
Earl of Suffolk. The earlier arms of Willoughby de Eresby were: *Gold,
fretty azure.*

Walter, Lord FitzWalter: *Gold, a fess between two chevrons, all gules* (60).
He was sixth in descent from Robert FitzWalter, mentioned in the chapter
on *King John.*

Sir Stephen Scrope (or Scroop) was the third son of Richard, first Lord
Scrope of Bolton, and a younger brother of William Scrope, Earl of
Wiltshire, who is referred to but does not appear in the play (see Table II).

[1] Shown in colour in Plate III.

FIG. 59. Willoughby
de Eresby.

FIG. 60. FitzWalter.

FIG. 61. Sir Stephen Scrope.

Sir Stephen bore, *Azure, a gold bend* with a difference for cadency, probably a molet (61).   Wiltshire, who was also Lord of Man, bore, *Quarterly Man and Scrope,* each coat differenced with a label, i.e. *Gules, three armoured legs joined at the thighs and bent at the knees, in proper colours, garnished and spurred gold, a label of three points,* for Man; and, *Azure, a gold bend and a label gules,* for Scrope (62). According to Holinshed, Sir Stephen Scrope bore the sword before Richard II at his meeting with Bolingbroke at Flint.

The Lord Marshal is referred to above in connection with the Duke of Surrey.

Sir John Bushy (or Bussey): *Silver, three bars sable* (63).

Sir William Bagot: *Silver, a chevron gules between three molets sable, with a crescent for difference on the chevron* (65).

Sir Henry Green (probably): *Azure, three gold bucks passant* (64). Rodway identifies him with a Green who bore: *Silver, a cross engrailed gules charged with five silver crescents.*

Sir Pierce of Exton: In *Shakespeareana Genealogica,* French suggests that this person may have been a near relative of Sir Nicholas Exton, Mayor of London, a violent opponent of Richard II.   He gives Sir Nicholas's arms as: *Gules, a gold cross between twelve gold cross-crosslets fitchy;* but Burke (*General Armory*) makes the field azure, the cross silver, and the crosslets gold (67).

The Bishop of Carlisle at this time was Thomas Merk, or Merkes.   His seal shows his arms to have been, *a canton, over all a label of five points* (Rodway).

FIG. 62. Scrope, Earl of Wiltshire.   FIG. 63. Sir John Bushy.   FIG. 64. Sir Henry Green.

The Abbot of Westminster in the play has been named as William de Colchester, but French thought his successor, Richard Harounden, or Harweden, was intended.

A number of persons are mentioned in act ii, scene 1, as having accompanied Bolingbroke on his return from exile, and while they have no speaking parts they may be represented in Bolingbroke's following. These are:

Rainald, Lord Cobham of Sterborough: *Gules, a gold chevron charged with three estoiles sable* (68).

Sir Thomas Erpingham, whose arms (114) are given in the chapter on *Henry V*.

Sir John Ramston, whom Holinshed names Thomas, (probably): *Gules, three silver rams' heads caboshed* (69).

Sir John Norberry: *Sable, a silver chevron between three silver bulls' heads caboshed, and on the chevron a fleur-de-lys sable* (70).

Sir Robert Waterton: *Barry of six pieces ermine and gules, over all three crescents sable* (71).

The Lord Beaumond, named in act ii, sc. 2 as having joined Bolingbroke on his return, was Henry, Lord Beaumont, who bore: *Azure, semé of gold fleurs-de-lys and a gold lion rampant* (72). Holinshed also mentions 'Lord Darcie' as among those who first joined Bolingbroke on his landing; this was John, Lord Darcy, who bore: *Azure, semé of silver cross-crosslets and three silver cinquefoils* (73).

FIG. 65.   Sir William Bagot.

FIG. 66.   Sir Simon de Felbrigge,
bearing Richard II's banner.

FIG. 67. Exton.   FIG. 68. Cobham.   FIG. 69. Ramston.

Holinshed also supplies the following names of those who joined Bolingbroke, and they may be shown in his train.

Ralph Nevill, first Earl of Westmoreland: *Gules, a silver saltire* (85).[1] He appears in *Henry IV* and *Henry V*.

Thomas FitzAlan[2], son of Richard, sixth Earl of Arundel who had been beheaded by Richard II in 1397: *Gules, a gold lion rampant.*

Ralph, Lord Greystoke: *Barry of six pieces silver and azure, three chaplets gules* (74).

Richard, Lord St Maur (or Seymour) may appear attending on the Duke of York in act ii, sc. 3, where he is named.   He bore: *Silver, two chevrons gules, a label of three points azure* (75).

The reference in the last scene of the play to Oxford's head having been sent to London after the conspiracy is unhistorical, as the Earl of Oxford was not involved. In the folio of 1623, the name 'Spencer' is substituted for 'Oxford'; this refers to Thomas Despencer, Earl of Gloucester, who was beheaded in 1400. He bore, *Quarterly, silver and gules, the gules fretty or, and over all a bend sable.* Blunt, mentioned in the same connection, was

---

[1] Shown in colour in Plate II.

[2] He is probably the person intended by the blank line in Act ii, scene 1, before the lines:
    That late broke from the Duke of Exeter,
    His brother, Archbishop late of Canterbury.
The Archbishop was Thomas, brother of Richard, sixth Earl of Arundel. Malone supplies as the missing line:
    The son of Richard, Earl of Arundel.
Thomas, son of Richard and nephew of the Archbishop, became seventh Earl of Arundel on the accession of Henry IV. He appears in 2 *Henry IV* as Earl of Surrey.

FIG. 70. Norberry.

FIG. 71. Waterton.

FIG. 72. Beaumont.

Sir Thomas of that name.   In the same scene, FitzWalter speaks of having sent to London

> The heads of Brocas and Sir Bennet Seely.

The former was Sir Bernard Brocas, Master of the Buckhounds, who bore: *Sable, a gold lion rampant guardant.*   The latter (whose name Holinshed gives as Cilie) cannot be identified.

In act i, sc. 1, Richard bids the Lord Marshal to command the officers of arms to be ready to direct the combat between Hereford and Norfolk, and in the lists at Coventry the heralds are seen escorting and announcing the contestants.

At this period, not only kings but also great nobles had heralds and

FIG. 73. Darcy.

FIG. 74. Greystoke.

FIG. 75. St Maur.

pursuivants of arms attached to their households. These officers wore their masters' arms or badges emblazoned on their garments, a practice to which Shakespeare refers in 2 *Henry VI*, *iv*, 10, where Alexander Iden, having slain Jack Cade, addresses his weapon,

> Sword, I will hallow thee for this thy deed,
> And hang thee o'er my tomb when I am dead:
> Ne'er shall this blood be wiped from thy point,
> But thou shalt wear it as a herald's coat,
> To emblaze the honour that thy master got.

The heralds who officiated at Coventry would be the King's own officers. These displayed the royal arms on their coats. The heralds' garments took various forms until the introduction of the tabard in the latter part of the fifteenth century. No. 139 gives examples.

D

TABLE II

SCROPE OR SCROOP

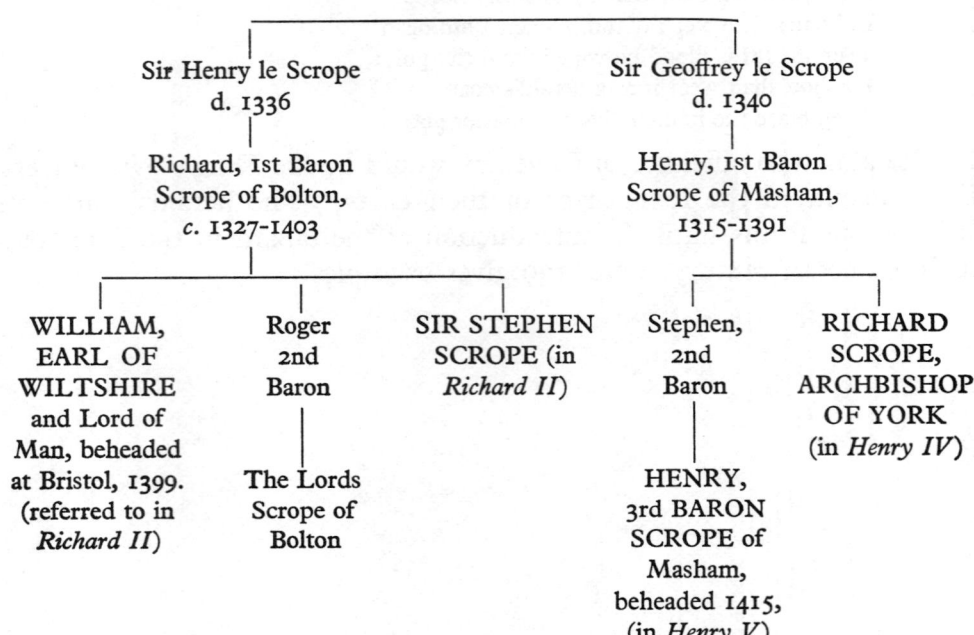

Sir William le Scrope
of Bolton

Sir Henry le Scrope
d. 1336

Richard, 1st Baron
Scrope of Bolton,
c. 1327-1403

Sir Geoffrey le Scrope
d. 1340

Henry, 1st Baron
Scrope of Masham,
1315-1391

WILLIAM,
EARL OF
WILTSHIRE
and Lord of
Man, beheaded
at Bristol, 1399.
(referred to in
Richard II)

Roger
2nd
Baron

The Lords
Scrope of
Bolton

SIR STEPHEN
SCROPE (in
Richard II)

Stephen,
2nd
Baron

HENRY,
3rd BARON
SCROPE of
Masham,
beheaded 1415,
(in *Henry V*)

RICHARD
SCROPE,
ARCHBISHOP
OF YORK
(in *Henry IV*)

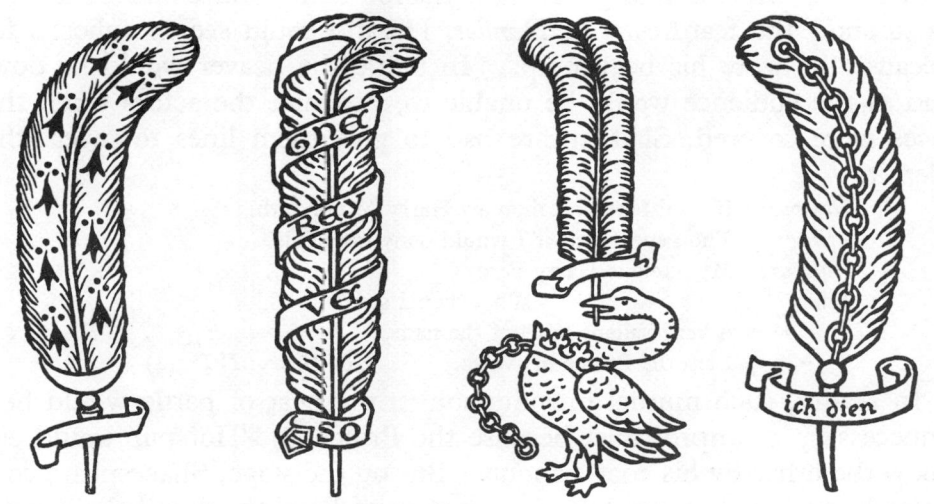

FIG. 76. John of Gaunt,
Duke of Lancaster, and
Thomas, Duke of
Clarence

FIG. 77. Henry IV

FIG. 78. Henry,
Prince of Wales
(Henry V)

FIG. 79. Edward,
Duke of York
(Aumerle in *Richard II*)

Ostrich Feather Badges.

CHAPTER V

KING HENRY IV

IN *Henry IV* Shakespeare described the armed knighthood of the
fifteenth century as no doubt he would have represented it on the stage
so far as the theatre's wardrobe permitted.   Sir Richard Vernon speaks
of the Prince of Wales and his comrades as 'all furnish'd, all in arms;
all plum'd like estridges ... baited [i.e. fluttering] like eagles ... glittering
in golden coats ... and gorgeous as the sun at midsummer.'

> I saw young Harry, with his beaver on,
> His cuisses on his thighs, gallantly arm'd ...

(Pt. 1, iv, 1)

While he had to rely a good deal on words to paint the scene, he would
scarcely risk disappointing his audience by promising so splendid a
spectacle if he was quite unable to provide it, and we may assume that
the wardrobe ran to plumed helms, some armour, and decorated surcoats
for at least the principal persons in the battle scenes.

A beaver was the face-guard of a visored helm, and could be lifted so as to show the features. In *Hamlet*, Horatio could see the ghost's face because 'he wore his beaver up.' In battle the beaver would be down, and as the audience would be unable to recognise the actors when their faces were covered, Shakespeare had to give them lines to reveal their identity:

> *Hotspur:* If I mistake not, thou art Harry Monmouth.
> *Prince:*   Thou speakst as if I would deny my name.
> *Hotspur:* My name is Harry Percy.
> *Prince:*   Why, then I see
> A very valiant rebel of the name;
> I am the Prince of Wales.   (I *Henry. IV*, v, 4)

In reality, such mutual introduction in the heat of battle would be as unnecessary as improbable, because the Prince and Hotspur would each know the other by his coat-armour. But on the stage, Shakespeare could not rely on his audience knowing enough of heraldry to tell the warriors by their arms, even supposing the wardrobe contained the proper surcoats.

However, we may assume that the Elizabethan audience knew the royal arms, and that the theatre possessed at least two shields and surcoats of these arms. In the Shrewsbury battle scene, which Shakespeare based on Holinshed, Sir Walter Blunt appears 'semblably furnish'd like the king himself,' and is slain by Douglas in mistake for the King. Hotspur tells Douglas that 'the king hath many marching in his coats'—that is, coats bearing the royal arms—whereupon Douglas swears,

> Now, by my sword, I will kill all his coats;
> I'll murder all his wardrobe, piece by piece,
> Until I meet the king.

Later Douglas encounters the King himself:

> Another king? they grow like Hydra's heads:
> I am the Douglas, fatal to all those
> That wear those colours on them: what art thou,
> That counterfeits the person of a king?
> *King:* The king himself; who, Douglas, grieves at heart
> So many of his shadows thou hast met
> And not the very king.   (I *Henry. IV*, v, 3 and 4)

We may take it that on Shakespeare's stage the King and Blunt wore surcoats of the royal arms (probably those of Elizabeth rather than Henry IV: the slight difference between them is dealt with below); and that for the other characters, the producer would find what he could in the wardrobe to redeem the playwright's promise of warriors 'glittering in golden coats,' though probably these would not be true to the heraldry of the persons represented.

FIG. 80.   Crown of Henry IV, and royal arms from 1405.

Royal Heraldry

At the beginning of his reign, Henry IV bore the royal arms in the form which had come down from Edward III: *France Ancient and England quarterly.*   He did not continue the practice of impaling the arms of the Confessor, perhaps because this was too closely associated with the king he had supplanted.

About 1365, Charles V of France had reduced the number of fleurs-de-lys in the French coat to three, producing the arms termed France Modern.   In 1405 Henry IV followed this example in the English royal arms. There is therefore a difference in the arms between the first and second parts of *Henry IV*: in Part I the French quarters are *Azure, semé-de-lys gold,* and in Part II they are *Azure, three gold fleurs-de-lys.* This difference should be observed in production. *France Modern and England quarterly* (80)[1] remained the English royal arms until the end of Elizabeth's reign.

Henry IV bore the same crest as his predecessor; that is, on a chapeau gules turned up ermine, a gold lion statant guardant with a gold crown on his head. When actually worn on a helm, the lion would not be guardant, but would look straight before it. The play contains several references to the lion as the royal emblem. Falstaff alludes to Prince Henry as 'the lion's whelp,' adding, 'the King himself is to be feared as the lion.'

Henry IV, referring to Hotspur, says,

> He doth fill fields with harness in the realm,
> Turns head against the lion's armed jaws;

and Hotspur says,

> the blood more stirs
> To rouse a lion than to start a hare.

As King, Henry used as badges not only the swan, antelope, fox's tail and tree-stock (already noticed in his earlier heraldry), but also a number of others, including an ostrich feather entwined with a scroll bearing the word SOVEREYGNE (77), the letters SS (probably alluding to the same word), the sun-in-splendour, the red rose of Lancaster, the last two combined to form a red rose *en soleil* (that is, irradiated), a crowned eagle, a columbine flower, a crowned panther, a cresset, *planta genista,* and a gennet (or civet) between two sprigs of the famous broom-plant, playing on the name Plantagenet. His colours were white and blue.

Associated with Henry IV's SS badge is the collar of SS, a decoration of honour conferred by the Lancastrian kings. This consisted of letters S linked together or set close on a blue and white ribbon, the ends being connected by a trefoil link. From the link sometimes hung a pendant, which in some cases consisted of the swan badge (142, 143).

Henry's four sons all bore the royal arms with the differences given below. In the case of Prince Henry and Prince John, who appear in both parts of the play, the change from France Ancient to France Modern should be made, as in the King's arms.

[1] Shown in colour in Plate IV.

Henry, Prince of Wales, following the practice which began with the Black Prince and continues to this day, differenced the royal arms and crest with a plain white label. His badge was the white swan with a gold coronet about its neck with a gold chain attached, holding in its beak an ostrich feather erect enfiled with a scroll (78).

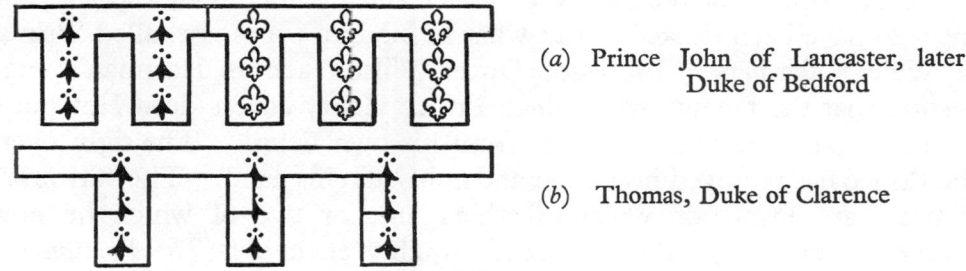

(a) Prince John of Lancaster, later Duke of Bedford

(b) Thomas, Duke of Clarence

FIG. 81. Labels of Henry IV's sons.

Prince John of Lancaster, a Knight of the Garter, had for difference a label of five points, two being ermine, and the other three azure each charged with three gold fleurs-de-lys—that is, the label *per pale Brittany and France* which his father had borne as Duke of Lancaster (81a). His badges included the gold tree-stock and an ostrich feather. His banner was *semé* of gold tree-stocks, and bore the motto, *A vous entier*, which appears to have been addressed to his wife, since her motto, *J'en suis contente*, seems to answer his. He was created Duke of Bedford in 1414, and appears under this title in *Henry V* and 1 *Henry VI*.

Thomas, Duke of Clarence and Earl of Albemarle (so created in 1411), bore the royal arms and crest with a label ermine charged on each point with a canton gules (81b). His badges were a greyhound with a plain collar, and an ostrich feather ermine (76). His effigy shows him wearing the Lancastrian collar of SS.

Prince Humphrey of Gloucester differenced the royal arms with a plain white bordure, and the lion in the crest with a plain silver collar and a silver crown. He also bore the ostrich feather as a badge, its quill studded with fleurs-de-lys, and his badges also included the swan and antelope. His motto was *Loyalle et belle*. He was created Duke of Gloucester in 1414, and appears by this title in *Henry V* and 1 *Henry VI*.

It will be observed that Henry IV and his four sons all used the ostrich feather as a badge, sometimes combining it with another emblem. It was also used by some other members of the royal house who do not appear

in this play.   The ostrich feather, though most famous for its appearance
in the Black Prince's 'shield for peace,' was not at this time specially
associated with the Prince of Wales.   The point is important, because
some commentators (taking 'estridge' to mean ostrich, and not goshawk)
have read an heraldic meaning into the words 'plum'd like estridges'
in the description of the Prince of Wales and his followers, and suppose
them to have been decked out in what in modern times are called 'Prince
of Wales's feathers.'   Professor Dover Wilson adopts Hartman's sug-
gestion that the favours with which Prince Henry covers dead Hotspur's
'mangled face' (v, 4) are feathers from his own helm.   'The fight over,
the Prince has removed his beaver and holds it in his hand.   The "favours"
it bears are Prince of Wales's feathers, one or two of which he now
reverently lays across the face of his mighty enemy.'   (*The Fortunes of
Falstaff*.)

It is an anachronism to speak of 'the Prince of Wales's feathers' in
connection with Henry of Monmouth.   He shared the feathers with too
many people for them to be particularly associated with him.   Furthermore, the Plantagenet ostrich feather was not used as a crest, but as a
badge on clothing, furnishings, seals etc.   Quite likely Prince Henry did
wear plumes on his helm, but the fashion was so common among armoured
knights that it was merely decorative and had no heraldic or distinctive
purpose.   I do not think the Prince would regard the feathers on his
helm as his personal and intimate 'favours.'

However, the real question is whether Shakespeare thought of the
ostrich feathers as the particular emblems of the Prince of Wales, and
whether he could use them in the play with confidence that his audience
would understand their significance.

When Shakespeare wrote *Henry IV* there was no Prince of Wales (nor
any acknowledged successor to the throne), and there had not been a
Prince of Wales for nearly ninety years.   Arthur Tudor (son of Henry
VII), Prince of Wales from 1489 to 1503, had used as a badge the three
ostrich feathers encircled by a coronet.   His brother Henry was Prince
of Wales from 1503 to 1509 (when he succeeded as Henry VIII), but he
does not appear to have used the feathers.   The latter's son Edward
(afterwards Edward VI) used the feathers during the period 1537-1547,
but not as Prince of Wales for he never held that title.

It therefore appears that in Tudor times the ostrich feathers formed a
badge of the heir apparent (not necessarily Prince of Wales) for two periods,

the latter ending fifty years before Shakespeare wrote *Henry IV*. The badge can scarcely have been familiar to Shakespeare's audiences. It had not become an inn-sign, or the badge of a famous regiment, or a sign over shops boasting royal custom. In fact, it was only in Stuart times that the feathers began to be used definitely and consistently as the badge of the heir apparent.

I do not think Shakespeare or his public can have associated the feathers particularly with the Prince of Wales, and I suppose that what Shakespeare intended the Prince to lay on dead Hotspur's face was not a feather, such as any armed man might wear, but a torse of silk of his own colours— white and blue—which he unbound from his helm for the purpose.

The Crown

In the reign of Henry IV, the royal diadem was the famous 'Harry crown,' consisting of a richly jewelled circlet heightened by six strawberry leaves and six fleurs-de-lys alternately (80). This crown was broken up and used as security for the loan which Henry V needed for his French expedition, its fragments being redeemed in Henry VI's reign. This was the crown which the King would keep by him for state use, and it should be represented in 2 *Henry IV*, iv, 5, where Prince Henry removes the 'polish'd perturbation, golden care' from his sick father's pillow.

It appears that at this time there was another crown of special sanctity which was used at the coronation, for Froissart, describing the crowning of Henry IV, states that the archbishop set on his head Saint Edward's crown 'which is close above'—other versions say 'arched in a cross,' or 'arched in three.' An ancient arched crown traditionally associated with Edward the Confessor continued in existence until the Commonwealth, when it was destroyed. The present St Edward's crown was made at Charles II's restoration on the model of the former one.

Mortimer, Percy and Glendower

The relations between the Mortimers, Percys and Owen Glendower, and their connection with the royal house, are shown in Table III, in which the names in capitals are those of characters which appear in Shakespeare's plays.

TABLE III

MORTIMER, PERCY AND GLENDOWER

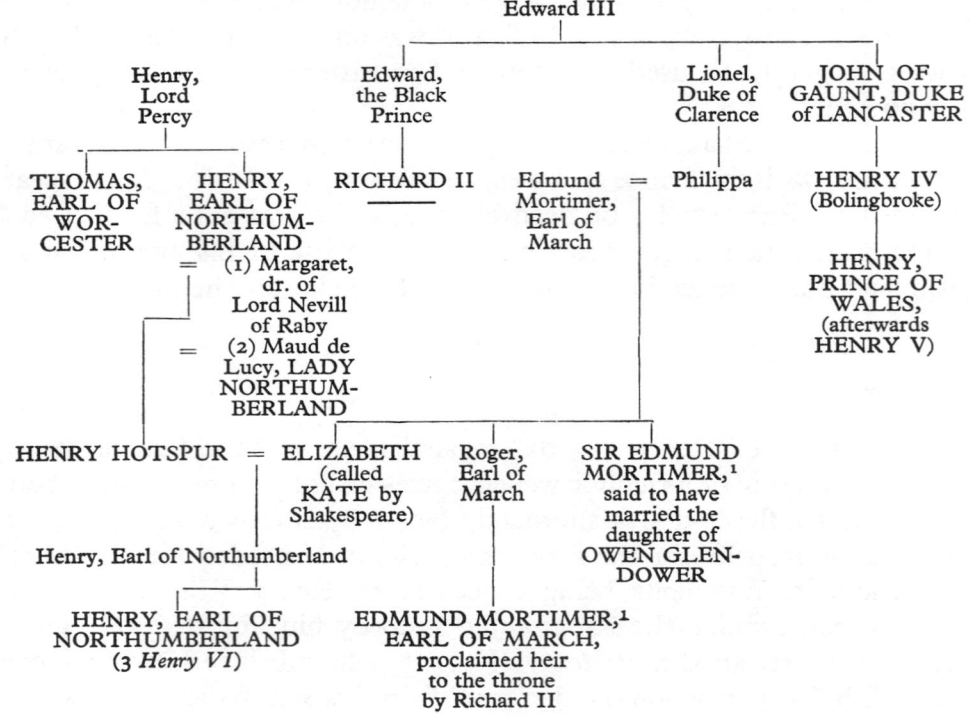

[1] Shakespeare confuses these two persons.

In *Richard II* Shakespeare makes it clear that Henry Bolingbroke, son of John of Gaunt, had no claim to be regarded as next in succession to the throne: The King says:

> Were he my brother, nay, my kingdom's heir,
> As he is but my father's brother's son . . .   (i, 1)

In 1 *Henry IV* (i, 3) it is noted that Edmund Mortimer, Earl of March, great-great-grandson of Edward III through Lionel, John of Gaunt's elder brother, was proclaimed heir to the throne by Richard when he left on the Irish expedition. Mortimer is referred to as Hotspur's brother-in-law, and is said to have fought Glendower and afterwards married his daughter. Here Shakespeare confused two Edmund Mortimers. It was the Earl of March of that name who was declared heir to Richard II. This Earl was born in 1391, and it therefore cannot be he who at the date of 1 *Henry IV* (1402-3) had fought Glendower and married his daughter; this was his uncle, Sir Edmund Mortimer. Hotspur's wife correctly refers to the latter as her brother, but is wrongly made to say,

> I fear my brother Mortimer doth stir
> About his title.

The important point about the Mortimer of the play is that he had been proclaimed

> By Richard that dead is, the next of blood.

We must disregard the discrepancies due to the confusion between the two Mortimers, and assign the character the arms of the Earl of March.

FIG. 82. Mortimer, Earl of March.　　FIG. 83. Percy, Earl of Worcester.　　FIG. 84. Owen Glendower.

These were the coats of Mortimer and Ulster quarterly; that is, for Mortimer, *Gold, three bars azure, and on a gold chief two pallets between two gyrons, also azure, and over all a silver inescutcheon;*[1] and for Ulster, *Gold, a cross gules* (82). The Ulster coat was derived from Lionel of Clarence's wife, the daughter and heir of De Burgh, Earl of Ulster. Mortimer's crest was a panache of blue feathers rising from a coronet. The badges of the house of Mortimer included a white wolf and a white rose. From the latter the Yorkist rose was probably derived. (Not yet, however, were the white and red roses the badges of rival factions.)

To the Percys—Northumberland and Hotspur—whose arms have been given in the last chapter, we have now to add Northumberland's younger brother, Thomas, Earl of Worcester. He bore *Gold, a lion rampant*

---

[1] This is the form of the Mortimer arms as they appear on Earl Edmund's seal. They are sometimes shown as barry of six instead of three bars, with three pallets on the chief.

azure, charged on the shoulder with a silver fleur-de-lys—the coat of Percy
with a difference (83). His crest was a lion passant, and his badge a
silver crescent.

The *mot* or *cri* of the Percys was *Esperance*, a remote play on the name
which is the more apparent when the final *e* is pronounced, as Shakespeare
meant it to be. Holinshed says, 'the kings part crying S. George upon
them, the adversaries cried *Esperance Persie*.' Shakespeare puts the word
into Hotspur's mouth when he is preparing to support Mortimer (ii, 3),
and again before the battle of Shrewsbury:

> Now, Esperance! Percy and set on.   (*v*, 2)

We find an echo of the Percy motto in 2 *Henry IV*, *i*, 3, when Lord
Bardolph says that Hotspur

> lin'd himself with hope,
> Eating the air, and promise of supply,
> Flattering himself in project of a power
> Much smaller than the smallest of his thoughts:
> And so, with great imagination
> Proper to madmen, led his powers to death,
> And, winking, leap'd into destruction.

The Earl of Northumberland had a private pursuivant with the title of
Esperance. It is possible that we have a glance at the Percy badge of a
silver crescent in Hotspur's words,

> By heaven, methinks it were an easy leap,
> To pluck bright honour from the pale-fac'd moon.   (1 *Henry IV*, *i*, 3)

An ancient legend of the Percy family identifies their crescent badge with
the moon, which, when their ancestor, Gernons, was attacked by night
in the land of Perse, shone in his shield by 'an hevynly mystery,' enabling
him to gain the victory.

Elizabeth Mortimer, as the wife, and later widow, of Hotspur, would
bear impaled arms, with her husband's coat on the dexter side and her
paternal coat of Mortimer in the sinister.

Lady Northumberland in the play is the Earl's second wife and
Hotspur's step-mother. She was Maud de Lucy, whose arms were
quartered with the Percy coat in the shield of Northumberland and
Hotspur (see *Richard II*).

Owen Glendower bore, *Quarterly gold and gules, four lions rampant
counterchanged* (84). His crest was a red dragon. These were derived

from the arms of Llewellin, Prince of North Wales, from whom he claimed descent. The arms are similar to those now appertaining to the principality of Wales, in which, however, the lions are passant guardant.

In the dragon crest of Glendower, the Percy lion, and the Mortimer badge of a wolf, we have the three emblems referred to by Holinshed, where he says that the partition of the realm between Glendower, Percy and Mortimer was done 'through a foolish credit given to a vaine prophesie, as though King Henrie was the mouldwarpe, curssed of Gods owne mouth, and they three were the dragon, the lion, and the woolfe, which should divide this realm betweene them.' The prophesy is referred to in Thomas Phaer's *Owen Glendower*, 1559:

> A prophet came (a vengeaunce take them all)
> Affirming Henry to be Gogmagog,
> Whom Merline doth a mouldwarp ever call,
> Accurst of God, that must be kept in thrall
>   By a wolfe, a dragon, and a lion strong,
>   Which should devide his kingdome them among.

Shakespeare shows Glendower, Hotspur and Mortimer discussing the division of the realm, but he does not appear to have known that the dragon, lion and wolf of the prophecy were their heraldic emblems, or he would surely have brought out the point. As it is, he refers only indirectly to the prophecy in Hotspur's contemptuous remarks about the 'skimble-skamble stuff' in Glendower's brain:

> Sometimes he angers me
> With telling me of the moldwarp and the ant,
> Of the dreamer Merlin and his prophecies,
> And of a dragon and a finless fish,
> A clip-wing'd griffin and a moulten raven,
> A couching lion and a ramping cat . . .
>   (1 *Henry IV, iii, 1*)

Other Historical Characters

Ralph Nevill, Earl of Westmoreland, K.G., bore, *Gules, a silver saltire* (85). His crest was a bull's head; this would only be used on his great helm. His monument shows him wearing a bascinet with a broad wreath, resting his head on his crested helm. He wore the collar of SS (143).

Richard Beauchamp, Earl of Warwick, K.G., bore until 1423, *Quarterly*

FIG. 85. Nevill,
Earl of Westmoreland.

FIG. 86. Beauchamp,
Earl of Warwick.

FIG. 87. FitzAlan,
Earl of Arundel and Surrey.

Beauchamp and Neubourg, i.e. *Gules, a gold fess between six gold cross-crosslets,* for Beauchamp, and *Checky gold and azure, a chevron ermine,* for Neubourg (86).[1] His later arms and badges are dealt with under *Henry VI.* Shakespeare was in error in making the King address Warwick as 'cousin Nevil.' The first Nevill Earl of Warwick was Beauchamp's son-in-law.

By the 'Earl of Surrey,' Shakespeare must have meant Thomas FitzAlan, Earl of Arundel and Surrey, K.G. He bore quarterly FitzAlan and Warrenne, i.e. *Gules, a gold lion rampant,* for FitzAlan, and *Checky gold and azure,* for Warrenne (87). On his effigy he wears the collar of SS.

Thomas, Lord Mowbray, was the eldest son of the Duke of Norfolk in *Richard II,* but himself never held the ducal title. This makes it strange that Westmoreland should suggest that he has not 'an inch of any ground to build a grief on' (2 *Henry IV, iv,* 1). He was usually styled Earl Marshal. He bore the arms of Mowbray, *Gules, a silver lion rampant.*

By the title of 'Lord Hastings,' Shakespeare presumably meant Ralph Hastings (son of Sir Ralph Hastings, of the family which became Lords Hastings and Earls of Huntingdon), who joined Glendower and was beheaded in 1410. He bore, *Argent, a maunch sable* (88). A maunch is a lady's sleeve with a baggy pendant from the wrist—a twelfth century fashion perpetuated as an heraldic charge. (Another branch of the Hastings family bore the maunch argent on gules, as it appears in Plate III.)

[1] Shown in colour in Plate III.

FIG. 88.   Hastings.   FIG. 89.   Bardolph.   FIG. 90.   Blunt.

Thomas, Lord Bardolph, bore, *Azure, three gold cinquefoils* (89).[1]

Sir Walter Blunt bore, *Barry nebuly of eight pieces gold and sable* (90); but at Shrewsbury he was one of those 'semblably furnish'd like the king himself,' and he must therefore appear with the royal arms of Henry IV on surcoat and shield.   In 2 *Henry IV* we read of

> both the Blunts
> Kill'd by the hand of Douglas.

The other Blunt slain at Shrewsbury was the King's standard-bearer; if represented on the stage, he should appear in the Blunt arms.   The Blunt mentioned in 2 *Henry IV*, iv, 3, was probably a member of the same family.

Douglas, addressing Sir Walter Blunt, thinking him to be the King, says:

> The Lord of Stafford dear to-day hath bought
> Thy likeness, for instead of thee, King Harry,
> This sword hath ended him.   (1 *Henry IV*, v, 3)

This was Edmund, Earl of Stafford.   Holinshed says he was " that daie made by the King constable of the realme", and Shakespeare makes him one of those dressed as the King. His own arms were, *Gold, a chevron gules* (124).[2]

---

[1] Shown in colour in Plate III.

[2] Shown in colour in Plate II.

FIG. 91.   Vernon.   FIG. 92.   Colevile.   FIG. 93.   Douglas.

Sir Richard Vernon, of Shipbrook, bore, *Gold, on a fess azure three gold garbs* (91).   The garbs, or wheatsheaves, were added to the original coat in token that the Vernons held the barony of Shipbrook from the Earls of Chester, who bore *Azure, three gold garbs.*

Sir John Colevile 'of the Dale' was of the Yorkshire family seated at Arncliffe.   He bore, *Gold, a fess gules, in chief three roundles gules* (92).

Archibald, Earl of Douglas, bore, *Argent, a heart gules, on a chief azure three silver molets* (93).   The original arms of Douglas did not contain the heart.   This was added to commemorate the mission of Sir James Douglas to carry the heart of King Robert the Bruce to the Holy Land for burial.   Later the heart in the arms was ensigned with a royal crown, as it is now borne.

FIG. 94.   Standard of Douglas.

FIG. 95. Gawsey.　　　FIG. 96. Clifton.　　　FIG. 97. Gascoigne.

Douglas may be given a standard based on the one preserved at Cavers. This is blue, with the white cross of St Andrew near the staff, two red hearts, a white lion passant, and the motto *Jamais arriere* in white (94).

Mordake, Earl of Fife, mentioned in 1 *Henry IV*, i, 1, as having been taken prisoner by Hotspur, and in ii, 4, as having joined the Percys and Glendower, was Murdach Stewart, son of Robert, Duke of Albany.   He bore, *Gold, a fess checky azure and silver*, with a difference, probably a label.

'Lord Mortimer of Scotland,' referred to in 1 *Henry IV*, iii, 2, was in no way connected with the English Mortimers: in fact, there was no such person. The introduction of this name seems to have been due to a mis-understanding of Holinshed's reference to 'the earle of March, the Scot,' who supported King Henry at the battle of Shrewsbury. Shakespeare confused him with the English Earls of March, and wrongly called him by their name of Mortimer. He was in fact a son of the Earl of Dunbar; having quarrelled with the Scottish King, he had attached himself to Henry IV.

At Shrewsbury, Prince Henry says:

> Sir Nicholas Gawsey hath for succour sent,
> And so hath Clifton.

These characters may therefore be introduced in the battle scenes. Gawsey bore, *Gold, three bars gules and a canton ermine* (95). Sir John Clifton, who was slain, bore, *Sable, semé of silver cinquefoils and a silver lion rampant* (96).

'Valiant Shirley,' mentioned as slain at Shrewsbury, was Sir Hugh Shirley, Henry IV's Master of Hawks. He bore, *Paly of six pieces gold and azure, a canton ermine.*

The Chief Justice at the period of 2 *Henry IV* was Sir William Gascoigne. He bore, *Silver, a pale sable charged with a gold luce's (or conger's) head* (97).

Richard Scroop, or Scrope, Archbishop of York, son of the first Lord Scrope of Masham, bore, *Azure, a gold bend and a silver label of three points.* Shakespeare makes Worcester say that the Archbishop

> bears hard
> His brother's death at Bristowe, the Lord Scrope;

but the Scrope who was executed at Bristol was the Earl of Wiltshire, son of the first Lord Scrope of Bolton, and the Archbishop's second cousin. The confusion seems to have arisen from the fact that the Archbishop was the godson of this Lord Scrope of Bolton, and in some documents was referred to as his son. The relationship between the two lines of Scrope is shown in Table II.

Gower and Harcourt cannot be certainly identified. They appear as messengers, and not in the battle scenes, so they need no personal heraldry, but they may wear on breast or shoulder the ostrich feather badge to denote their adherence to the king. French suggests that Gower is intended for Thomas Gower, son of Sir Thomas Gower of Stitenham, who bore, *Barry of eight pieces silver and gules, a cross paty sable* (98); and that Harcourt was Sir Thomas Harcourt of Stanton, Sheriff of Berkshire, whose arms were, *Gold, two bars gules*—others of the name reversed the tinctures.

Travers and Morton, as retainers of Northumberland, might wear as their household badge the silver crescent of the Percys.

Falstaff and Others

Sir John Falstaff, for all his knighthood, is scarcely a figure of chivalry. To him 'honour is a mere scutcheon'—that is, a funeral scutcheon, or hatchment, dignifying only him 'that died o' Wednesday.' Although there was a real Sir John Falstaff, or Fastolfe (who appears in *Henry VI*), Shakespeare evidently did not intend the fat knight to be identified with him, or any historical person. It is well known that he first named the character 'Oldcastle,' but changed the name because of objections raised by descendants of the true Sir John Oldcastle. It has been suggested that he hit on the name Falstaff as allusive—a false staff for the Prince to lean on. It would clearly be improper to assign to Sir John the arms of any historical person; yet, as he appears in armour, some insignia he should have. The early arms of the Falstaff family appear to have been, *Quarterly gold and azure*, to which the historical Sir John (in *Henry VI*) added *a bend gules charged with three silver cross-crosslets* (171).

FIG. 98.   Gower.   FIG. 99.   Sir John Falstaff   FIG. 100.   Lucy.
(suggested arms).

I suggest that the Falstaff of *Henry IV* and *The Merry Wives of Windsor* should bear the early arms of the Falstaff family with the tinctures reversed, and some sufficient and suitable difference—and what more suitable than the sign of the tavern that he wished his drum? This was the Boar's Head in Eastcheap. With this house, as landed knights with their manors, Falstaff was associated by his fellows:

> *Prince:* Doth the old boar feed in the old frank?[1]
> *Bardolph:* At the old place, my lord, in Eastcheap.
>
> (*2 Henry IV, ii, 2*)

Again, in act ii, sc. 4, Doll Tearsheet addresses Falstaff with affectionate sarcasm as 'thou whoreson little tidy Bartholomew boar-pig.' The indications point clearly to the boar's head as Falstaff's proper emblem. Let him bear it next his heart; let his arms be, *Quarterly azure and gold, in the second quarter a boar's head azure* (99).

[1] Sty.

Poins is thought to have been intended by Shakespeare as a cadet of the Gloucestershire family of Pointz, Poyntz, or Poynes, which bore, *Barry of six pieces gules and gold*. Peto's name may have been suggested by the Warwickshire Petos, whose arms were, *Per pale indented and barry of six pieces silver and gules all counter-changed*.

Justice Shallow

Though Justice Shallow does not appear in coat-armour, he is nevertheless important from the heraldic viewpoint. The allusion to his arms occurs in *The Merry Wives of Windsor*, but may be conveniently dealt with here. The arms attributed to him by Shakespeare suggest that Shallow was a caricature of Sir Thomas Lucy, of Charlecote, Warwickshire, whom Shakespeare thus pilloried in retaliation for an old grudge. The tradition is well known that as a young man Shakespeare was involved in a poaching escapade in Lucy's park. It is referred to by Richard Davies (1688-1709) in a memorandum[1] which states that Shakespeare was

> much given to all unluckinesse in stealing venison and Rabbits particularly from Sᵣ Lucy who had him oft whipt & sometimes Imprisoned & at last made Him fly his Native Country to his great Advancemᵗ. but his reveng was so great that he is his Justice Clodpate and calls him a great man and yᵗ in allusion to his name bore three lowses rampant for his Arms.

The arms of Lucy of Charlecote were, *Gules, semé of cross-crosslets and three luces (pike-fish) hauriant argent* (100); the crosslets differenced the arms from the old coat of Lucy as quartered by the Percys (see above). In *The Merry Wives* Slender, boasting his cousin Shallow's gentility, says his ancestors 'may give the dozen white luces in their coat.' In making the number a dozen instead of three in the actual shield of Lucy, Shakespeare was providing for Sir Hugh Evans's blundering impression that the reference was to a verminous garment:

> The dozen white louses do become an old coat well; it agrees well, passant; it is a familiar beast to man, and signifies love.

In introducing the word 'passant,' Shakespeare is merely having fun with an heraldic term. Evans simply means 'passing well.' He does not use the word with any heraldic significance. In fact, he is clearly unaware

[1] Quoted and shown in replica in Sir E. K. Chambers's *William Shakespeare*, 1930.

that the others are speaking of a coat of arms, for in the following dialogue
he continues to misunderstand the terms of heraldry:

Slender: I may quarter, coz.
Shallow: You may, by marrying.
Evans: It is marring indeed if he quarter it.
Shallow: Not a whit.
Evans: Yes, py'r lady; if he has a quarter of your coat, there is but
three skirts for yourself in my simple conjectures.

Here again Shakespeare is merely playing with heraldic words without
much regard to the sense of the passage. Slender remarks with some
pride that he is entitled to include the arms of his cousin Shallow in a
quarter of his own shield. Shallow agrees that this is so 'by marrying'—
not by Slender's own marriage with a Shallow heiress (which would give
the children, but not Slender himself, the right to quarter the arms),
but because some ancestor of Slender has in the past married an heiress of
some branch of the Shallows. 'By marriage' would have been clearer,
but Shakespeare used the word 'marrying' to give Evans a chance for
another blunder.

This reference to Sir Thomas Lucy in *The Merry Wives* may have been
Shakespeare's second literary dig at him. Nicholas Rowe, in the life
appended to Shakespeare's works (1709), says that when young Shakespeare
was prosecuted by Lucy,

he made a Ballad upon him. And tho' this, probably the first Essay of
his Poetry, be lost, yet it is said to have been so very bitter that it redoubled
the Prosecution against him . . .

Probably the loss of this ballad is not to be lamented. Its first stanza
is said to have been remembered by an old man living near Stratford,
and was put on record by William Oldys (1696-1761); and as interest in
Shakespeare grew, someone conveniently discovered the rest of the verses.
The first and one other stanza may be quoted as a sample of the whole:

A parliament member, a justice of peace,
At home a poor scarecrow, in London an asse;
If Lucy is lowsie, as some volke miscall it,
Sing lowsie Lucy, whatever befall it.

Though luces a dozen he paints in his coat,
His name it shall lowsie for Lucy be wrote;
For Lucy is lowsie, as some volke miscall it,
Sing lowsie Lucy whatever befall it.

The thing is, of course, suspect, but the two lines forming the refrain
may be genuine. If Shakespeare wrote such a ballad, it probably harped

on the theme of 'lowsie Lucy' (or should we say 'loozie Lucy'?), an obvious jingle which may may well have been current in Warwickshire before the ballad was written.

The identification of Shallow with Lucy has been challenged. An alternative theory represents Shallow as a lampoon on Justice Gardiner, who was hostile to Shakespeare and his fellows, and who, having married Frances Luce or Lucy, impaled a version of the Lucy arms with his own coat, *Azure, a gold griffin passant*.[1] From the heraldic point of view, the theory is not well founded, for Shallow-Gardiner, bearing the luces in right of his wife, could not have claimed that they were his ancestral coat; the wife in respect of whom he bore them died in 1576, nearly twenty years before the reference in *The Merry Wives*.

It is possible that Shakespeare derived Evans's blunder about 'the dozen white louses' from Holinshed's *Chronicles of Ireland*, where it is told that the King, noting the ermine of the charges on Sir William Wise's seal, remarked, 'Why, how now Wise, what, hast thou lice here?' 'And, if it like your majesty,' quoth Sir William, 'a louse is a rich coat, for by giving the louse I part arms with the French King, in that he giveth the flower-de-lice.'

---

[1] Leslie Hotson, *Shakespeare versus Shallow*, 1931.

FIG. 101.   Henry V, from his Great Seal.

CHAPTER VI

KING HENRY V

IN THE PROLOGUE of *Henry V*, which Shakespeare himself may have spoken,[1] the playwright laments the shortcomings of his stage and wardrobe to present 'so great an object':

> Can this cockpit hold
> The vasty fields of France? Or may we cram
> Within this wooden O the very casques
> That did affright the air at Agincourt?

He begs his audience to 'piece out our imperfections with your thoughts'—

> For 'tis your thoughts that now must deck our kings.

He is specially aware of the inadequacy of the battle scene,

> Where—O for pity!—we shall much disgrace
> With four or five most vile and ragged foils
> (Right ill-dispos'd, in brawl ridiculous)
> The name of Agincourt.

[1] See J. Dover Wilson, *Henry V* (Cambridge).

But if he cannot dress the scene he paints it in vivid words, giving us glimpses of the 'fair show' of the French chivalry with the sun glinting on their armour, in contrast with the English in war-worn coats, rusty and plumeless helms, and banners like 'ragged curtains.'   Mars may be 'bankrupt in their beggar'd host,' but their King speaks proudly:

> We are but warriors for the working-day;
> Our gayness and our gilt are all besmirch'd
> With rainy marching in the painful field;
> There's not a piece of feather in our host—
> Good argument, I hope, we will not fly—
> And time hath worn us into slovenry:
> But, by the mass, our hearts are in the trim;
> And my poor soldiers tell me, yet ere night
> They'll be in fresher robes, or they will pluck
> The gay new coats o'er the French soldiers' ears
> And turn them out of service.

We may therefore imagine the nobles and knights with their arms blazoned on their shields, surcoats and horse-bardings, and with heraldic pennons and guidons on their lances, the leaders attended by a knight or esquire bearing their armorial banners—the French colours all fresh and gay, the English dingy and tattered.   On neither side would heraldic crests be worn, since a man going into battle would not cumber himself with unnecessary weight, but the French helms would be topped with plumes of various colours.

Royal Heraldry

Henry V bore the same arms as his father had used during the latter part of his reign: *Quarterly France Modern and England*.[1] His crest also was the same, and as his Great Seal shows (101), this was placed not only on his great helm, but also on his horse's head—this in tournaments and pageantry; in battle he wore a bascinet encircled with a jewelled coronet. At Agincourt, the coronet round his helm contained the famous ruby given by Pedro of Castile to the Black Prince, and now part of the State Crown.   This was in danger of loss when part of Henry's coronet was hewn off by the axe of the Duke of Alençon.

There is a reference to the lion as the emblem of English royalty in act 1, sc. 2, where Exeter, urging the French expedition on Henry, says,

---

[1] Shown in colour in Plate IV.

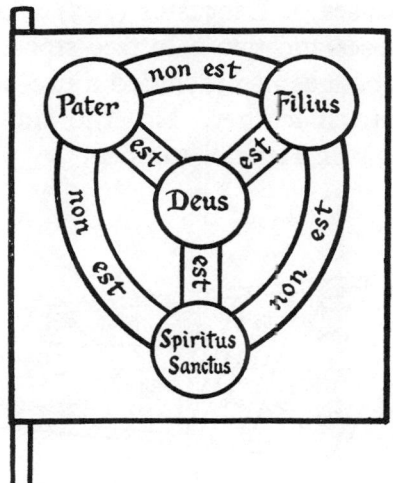 

FIG. 102. Banner of the Holy
Trinity.

FIG. 103. Banner of St Edward
the Confessor.

> Your brother kings and monarchs of the earth
> Do all expect that you should rouse yourself,
> As did the former lions of your blood.

Again, in act iv, sc. 3, Henry, rejecting France's offer to accept his ransom, says:

> The man that once did sell the lion's skin
> While the beast liv'd, was kill'd with hunting him.

The importance which Henry V attached to his arms, as symbolising his honour, is shown by an incident two nights before Agincourt. By mistake, the King had ridden half a league beyond the place fixed for his night's lodging, and found himself in advance of his army. He refused to turn back, because he was wearing his coat of arms.

At Agincourt, Henry displayed a banner bearing his royal arms, together with banners showing the symbol of the Holy Trinity (102), the cross of St George, the crowns of St Edmund, and the arms attributed to Edward the Confessor (103). Henry also had several personal standards—tapering flags with the cross of St George next the staff, the fly divided lengthwise in his colours, white and blue, crossed with the motto, DIEU ET MON DROYT, and charged with his badges: one bearing the white swan of Bohun and gold tree-stocks of Woodstock (104), and another a white antelope and the red roses of Lancaster (105). Another standard bore the swan with four red roses and two gold tree-stocks, with the motto, UNE SANZ PLUS. The King's badges also included a fire-beacon, or cresset, a fox's tail, and a white ostrich feather. No. 140 shows the antelope, beacon and swan as they appear on Henry's tomb.

FIG. 104.   Standard of Henry V with swan and tree-stocks.

FIG. 105.   Standard of Henry V with antelope and roses.

In the prologue to act ii of the play, Shakespeare uses a piece of imagery which may have been suggested by a royal badge of Edward III:

> For now sits Expectation in the air,
> And hides a sword, from hilts unto the point,
> With crowns imperial, crowns and coronets,
> Promis'd to Harry and his followers.

A sword erect, the blade encircled by three crowns (106), was a device of Edward III, perhaps assigned to him at some later period, 'either in allusion to the three great victories of his reign—Cressy, Neville's Cross, and Poictiers—or to the kingdoms of England, France, and of the Romans, the latter crown having been offered to him by the Electors.'[1]   Professor Dover Wilson notes a woodcut of Edward III holding a sword encircled by two crowns found in Holinshed (ed. i) p. 885.[2]

FIG. 106.   Device
attributed to Edward III.

FIG. 107.   Crown of Henry V.

At the beginning of his reign, Henry V no doubt used the 'Harry crown' he had inherited from his father (80), and he may be represented as wearing in it act i, sc. 2.   When this was broken up to provide security for the loan for the French war, it was replaced by a crown which was presumably less costly.   The new crown differed in design from those of previous reigns, the circlet being heightened by crosses and fleurs-de-lys, and arched over with two bands, broadening to the point of their intersection, where they were surmounted by a mound and cross (107). Possibly the design of the new crown was suggested by the ancient 'crown of St Edward' which was used at the coronation of Henry IV and perhaps of his son.

The heraldry of the King's brothers, Clarence, Bedford and Gloucester, has been dealt with in the Chapter on *Henry IV*.

[1] Mrs. Bury Palliser, *Historic Devices*.

[2] *Henry V* (Cambridge).

Edward, Duke of York—the 'Aumerle' of *Richard II*—bore, as his father had done, *France and England quarterly, with a silver label charged on each point with three roundles gules* (40d). (The Rouen roll of arms assigns him the coat of England alone with this label, and these may have been the arms he placed on his war shield.)   His badge was an ostrich feather with a chain laid along the quill (79).   His brother Richard, Earl of Cambridge, bore the same arms and label with the addition of *a silver bordure charged with eight (or twelve) lions rampant purpure*— that is, a bordure of Leon, derived from his mother, Isabella of Castile and Leon (108).

FIG. 108.   Richard, Earl of Cambridge.

Thomas Beaufort, Duke of Exeter, K.G., the King's uncle, was a natural son of John of Gaunt by Catherine Swynford.   The first arms of the Beauforts, denoting their illegitimate origin, were *Per pale silver and azure, a bend gules charged with three gold lions passant guardant and a label azure semé of gold fleurs-de-lys* (109)—that is, a shield of the Lancastrian colours with the arms of the Duchy of Lancaster on a bend. On their legitimation, the Beauforts bore the royal arms with a distinctive bordure.   In the case of theeldestson, John, Earl of Somerset, the bordure was *compony silver and azure;* Thomas made it ermine and azure. He therefore bore, until 1417, *Quarterly France Modern and England within*

FIG. 109. Beaufort,   FIG. 110.   Before 1417   FIG. 111.   After 1417
before legitimation.   Thomas Beaufort, Duke of Exeter.

a bordure compony ermine and azure (110). In 1417, after his creation as
Duke of Exeter, he altered the bordure to silver and azure, charging each
of the azure pieces with a gold fleur-de-lys (111). His badge was the
Beaufort portcullis (152).

John Holland, Earl of Huntingdon, K.G., who is present in act v, sc. 2,
but does not speak, was descended through his grandmother, Joan of
Kent, from Edward I, and bore the arms of England with a bordure of
France, i.e. *azure, semé-de-lys gold*, and also the royal crest, the lion being
differenced with an azure crown. He was created Duke of Exeter in 1443
in succession to Thomas Beaufort.

The English Nobles and Knights

Thomas de Montagu, Earl of Salisbury, K.G., son of the Salisbury of
Richard II, bore the same arms: *Quarterly Montagu and Monthermer* (55).

The Earls of Warwick and Westmoreland are the same as those who
appear in *Henry IV*, and their heraldry has already been noted. Westmoreland's helm with wreath (but no crest) and SS collar is shown in
fig. 143.

Henry, Lord Scrope of Masham, nephew of the Archbishop of York
in *Henry IV*, bore, *Azure, a gold bend and a silver label* (112). He was a
Knight of the Garter. 'It appears to have been thought necessary to
absolve the Order from any disgrace that might attach to it in conse-
quence of the offence of one of its companions. The record of Scrope's

FIG. 112. Lord Scrope of   FIG. 113. Sir Thomas Grey.   FIG. 114. Sir Thomas
          Masham.   Erpingham.

attainder in Parliament, therefore, recites that "whereas he was a knight of the renowned and excellent military Order of the Garter, which had been laudably instituted in support of the faith, the king, the realm, and the law, no person shall presume to vilify or reflect upon those who are worthy members of that venerable body, because the said Henry Scrope has dishonoured himself by the crime which he has committed".' (Beltz, *Memorials of the Most Noble Order of the Garter.*)

Sir Thomas Grey, or Gray, of Heton and Warke, Northumberland, bore, *Gules, a silver lion rampant within a silver bordure engrailed* (113).

Sir Thomas Erpingham, K.G., bore, *Vert, a silver inescutcheon within an orle of silver martlets* (114).

Michael de la Pole, Earl of Suffolk, referred to in act iv, sc. 6, as having been slain at Agincourt, bore, *Azure, a gold fess between three gold leopards' faces* (115). In his full achievement he quartered this with, *Silver, on a bend gules between cotices sable, three pairs of wings cojoined argent* (for Wingfield).

'Sir Richard Ketly, Davy Gam esquire,' who were also among the slain, cannot be identified. The former, whose name is given as 'Kikelie' by Holinshed, may have been one of the Keighley family, which bore, *Argent, a fess sable.* There is a Welsh family of Gam or Gamme, bearing, *Argent, three cocks gules, with gold combs.*

Talbot, one of the names mentioned by King Henry as to be 'freshly remembered,' refers to Gilbert, Lord Talbot (brother of Shrewsbury in

FIG. 115. De la Pole,
Earl of Suffolk.

FIG. 116. Gilbert,
Lord Talbot.

FIG. 117. Thomas,
Lord Camoys.

Henry VI), who bore, *Quarterly*, 1 *and* 4, *Gules, a gold lion rampant within a gold bordure engrailed*, for Talbot; 2 *and* 3, *Silver, two lions passant gules*, for Le Strange (116).

Others who might appear in the battle scenes, though not mentioned by Shakespeare in *Henry V*, are:

Edmund Mortimer, Earl of March: arms as in *Henry IV* (82). He appears to have been loyal to Henry V, notwithstanding the conspiracy of his brother-in-law, the Earl of Cambridge, to place him on the throne.

John, Lord Mowbray, Earl of Nottingham and Earl Marshal (brother of the Mowbray in *Henry IV*): *Gules, a silver lion rampant*. He was created Duke of Norfolk in the reign of Henry VI.

Thomas, Lord Camoys: *Gold, on a chief gules three silver roundles* (117).

Sir Walter Hungerford: *Sable, two silver bars, in chief three silver roundles* (118).

Sir Louis Robsert, esquire of the body to Henry V: *Vert, a gold lion rampant*.

William, Lord Ferrers of Groby: *Gules, seven gold mascles cojoined* (119).

William, Lord FitzHugh: *Azure, three gold chevrons interlaced and a gold chief* (120).

Edward Courtenay, Earl of Devon: *Gold, three roundles gules, a label of three points azure* (121).

Sir Gilbert Umfraville, Lord Kyme: *Gules, a gold cinquefoil in an orle of gold cross-crosslets* (122).

FIG. 118. Hungerford.

FIG. 119. Ferrers of Groby.

FIG. 120. FitzHugh.

James le Boteler, Earl of Ormonde, K.G.: *Gold, a chief dancetty of three indents azure* (123).

Humphrey, Earl of Stafford (later Duke of Buckingham): *Gold, a chevron gules* (124).

Sir Hugh Stafford: *Gold, a chevron and a bordure gules* (125).

Sir William Bourchier: *Silver, a cross engrailed gules between four water-budgets sable* (126).

The Lords Berkeley, Fitz Walter, de Ros, and Willoughby, and Sir John Norberry, as in *Richard II*; Lord Bardolph as in *Henry IV*; John de Vere, Earl of Oxford, and the Lords Clifford and Scales as in *Henry VI*.

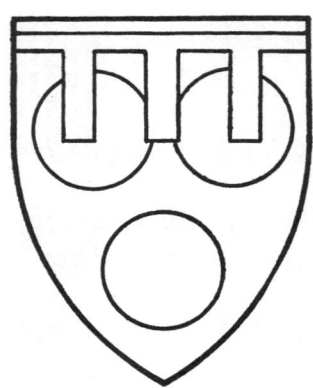

FIG. 121.   Courtenay,
Earl of Devon.

FIG. 122.   Umfraville,
Lord Kyme.

FIG. 123.   Le Boteler,
Earl of Ormonde.

FIG. 124. Earl of Stafford.   FIG. 125. Sir Hugh Stafford.   FIG. 126. Bourchier.

The French Nobility

The royal arms of France were at this time, *Azure, three gold fleurs-de-lys*. King Charles VI used as a device a winged stag with a crown round its neck. He also bore the sun as a badge. His crown was an open circlet heightened with fleurs-de-lys, alternately large and small.

Louis the Dauphin bore the royal arms of France quarterly with the arms of the Dauphiné, *Gold, a dolphin hauriant and embowed azure* (127). In armour, he would wear a coronet of fleurs-de-lys round his bascinet.

The arms of the Duke of Burgundy were, *Quarterly, 1 and 4, France Ancient within a bordure compony silver and gules; 2 and 3, Bendy of six pieces gold and azure within a bordure gules* (128). The Duke mentioned

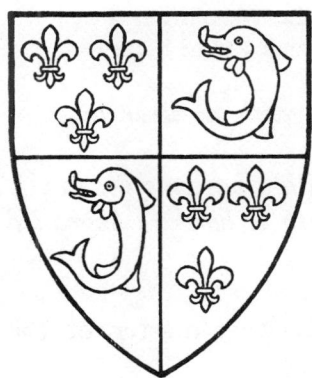  

FIG. 127. The Dauphin of France.   FIG. 128. The Duke of Burgundy.   FIG. 129. D'Albret, Constable of France.

E

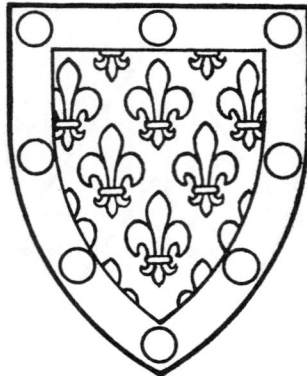

FIG. 130. The Duke of Orleans.   FIG. 131. The Duke of Bourbon.   FIG. 132. The Duke of Alençon.

in the list of French lords in act iii is John the Fearless. He died in 1418, and the Duke who appears in act v is his son Philip, the Count of Charolois in the earlier list. Duke John's brother, Anthony, Duke of Brabant, who is mentioned in the play as having been slain at Agincourt, bore *Quarterly, 1 and 4, France Ancient within a bordure compony silver and gules; 2 and 3, Sable, a gold lion rampant*, for Brabant.

Charles Delabreth (d'Albret), Constable of France, bore the arms of France quarterly with plain gules (129). The reference to stars on his armour in act iii does not appear to have any heraldic significance. In act iv, sc. 2, in his haste to join the battle, he takes a banner from a trumpet to serve as a guidon, or flag. Holinshed attributes this incident to the Duke of Brabant, who,

> when his standard was not come, caused a baner to be taken from a trumpet and fastened to a speare; the which he commanded to be borne before him in stead of his standard.

Charles, Duke of Orleans, bore *France Modern with a silver label of three points* (130).

John, Duke of Bourbon, bore: *France Modern with a baston gules* (131).

John, Duke of Berri, bore : *France Modern with a bordure engrailed gules.*

John, Duke of Bretagne, bore: *Ermine.*

Lord Rambures, who, according to Holinshed, was 'master of the crossbowes,' probably bore: *Gules, three gold bars.*

Lord Grandpré cannot be identified with certainty, but may have borne: *Barruly gold and gules.*

FIG. 133. The Duke of Bar.   FIG. 134. Chatillon,   FIG. 135. d'Estouteville.
                              Lord Dampierre.

A number of French nobles are mentioned without being introduced as characters in the play. They may appear in the battle scenes with their appropriate shields and surcoats. These include:

The Duke of Alençon: *France Ancient with a bordure gules charged with golden roundles* (132). By the name 'Alanson,' he is referred to in the play as having been in personal combat with Henry V.

The Duke of Bar: *Azure, semé of gold cross-crosslets pointed at the foot, two gold barbels hauriant back to back* (133).

Jacques de Chatillon, Lord Dampierre, Admiral of France: *Gules, three pallets vairé, a gold chief charged with two lions passant sable* (134).

The Count of Vaudemont: *Barruly silver and sable.*

The Count of Foix: *Gold, three pallets gules.*

Lord Bouciqualt, Marshal of France: *Silver, an eagle displayed gules, with beak and legs azure.*

Monsieur le Fer, whom Pistol takes prisoner, may be regarded as a member of the family which bore: *Checky gold and gules.*

The Governor of Harfleur at the time of the siege was Jean, Sieur d'Estouteville, who bore: *Barry of eight pieces, silver and gules, a lion rampant sable with a gold crown* (135).

At Agincourt, the French fought under the *oriflamme*. This has been variously described, but is generally conceived to have been at this period a long flag with three points, red throughout and bearing no device but fringed and tasselled with green, suspended from its staff by a cross-bar. Other flags borne by the French probably included a banner of the royal arms, while Rodway gives the crosses of St Denis and St Martin (see *King John*), the banner of Bretagne (*Gold, a cross sable*), the Constable's banner (*plain gules*), and the banner of Burgundy (*Bendy of six, gold and azure*). The oriflamme was borne by the Seigneur Martel de Bacqueville, whose arms were, *Or, three hammers (marteaux) gules.*

The heraldic standards of the French consisted of the cross of St Denis (white on blue) next the staff, the fly bearing badges and crossed by a motto. For example, that of the Duke of Bourbon was parted white and green, and was charged with a gold flying stag with a collar bearing the word 'Esperance,' above flames of fire; three thistles counterchanged, and the *cri*, ESPERANCE—ESPERANCE (136).

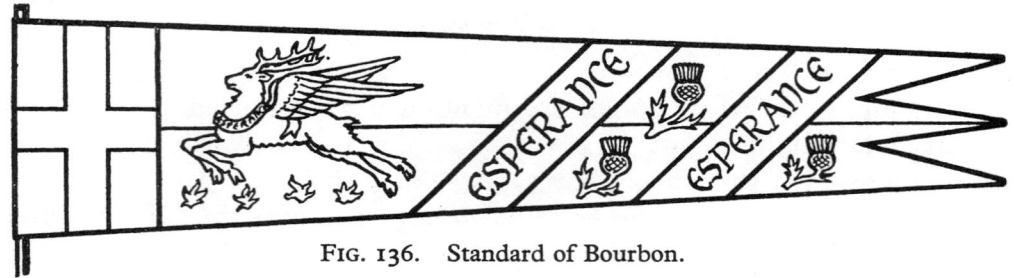

FIG. 136.   Standard of Bourbon.

Other Characters

While at this period there was no military uniform in the modern sense, it was ordained that every man in the English host should wear a large red cross of St George. Such a one as Pistol 'that now and then goes to the wars, to grace himself at his return into London, under the form of soldier,' would probably wear the red cross over his ordinary garments, and pick up what he could in the way of clothing and equipment on the battlefield. So far as there was a uniform device among the French, it seems to have been a white cross on blue.

The play gives us an early instance of a national emblem displayed on commemorative occasions, in the leek which Fluellen wears on St David's day, and Captain Gower commends as 'an ancient tradition, begun upon an honourable respect, and worn as a memorable trophy of predeceased valour.' Fluellen recalls that it originated at Cressy, where

> the Welshmen did good service in a garden where leeks did grow, wearing leeks in their Monmouth caps, which your majesty know to this hour is an honourable badge of the service; and I do believe your majesty takes no scorn to wear the leek upon Saint Tavy's day.
>
> *Henry:* I wear it for a memorable honour.

The producers of the film of *Henry V*,[1] feeling, no doubt, that as Fluellen had his national emblem, Gower, Jamy and Macmorris should display theirs, gave them respectively a red rose, thistle, and shamrock as badges on their garments.   As to the rose and thistle, their use in the production may be justified by the fact that they were already national emblems of England and Scotland in Shakespeare's time (though not in the reign of Henry V).   The adoption of the shamrock as the emblem of Ireland appears to be more modern, though the plant is associated with the legend of St Patrick.

Fig. 137. Chichele, Archbishop   Fig. 138. Fordham, Bishop
        of Canterbury.   of Ely.

While there is no stage occasion to show the arms of Henry Chichele, Archbishop of Canterbury, it may be noted that they were: *Gold, a chevron gules between three cinquefoils gules*.   These are now the arms of his foundation of All Souls College, Oxford.   They might have been impaled with the arms of the archbishopric (137), *Azure, an archbishop's staff of silver, the cross gold, surmounted by a pall of silver, edged and fringed with gold and charged with four crosses formy fitchy sable*.

The Bishop of Ely in the play was John Fordham.   He bore: *Sable, a gold chevron between three gold crosses paty*, and he might have impaled these arms with those of the See of Ely (138), *Gules, three gold crowns*.

[1] The heraldry of the film was generally excellent. It was, however, spoiled by the use of round and oval targes instead of the shield-form proper to the period.   One result was that some of these targes were accidentally carried upside down (which could not have happened had true shields been used), and we had the strange sight of a proud noble of France riding into battle with his arms reversed —a traditional sign of disgrace.

FIG. 139. Garter King of Arms, and English and French Heralds.

The Heralds

The play gives us a glimpse of the heralds on both sides carrying out their war-time duties of bearing messages between armies, and meeting after the battle to identify the fallen nobility and to estimate the number of the slain.   According to French,[1] 'three heralds attended Henry V at Agincourt, namely Lancaster, Guienne, and Ireland, Kings at Arms.' Holinshed mentions Antelope Pursuivant of Arms as having been sent by Henry to the French King to deliver his claim to the throne and his intention to prosecute it by war.   In the play this task is entrusted to Exeter, but the pursuivant may be represented in his train.

The heralds wore tabards emblazoned on back and front, and on the elbow-length sleeves, with their Sovereign's arms. They were thus clearly recognizable. The French Herald, Montjoy King of Arms (whose name came from the French war-cry, 'Montjoie, St Denis!') introduces himself to Henry merely with the words, 'You know me by

[1] *Shakespeareana Genealogica.*

my habit.' Notwithstanding the blunt defiance of his message, the way he delivers it earns Henry's approval: 'Thou dost thy office fairly. . . . There's for thy labour, Montjoy,' the last words referring to the 'princelie reward' which Holinshed says the King gave the herald.

In the midst of the battle, the King says:

> Take a trumpet, herald,
> Ride thou unto the horseman on yon hill.
> If they will fight with us, bid them come down,
> Or void the field; they do offend our sight.

For 'trumpet' we must understand 'trumpeter.' As has been mentioned in the chapter on *King John*, it was no part of a herald's duty to blow fanfares.

After the battle, it is Montjoy who tells Henry that the day is his, and asks for:

> charitable license,
> That we may wander o'er this bloody field,
> To book our dead, and then to bury them,
> To sort our nobles from our common men. (*iv*, 7)

In commemoration of the victory, the title of Agincourt was conferred on an English herald.

We may here notice that Agincourt became a landmark in heraldic history. In 1418, Henry V issued a writ referring to the fact that heretofore 'divers men . . . assumed unto themselves Arms and Coats of Arms, called Coat-Armours, in cases where neither they nor their ancestors in times gone by used such Arms;' and proclaiming 'that no one, of whatsoever rank, degree or condition he may be, shall assume such Arms or Coats of Arms, unless he possess or ought to possess the same in right of his ancestors, or by the gift of some person having adequate power for that purpose; and that he shall plainly show forth, on the day of his mustering, by whose gift he hold those Arms . . . those excepted who bore arms with us at the battle of Agincourt.' In other words, if a veteran of Agincourt assumed heraldic arms, no questions would be asked. It seems likely that Shakespeare was aware of this, and had it in mind when he gave the King the words:

> We few, we happy few, we band of brothers;
> For he to-day that sheds his blood with me
> Shall be my brother; be he ne'er so base,[1]
> This day shall gentle his condition. (*iv*, 3)

[1] For 'base' the folio reads 'vile': each word means here merely low-born, and has no defamatory sense.

The 'Rouen' roll of arms, compiled about 1415 and giving the names and arms of 107 English nobles and knights, is a contemporary source of information on the heraldry of this period. (It was so named because it was formerly believed to be a roll of the arms of those present at the siege of Rouen in 1418.) The original is lost, but copies exist, and a version was printed in *Notes and Queries*, 6th series, vols. 2 and 3, 1880.

FIG. 140. Antelope, Beacon and Swan, on Henry V's tomb.

FIG. 141.   Arms, Crown and Supporters of Henry VI.

CHAPTER VII

KING HENRY VI

ABOUT THE time of Agincourt the close-fitting heraldic surcoat called a jupon began to go out of fashion.   Armour was becoming more elaborate, and was often richly decorated, so that knights were unwilling to hide its magnificence.   However, they could not altogether dispense with a surcoat, and about the middle of the fifteenth century an early form of tabard appeared.   This was open at the sides, and had flap-sleeves half way to the elbow, so that it could be easily put on and off.   The wearer's arms were emblazoned on front, back and sleeves.   It is unlikely that the tabard was worn in action.

As plate armour developed there was a tendency to discard the shield, except at jousts, but for stage purposes the heraldic shield may be used.

The Great Seal of Edward IV shows him in a tabard and bearing a shield of his arms.

A feature of fifteenth century costume was the heraldic mantle, which was worn by both men and women of rank on state occasions. This frequently displayed the arms of husband and wife impaled, and any quarterings accruing to the main coats (192).

Badges were commonly worn by both men and women, whether as their personal devices, or tokens of their political sympathies, or signs of the household to which they belonged. For the purposes of the play, the

FIG. 142. Lancastrian Collar of SS with Swan pendant.

FIG. 143. Ralph Nevill, Earl of Westmoreland.

badges of York and Lancaster are specially important, particularly the white and red roses.

A development of the badge was the collar, which was worn by some persons of rank and official standing. The collar of SS, derived from a badge of Henry IV, has already been noticed (142, 143). It sometimes had a pendant swan, the badge of Henry V in allusion to his Bohun descent. The Yorkists devised a collar of alternate suns and white roses, with the white lion of the earldom of March as a pendant (144).

The Royal Arms

Whether Henry VI or Edward IV sat on the throne, the royal arms remained the same: *Quarterly France Modern and England;* with the crest of a gold crowned lion standing on a chapeau, as used by Henry V.

Edward, Prince of Wales, son of Henry VI, differenced the shield and crest with a plain white label.

There is an allusion to the arms of England in 1 *Henry VI, i, 5,* where Talbot, rousing his men before Orleans, exclaims:

> Hark, countrymen, either renew the fight,
> Or tear the lions out of England's coat:
> Renounce your soil, give sheep in lions' stead:
> Sheep run not half so treacherous from the wolf,
> Or horse or oxen from the leopard,
> As you fly from your oft-subdued slaves.

The word 'give' is here used in its heraldic sense, 'to display as an armorial

FIG. 144. Yorkist Collar of Suns and White Roses, with the Lion of March as pendant.

bearing' (O.E.D.), and indicates Shakespeare's familiarity with the language of armory.

The King is referred to several times by allusion to the royal lion. Queen Margaret, urging her husband to take strong measures against Gloucester, says:

> Small curs are not regarded when they grin,
> But great men tremble when the lion roars;
> And Humphrey is no little man in England.   (2 *Henry VI, iii, 1*)

In Henry VI's reign, heraldic supporters came into general use by the king and great nobles. These flanked and upheld the shield in representations of arms. Henry variously used as supporters two white antelopes, a lion and a panther, and a lion and an antelope (141). The panther and antelope also appear as royal badges; both were the heraldic, and not the natural, beasts, the panther being shown as spotted and breathing flames, and the antelope as here illustrated. Henry also used as a badge two ostrich feathers crossed saltire-wise, one silver and the other gold. His colours were the white and blue of Lancaster.

It would be appropriate, and add to the heraldic interest of the production, to display the royal arms with the supporters of whichever king occupied the throne at the time, in court scenes. Henry VI's arms may be shown impaled with those of Queen Margaret of Anjou, which are given later in this chapter (191).

Henry VI's first rival for the possession of the crown was Richard Plantagenet, Duke of York, heir of Edmund Mortimer, Earl of March.

Mortimer (whose heraldry has been dealt with under *Henry IV*) died in 1424. The account of his life which Shakespeare puts into his mouth in I *Henry VI*, ii, 5, is far from the facts. Certainly he was imprisoned for a time by Henry IV, but since he never pressed his claim to be Richard II's heir, he was on excellent terms with Henry V, and had not only his liberty but also responsible and honourable employment. His sister and heir married the Earl of Cambridge (who appears in *Henry V*), son of Edmund Langley, Duke of York. Accordingly, Cambridge's son, Richard Plantagenet, succeeded Mortimer in the earldom of March and Ulster and the lordship of Clare (or Clarence), and inherited the claim to the throne which Mortimer had allowed to lie dormant. Richard was created Duke of York and made a Knight of the Garter in 1433. Like his two predecessors in the dukedom, he bore the royal arms and crest with the label of York: white, charged with nine red roundles (150a). As supporters he used a white falcon and a white lion, for York and March respectively. His badges were a silver falcon in a gold fetterlock derived from Edmund Langley, the white rose (of which presently), the white lion of March, the black dragon of Ulster, and the black bull of Clarence. He also used the Plantagenet ostrich feather with a chain laid along the quill (79).

Duke Richard seems to have been particularly associated in the public mind with the badge of the falcon and fetterlock. Political verses written in 1449 refer to him in the lines:

> The Fawkon fleyth and hath no rest
> Tille he witte wher to bigge his nest.

It is said that he symbolized his hope of attaining the crown for himself or his heirs by showing the fetterlock open, so that the falcon was no longer locked up as Edmund Langley had borne it; and certainly later representations of the badge show the fetterlock a little open (145).

It seems probable that Shakespeare had noted York's badge of a falcon, but had taken it for an eagle, for in 3 *Henry VI* he refers to York as a

FIG. 145.   Falcon and Fetterlock.

FIG. 146.   White Rose *en soleil*, Fleurs-de-lys, Lion of March, and Suns of York.

'princely eagle.'   In act ii, sc. 1, Richard of Gloucester addresses his brother Edward, then Earl of March:

> Nay, if thou be that princely eagle's bird,
> Show thy descent by gazing 'gainst the sun—

an allusion to the reputed ability of the eagle to meet unwinking the sun's full rays.   In act v, sc. 2, dying Warwick says:

> Thus yields the cedar to the axe's edge,
> Whose arms gave shelter to the princely eagle,
> Under whose shade the ramping lion slept.

Here again the eagle probably refers to York, while the lion is Henry VI, who enjoyed a brief spell of quietude while Warwick bore the burden of government.

Richard, Duke of York, had four sons: Edward (who succeeded as Edward IV; Edmund, Earl of Rutland; George, Duke of Clarence; and

Richard, Duke of Gloucester, who became Richard III.   Their heraldry
follows.

Edward 'of Rouen,' Earl of March at the beginning of 3 *Henry VI*,
became Duke of York on the death of his father, and later Edward IV.
As Earl, he would bear the royal arms with a differencing label, but it is
uncertain what form the label took; it may have been white charged with
three purple lions rampant, such as his father had used when Earl of March
(150b).   In Pt. 3, act ii, sc. 1, Edward became 'no longer Earl of March, but

FIG. 147. Arms, Crown and Supporters of Edward IV

Duke of York,' and in the following scenes he should bear the royal arms
differenced with the white label charged with nine red roundles, on shield
and surcoat.   His banner would show these arms quartered in the first
and fourth quarters with 2 Ulster, and 3 Mortimer.   In act iii, sc. 2,
he appears as king, and bears the royal arms without any differencing mark.

According to Speed, when Edward (having been turned off the throne)
returned from France in 1471, he pretended to claim nothing but his
dukedom of York, and 'in every place where hee came, proclaimed King
Henry himselfe, wearing an ostrich feather, which was Prince Edward's
livery.'   So Shakespeare (Pt. 3, iv, 7) makes Edward assure the Mayor

of York, 'I challenge nothing but my dukedom.' There is thus good authority for making him appear in this scene not in the royal arms, but in a garment of his livery colours, murrey and blue, embroidered with his ostrich feather. In the later scenes of the play, where he appears in armour he may wear a tabard of the royal arms.

Edward IV's supporters were two white lions of March, a silver or gold lion and a black bull of Clarence (147), and a lion and a white hart— the last perhaps derived from Richard II's badge, indicating that Edward was that king's legitimist successor. He also used the lion, bull and hart as badges, together with the white rose of York, the sun-in-splendour,

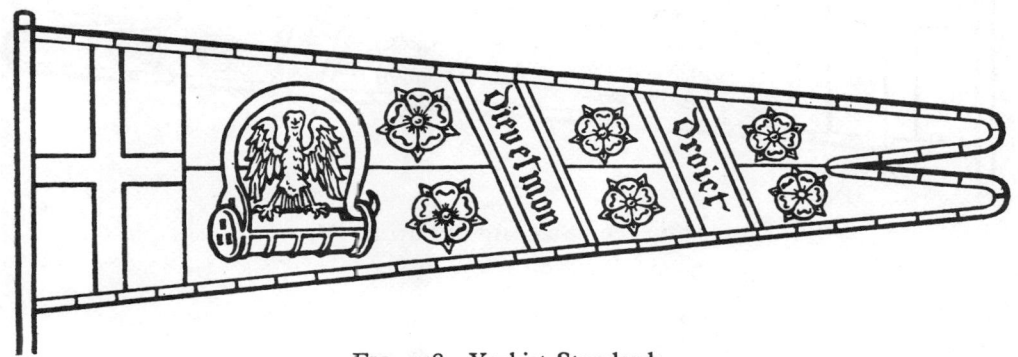

FIG. 148. Yorkist Standard.

and a white rose *en soleil*, i.e. irradiated, a combination of the last two badges (146). The rose and sun badges figure prominently in the play, and are fully dealt with below. Edward also used the falcon and fetter-lock of the dukedom of York, a black dragon with a gold crown as Earl of Ulster, and a white wolf, probably derived from the Mortimers. On his marriage with the Lancastrian Elizabeth Widville, he took the red rose of Lancaster and set it *en soleil* among his badges; and he also devised a rose parti-coloured white and red, anticipating the Tudor rose in which the rival blooms of York and Lancaster were eventually united. The impaled arms of Edward and his queen are shown in no. 193.

One of Edward's standards bore the cross of St George next to the staff, the fly being divided lengthwise into blue and murrey, and edged compony of the same colours, charged with a silver falcon in a gold fetterlock and six white roses, and crossed with the motto, DIEU ET MON DROICT (148). This may be used as the standard of the Yorkists in the battle scenes. Another standard was similar as regards the cross, motto and colours, but bore a gold lion of England, with six red roses on the blue part of the fly, and six white roses on the red (149). This appears to belong to the period after his marriage with Elizabeth Widville.

FIG. 149. Standard of Edward IV.

Edmund, Earl of Rutland, differenced the royal arms and crest with a label of five points, two gold each charged with a red lion rampant, and three silver each charged with three red roundles (150c). In his full achievement of arms he quartered this coat with Ulster and Mortimer quarterly. Edmund, who was York's second son, was seventeen years old at the time of his death at Wakefield; but Shakespeare represents him as a young boy, and it would therefore be inappropriate to show him on the stage in armour with an heraldic shield or tabard.

George, created Duke of Clarence in 1461 and a Knight of the Garter, differenced the royal arms and crest with a silver label of three points charged on each point with a canton gules (150d). In his full achievement this was impaled with the arms of his wife, a daughter of Nevill, Earl of Warwick: *Gules, a silver saltire and a label compony silver and azure.* His supporters were two black bulls of Clarence, and his badges were a black bull with gold horns and a label about its neck, and a silver gorget of chain edged and clasped with gold and lined with red.

Richard, created Duke of Gloucester in 1461 and dubbed a Knight of the Garter in 1465, bore the royal arms and crest with a label ermine charged on each point with a canton gules (150e). His heraldry as king is dealt with in the chapter on *Richard III*. His well-known badge of a white boar, to which there are several allusions in that play, may appear on his garments in *Henry VI* in scenes where he is not in armour.

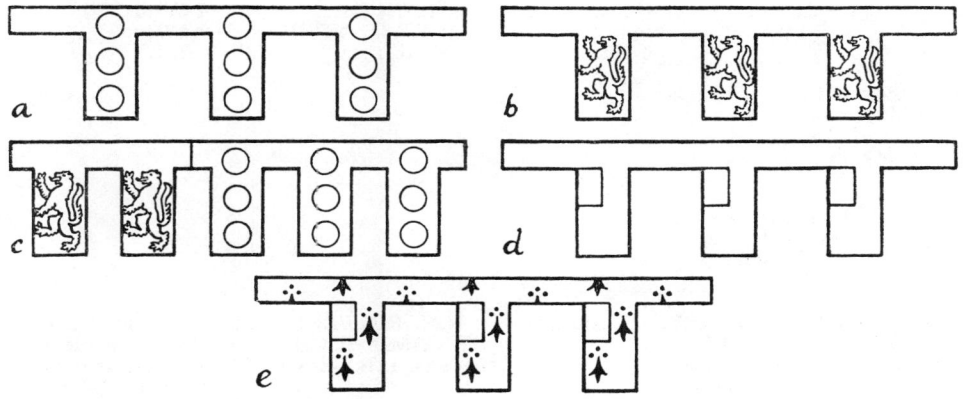

FIG. 150. Labels of the House of York:

(a) The Duke of York; (b) The Earl of March ;
(c) Edmund, Earl of Rutland; (d) George, Duke of Clarence;
(e) Richard, Duke of Gloucester.

Henry VI's uncles, the Dukes of Bedford and Gloucester, bore the arms already given in the chapter on *Henry V*. There is an echo (probably unintentional) of Gloucester's motto, *Loyalle et Belle*, in King Henry's words:

Ah, uncle Humphrey, in thy face I see
The map of honour, truth, and loyalty.   (*Pt. 2, iii, 1*)

Eleanor, Duchess of Gloucester, was the daughter of Rainald, Lord Cobham of Sterborough; her married arms were: *Quarterly France and England within a silver bordure* (for Gloucester) impaling: *Gules, on a gold chevron three estoiles sable* (for Cobham—68).

TABLE IV

THE HOUSE OF YORK

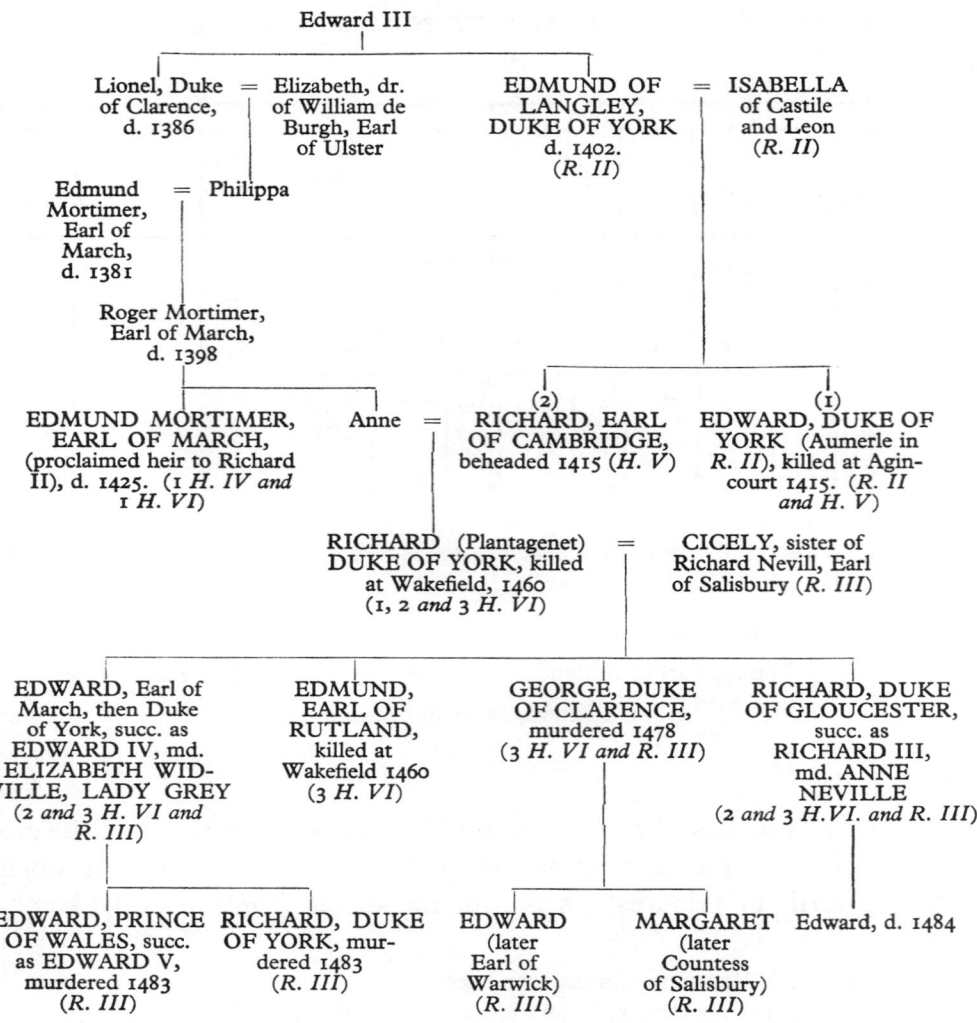

Edward III

Lionel, Duke = Elizabeth, dr.
of Clarence, | of William de
d. 1386 | Burgh, Earl
of Ulster

EDMUND OF = ISABELLA
LANGLEY, | of Castile
DUKE OF YORK | and Leon
d. 1402. | (R. II)
(R. II)

Edmund = Philippa
Mortimer,
Earl of
March,
d. 1381

Roger Mortimer,
Earl of March,
d. 1398

EDMUND MORTIMER,   Anne = RICHARD, EARL
EARL OF MARCH,   OF CAMBRIDGE,
(proclaimed heir to Richard   beheaded 1415 (H. V)
II), d. 1425. (1 H. IV and
1 H. VI)

(2)   (1)
RICHARD, EARL   EDWARD, DUKE OF
OF CAMBRIDGE,   YORK (Aumerle in
beheaded 1415 (H. V) R. II), killed at Agin-
                     court 1415. (R. II
                     and H. V)

RICHARD (Plantagenet) = CICELY, sister of
DUKE OF YORK, killed   Richard Nevill, Earl
at Wakefield, 1460   of Salisbury (R. III)
(1, 2 and 3 H. VI)

EDWARD, Earl of   EDMUND,   GEORGE, DUKE   RICHARD, DUKE
March, then Duke   EARL OF   OF CLARENCE,   OF GLOUCESTER,
of York, succ. as   RUTLAND,   murdered 1478   succ. as
EDWARD IV, md.   killed at   (3 H. VI and R. III) RICHARD III,
ELIZABETH WID-   Wakefield 1460   md. ANNE
VILLE, LADY GREY   (3 H. VI)   NEVILLE
(2 and 3 H. VI and   (2 and 3 H.VI. and R. III)
R. III)

EDWARD, PRINCE RICHARD, DUKE   EDWARD   MARGARET   Edward, d. 1484
OF WALES, succ. OF YORK, mur-   (later   (later
as EDWARD V,   dered 1483   Earl of   Countess
murdered 1483   (R. III)   Warwick)   of Salisbury)
(R. III)   (R. III)   (R. III)

TABLE V

THE HOUSE OF LANCASTER

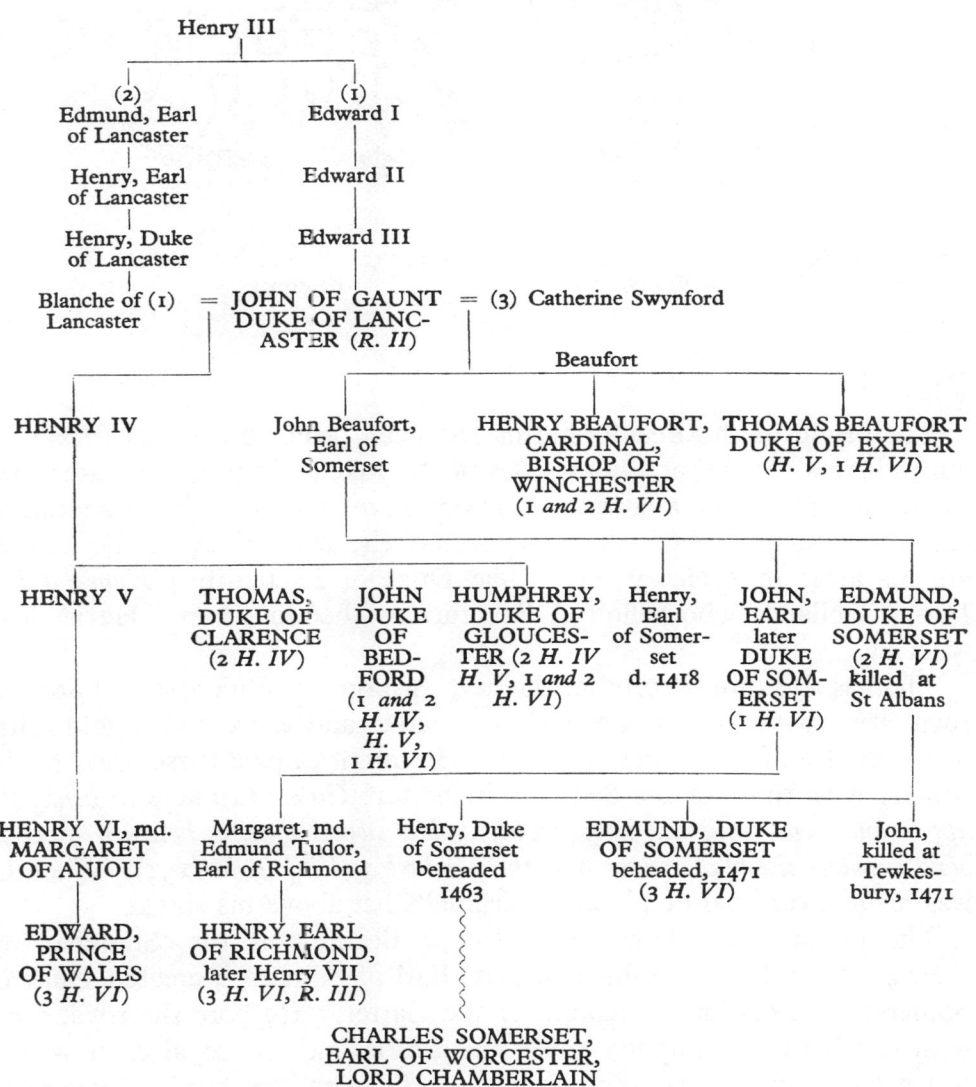

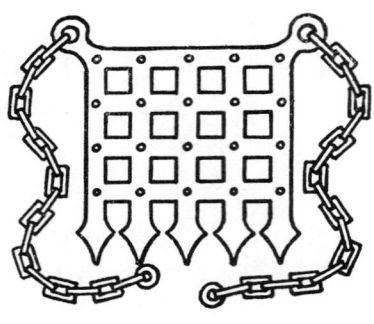

FIG. 151. Henry Beaufort,
Bishop of Winchester.

FIG. 152. Portcullis badge of
Beaufort.

Beaufort

The origin of the Beaufort arms has been dealt with under *Henry V*,
where it was noted that Thomas Beaufort, Duke of Exeter, bore after 1417
the royal arms within a bordure compony silver and azure (the Lancastrian
colours) with a gold fleur-de-lys on each of the azure pieces (111). These
are his arms in 1 *Henry VI*. (The Duke of Exeter in 3 *Henry VI* is
Henry Holland, who followed Beaufort in the dukedom. He is dealt
with later.)

Thomas Beaufort's brother Henry, Bishop of Winchester, bore the
royal arms with the bordure compony silver and azure and a gold mitre
in the centre of the upper bordure. He might impale these arms to the
sinister with those of the See of Winchester: *Gules, two keys in bend, the
upper one silver and the lower gold, and a sword passing between them in
bend sinister, the blade silver and the pommel and hilt gold* (151). When he
was made a cardinal he placed a cardinal's hat above his shield.

The nephew of Thomas and Henry Beaufort is the 'Somerset' of
1 *Henry VI*. He was John Beaufort, Earl of Somerset, created Duke of
Somerset in 1443, and a Knight of the Garter. He bore the royal arms
with the bordure compony silver and azure, and the royal crest with a
collar compony of the same colours. He bore the bordure compony
without any addition such as his uncles made, because as the son of their
elder brother, he was the head of the family. Somerset's livery colours
were red, green, and white; his badge was a white ostrich feather, the quill

compony silver and azure; and his supporters were a gold crowned eagle, and a silver yale with gold spots and horns. The drawing of his arms (5) is from his Garter stall-plate. His effigy shows him wearing a collar of SS.

John was succeeded as Duke of Somerset by his brother Edmund, who is the 'Somerset' in 2 *Henry VI*. He bore the same arms and crest. His badges were a steel bonnet, a portcullis (152), a cresset, and a beanstalk. He also was a Knight of the Garter.

Edmund was succeeded in the dukedom by his two sons: Henry (who does not appear in the plays) and Edmund, the Duke in 3 *Henry VI*. The last bore the same arms and crest as his predecessors. Him Gloucester addresses:

> Two of thy name, both Dukes of Somerset,
> Have sold their lives unto the house of York,
> And thou shalt be the third if this sword hold.   (*v*, 1)

The two were the first Edmund, slain at St Albans, and Henry, beheaded after Hexham. The second Edmund was beheaded after Tewkesbury, where his younger brother, John, was slain.

Margaret, daughter of John, first Duke of Somerset, married Edmund Tudor, Earl of Richmond. Henry, Earl of Richmond (afterwards Henry VII), was their son. In 3 *Henry VI* he appears only as a youth, to be greeted by the King as 'England's hope'—

> Likely in time to bless a regal throne.

His heraldry is dealt with in the chapter on *Richard III*.

The Regalia

In the reign of Henry VI, the crown advanced a stage further towards its modern form. Henry V had the circlet heightened with pairs of fleurs-de-lys between plain crosses. On his son's crown, single fleurs-de-lys alternated with crosses paty; moreover, the crown appears to have had more than two arches, though it is difficult to determine from representations how many arches there were (141). Edward IV reverted to two arches (147). Unarched crowns are still found in these reigns. Probably there was more than one crown: the principal one, used on great occasions of state, being arched; and the minor crown, worn by the king in semi-state, being a light unarched circlet. It does not seem likely that Edward, resting at night in a chair in his camp near Warwick (Pt. 3, iv, 3), would wear his state crown, and it would be more natural to show him in a light

open coronet of crosses paty and fleurs-de-lys, which Warwick removes
with the words:

> . . . Henry now shall wear the English crown,
> And be true king indeed; thou but the shadow.

In Pt. 2, v, 1, York says:

> This hand was made to handle nought but gold.
> I cannot give due action to my words,
> Except a sword or sceptre balance it:
> A sceptre shall it have, have I a soul,
> On which I'll toss the flower-de-luce of France.

From the reign of Edward III, English kings are shown on their Great
Seals bearing two sceptres, one usually topped with a cross, the other
sometimes with a shrine and sometimes with a trifoliate form. The
latter took the form of a fleur-de-lys on Henry V's seal, perhaps in allusion
to his claim to the French throne, and this is clearly the sceptre York has
in mind in the above speech. On Henry VI's seal, one sceptre bears a
floral top resembling a lily rather than a fleur-de-lys, and the other has
the *manus Dei*, a hand with the thumb and two fingers raised in
benediction.

The Roses

The heraldic theme of the rival roses runs through *Henry VI* and
Richard III, from the scene in the Temple garden where the flowers are
plucked as emblems of the factions, to the final speech in the latter play,
in which Henry of Richmond promises to 'unite the white rose and the
red.' To Elizabethan audiences the Tudor rose was, of course, familiar,
and was well known to have been produced by the union of the roses of
York and Lancaster, so that Shakespeare could use the flowers in his
imagery with confidence that the allusions would be understood.

The red rose, sprung from the same stem as Edward I's golden rose,
was a badge of the house of Lancaster from the time of Earl Edmund
'Crouchback' (son of Henry III) who died in 1296. The white rose was
originally a badge of the Mortimer Earls of March, and was used by Earl
Roger who died in 1360. The Yorkists chose it as the emblem of their
party, probably because it was through his Mortimer descent that Richard
Plantagenet (later Duke of York) claimed to be in the line of succession to
the throne, and also because it was the obvious and appropriate badge to

set against the red rose. The Plantagenet colours were white and red, and the hues of the rival roses thus symbolized the cleavage in the royal house.

At the time of the scene in the Temple garden (1 *Henry VI*, *ii*, 4) the roses already existed as badges, the red rose being definitely that of the house of Lancaster. We must not think of the episode as having given rise to the roses as badges, but only as having focused their rivalry.

Shakespeare does not tell us the nature of the wrangle which had begun in the Temple-hall and was continued in the garden; it could have been no mere academic point of law which engendered such heat, but something that touched the contestants nearly. Since the leaders in the argument were Richard Plantagenet and John Beaufort, Earl of Somerset, we may assume that it was indirectly concerned with the question of the succession to the throne—indirectly, because there could be no open discussion of possibilities which envisaged the death of the king without an heir.

Richard Plantagenet was the nephew and heir of the childless Mortimer, Earl of March, who was the senior descendant of Edward III, through Lionel, Duke of Clarence, and had been acknowledged by Richard II as heir to the throne. (In the play, Richard does not appear to realise his position fully until his interview with the dying Mortimer—a device of Shakespeare's to give an opportunity of explaining to the audience, through Mortimer, the dynastic issues involved.) Though in the senior line, Richard's descent from Edward III was through two women. On the other hand, Somerset was descended in a direct male though junior line from Edward III, being a grandson of John of Gaunt by Catherine Swynford. True, he was not the senior lineal descendant, but the only persons who stood between him and that position were the infant Henry VI and his childless uncles.

Either Richard or Somerset might some day find himself in a position to claim the throne; but in each potential claim there was a flaw. Richard's father, the Earl of Cambridge (see *Henry V*) had been executed for treason: Somerset refers contemptuously to Richard as 'yeoman.' Warwick, supporting Richard, protests:

> His grandfather was Lionel, Duke of Clarence,
> Third son to the third Edward King of England:
> Spring crestless yeomen from so deep a root?

(In fact, Clarence was Richard's great-great-grandfather.) Somerset, maintaining his words, demands of Richard:

Was not thy father, Richard, Earl of Cambridge,
For treason executed in our late king's days?
And by his treason stand'st thou not attainted,
Corrupted, and exempt from ancient gentry?
His trespass yet lives guilty in thy blood,
And, till thou be restor'd, thou art a yeoman.

On the other hand, Somerset himself, a Beaufort and of illegitimate origin, was debarred from the succession by the very act that had legitimated his family. In the play, the irregularity of the Beaufort descent is emphatically recalled by Gloucester, who addresses the Bishop of Winchester as 'thou bastard of my grandfather.'

In these rivalries, many 'nice sharp quillets of the law' were involved; and while we do not know, nor need to know, the particular point that gave rise to the dispute in the Temple, it was clearly a dynastic one.

Let us suppose that in the Temple garden Somerset is wearing a gown embroidered with the heraldic red roses of Lancaster, indicating his descent from John of Gaunt. To Richard Plantagenet, these red roses symbolise the obstacle to his own budding ambitions. Beside him is a rose bush with white blooms: what more appropriate to set against Somerset's red heraldic rose than one of these contrasting flowers? Indeed, the white rose is the more suited to this purpose because it is already a badge of the Mortimers, through whom Richard descends from Edward III in a senior line to that represented by Somerset's red roses. In picking a white rose, he is not taking an emblem at random but one which has a significance which, in an era of heraldic devices, Somerset, Warwick and the rest cannot miss.

I do not suggest that Shakespeare knew the history of the roses, or imagined these thoughts to pass through his character's mind; but the fact remains that a good heraldic reason can be read into Richard's action in choosing a white rose, and calling on his sympathisers:

Let him that is a true-born gentleman,
And stands upon the honour of his birth,
If he suppose that I have pleaded truth,
From off this brier pluck a white rose with me.
Somerset: Let him that is no coward nor no flatterer,
But dare maintain the party of the truth,
Pluck a red rose from off this thorn with me.

Vernon proposes that the majority opinion shall prevail, and Somerset agrees.   The Earl of Warwick, Vernon and the Lawyer pluck white roses, and the Earl of Suffolk picks a red one.

Plantagenet: Now, Somerset, where is your argument?

Somerset. Here in my scabbard, meditating that
         Shall dye your white rose in a bloody red.

Pla.: Meantime your cheeks do counterfeit our roses,
         For pale they look with fear, as witnessing
         The truth on our side.

Som.:   No, Plantagenet;
         'Tis not for fear, but anger, that thy cheeks
         Blush for pure shame, to counterfeit our roses,
         And yet thy tongue will not confess thy error.

Pla.: Hath not thy rose a canker, Somerset?

Som.: Hath not thy rose a thorn, Plantagenet?

Pla.: Ay, sharp and piercing, to maintain his truth,
         Whiles thy consuming canker eats his falsehood.

Som.: Well, I'll find friends to wear my bleeding roses
         That shall maintain what I have said is true . . .

Pla.: And, by my soul, this pale and angry rose,
         As cognizance of my blood-drinking hate,
         Will I for ever and my faction wear,
         Until it wither with me to my grave,
         Or flourish to the height of my degree.

The scene closes with Warwick's prophesy:
                         this brawl to-day,
         Grown to this faction in the Temple-garden,
         Shall send between the red rose and the white
         A thousand souls to death and deadly night.

The roses were not yet openly avouched as emblems of rival claims to the throne.   Henry VI's life lay before him: he might have an heir of his blood to nullify the pretensions of both Plantagenet and Somerset; also his uncles, Bedford and Gloucester, were still alive.   They who wore the roses must do so as tokens of a rivalry whose origin might not be declared —least of all in the presence of the king.   This comes out in the scene (1 *Henry VI, iv,* 1) where Vernon and Basset, wearing red and white roses respectively, beg the King's leave to fight:

King: What is that wrong, whereof you both complain?
         First let me know, and then I'll answer you.

Basset: Crossing the sea from England into France,
         This fellow here, with envious carping tongue,
         Upbraided me about the rose I wear,

> Saying, the sanguine colour of the leaves
> Did represent my master's blushing cheeks,
> When stubbornly he did repugn the truth
> About a certain question in the law
> Argued betwixt the Duke of York and him . . .
>
> *Vernon:*   I was provok'd by him,
> And he first took exceptions at this badge,
> Pronouncing that the paleness of this flower
> Bewray'd the faintness of my master's heart.

Here York and Somerset join in the quarrel and, wholly ignorant of what underlies it, Henry exclaims:

> Good Lord, what madness rules in brainsick men,
> When for so slight and frivolous a cause
> Such factious emulations shall arise!
>
> .   .   .   .   .   .
>
> I see no reason, if I wear this rose, (*putting on a red rose*)
> That anyone should therefore be suspicious
> I more incline to Somerset than York.

The white rose definitely appears as the symbol of York's claim to the throne in 2 *Henry VI, i,* 1, where York advises himself in soliloquy:

> Watch thou, and wake when others be asleep,
> To pry into the secrets of the state,
> Till Henry, surfeiting in joys of love,
> With his new bride, and England's dear-bought queen,
> And Humphrey with the peers be fall'n at jars:
> Then will I raise aloft the milk-white rose,
> With whose sweet smell the air shall be perfum'd,
> And in my standard bear the arms of York,
> To grapple with the house of Lancaster,
> And, force perforce, I'll make him yield the crown,
> Whose bookish rule hath pull'd fair England down.

We need not suppose Shakespeare to have been ignorant of the terms of heraldry because he here refers to the white rose as the *arms* of York. His correct use of the terms elsewhere shows that he must have known that the rose was a badge, and properly displayed on a standard; but he needed the word 'arms' to play on the idea of grappling in the next line.

York again alludes to the rose in act iii, sc. 1, where, hearing of the loss of the French territories, of which he had hopes equally with England, he says:

> Thus are my blossoms blasted in the bud,
> And caterpillars eat my leaves away.

In 3 *Henry VI* the roses are at open war. The factions of York and Lancaster appear in the first scene with their roses in their hats. Richard of Gloucester exclaims:

> I cannot rest
> Until the white rose that I wear be dyed
> Even in the luke-warm blood of Henry's heart. (*i*, 2)

And Richard again, on finding the body of Clifford, who had slain York and his son, Rutland:

> 'tis Clifford,
> Who not contented that he lopp'd the branch,
> In hewing Rutland, when his leaves put forth,
> But set his murdering knife unto the root,
> From whence that tender spray did sweetly spring,
> I mean our princely father, Duke of York. (*ii*, 6)

The tragedy of the War of the Roses is expressed by King Henry at the sight of a father weeping over the body of his son whom he has slain in battle:

> O that my death would stay these ruthful deeds!
> O pity, pity, gentle heaven, pity!
> The red rose and the white are on his face,
> The fatal colours of our striving houses:
> The one his purple blood right well resembles;
> The other his pale cheeks, methinks, presenteth:
> Wither one rose, and let the other flourish;
> If you contend, a thousand lives must wither. (*ii*, 5)

The Sun

Another badge worked into the imagery of 3 *Henry VI* is the Yorkist sun-in-splendour. As has been shown in an earlier chapter, the sun was the badge of Richard II, and figures prominently in the play about him. It was also among the badges of Henry IV, but he did not make much use of it (perhaps because it was too strong a reminder of Richard), and neither Henry V nor Henry VI seems to have used it. Probably it was revived by the house of York as an indication of their claim to be in the true line of succession to Richard II. Perhaps with Richard's sun-burst badge in mind, Shakespeare hints at a device consisting of the sun breaking through clouds against their will as a badge of the Yorkist supporters. This occurs in the scene in which Suffolk is murdered (2 *Henry VI*, iv, 1):

Captain: And now the house of York, thrust from the crown
　　　　By shameful murder of a guiltless king,
　　　　And lofty proud encroaching tyranny,
　　　　Burns with revenging fire, whose hopeful colours
　　　　Advance our half-fac'd sun, striving to shine;
　　　　Under the which is writ, 'Invitis nubibus.'

Of York's fall, Clifford says, 'Now Phaeton hath tumbled from his car'—a natural classical allusion, but with a double meaning in view of its heraldic significance.

Shakespeare, following Holinshed, attributes the adoption of the sun-badge by the house of York to the phenomenon at Mortimer's Cross, where three suns appeared in the sky:

Edward: Dazzle mine eyes, or do I see three suns?
Richard: Three glorious suns, each one a perfect sun,
　　　　Not separated with the racking clouds,
　　　　But sever'd in a pale clear-shining sky.
　　　　See, see, they join, embrace, and seem to kiss,
　　　　As if they vowed some league inviolable:
　　　　Now are they but one lamp, one light, one sun;
　　　　In this the heaven figures some event.

(3 *Henry VI, ii,* 1)

'For this cause,' wrote Holinshed, 'men imagined that he [Edward] gave the sunne in his full brightnesse for his badge or cognisance.'   So Shakespeare makes Edward say:

Whate'er it bodes, henceforward will I bear
Upon my target three fair-shining suns.

In fact Edward used not three suns but one, and not on his target or shield but merely as a badge.   Shakespeare took a liberty with Holinshed's text, and heraldic accuracy, to give Richard the chance of retorting:

Nay, bear three daughters: by your leave I speak it,
You love the breeder better than the male.

At Towton 'Edward's sun is clouded,' until the tide of battle turns, and Lancastrian Clifford laments:

The common people swarm like summer flies;
And whither fly the gnats but to the sun?
And who shines now but Henry's enemies?   (*ii,* 6)

After Barnet, Edward, now king, says:

> . . . in the midst of this bright-shining day,
> I spy a black, suspicious, threatening cloud,
> That will encounter with our glorious sun,
> Ere he attain his easeful western bed:
> I mean, my lords, those powers that the queen
> Hath rais'd in Gallia have arriv'd our coast,
> And, as we hear, march on to fight with us.
> *Clarence:* A little gale will soon disperse that cloud,
> And blow it to the source from whence it came:
> The very beams will dry those vapours up . . . (*v*, 3)

King Henry, likening his dead son to Icarus, describes Edward IV as:

> The sun that sear'd the wings of my sweet boy. (*v*, 6)

The White Rose en Soleil

Edward IV combined the two Yorkist badges of the white rose and the sun-in-splendour to form the badge of a white rose *en soleil*, or surrounded by golden rays. Though Shakespeare does not mention it, this badge played an important part at the second battle of Barnet (Pt. 3, v, 2 and 3), where it was worn as a badge by Edward's followers. On Warwick's side was De Vere, Earl of Oxford, whose men were wearing his silver star as their cognizance. Warwick, seeing through a mist the star of Oxford, mistook it for Edward's irradiated rose, and charged against his own supporters. In the confusion which resulted, the Lancastrians lost the battle.

Montagu, Nevill, and Beauchamp

Table VI shows the links between these families, and enables the different holders of the titles of Salisbury, Westmoreland and Warwick in the plays to be identified.

Thomas Montagu, Earl of Salisbury, killed at Orleans in 1 *Henry VI*, was the same earl that appears in *Henry V*. He was the son of Earl John in *Richard II*, and bore the same arms: *Quarterly Montagu and Monthermer* (55). He was an indirect descendant of Edward I, which is presumably why Shakespeare makes Talbot address him as 'Plantagenet' (i, 4).

Richard Nevill, a younger son of Ralph, Earl of Westmoreland, married Earl Thomas's heiress, and became Earl of Salisbury, as he appears in 2 *Henry VI*. His paternal arms were: *Gules, a silver saltire*, which, as a

TABLE VI

MONTAGU, NEVILL, BEAUCHAMP AND TALBOT

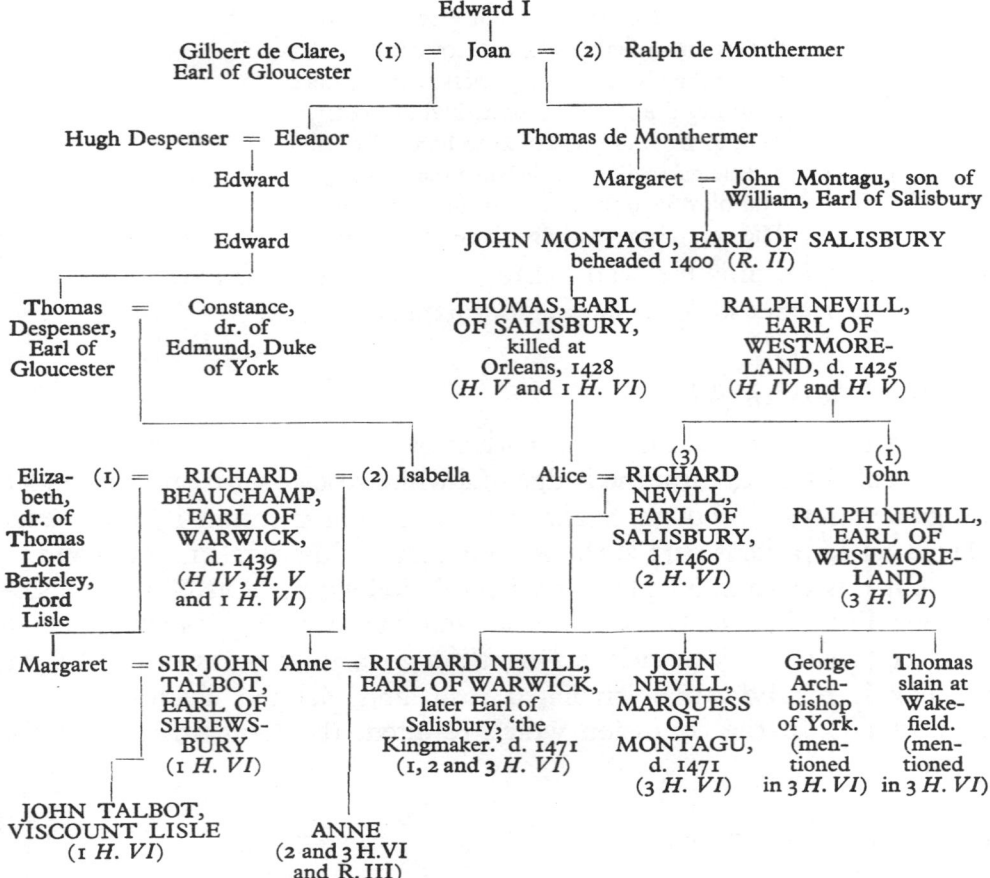

cadet, he differenced with *a label compony silver and blue*, choosing the Lancastrian colours for the purpose because his mother was a daughter of John of Gaunt. He quartered this paternal coat with *Quarterly Montagu and Monthermer*, placing the latter coats in the first and fourth quarters because they represented the earldom he held. His crest was a demi-griffin (153).

The undifferenced arms of Nevill (*Gules, a silver saltire—85*) were borne by Richard Nevill's nephew, Ralph, who succeeded to the earldom of Westmoreland, and appears in 3 *Henry VI*.

FIG. 153. Richard Nevill, Earl of
Salisbury.

FIG. 154. Richard Beauchamp,
Earl of Warwick.

Richard Nevill was the father of another Richard, famous as 'the
Kingmaker,' to whom the title of Salisbury passed in due course. The
Kingmaker is known in Shakespeare's plays by the title of Earl of Warwick,
which he obtained by marriage with the heiress of the last Beauchamp
Earl.

Richard Beauchamp, the Earl of Warwick in 1 *Henry VI*, is the same
earl as appears in *Henry IV* and *Henry V*. His paternal arms were:
Quarterly Beauchamp and Neubourg (blazoned in the chapter on *Henry IV*),
and after 1423 he bore thereon an inescutcheon with the arms of his second
wife, *Quarterly Clare and Despenser*, i.e.: *Gold, three chevrons gules*, for
Clare, and *Quarterly silver and gules fretty gold, over all a bend sable*, for
Despenser (154). In battle Warwick would probably bear only the coat
of Beauchamp on his shield. His crest was a white swan's head and
neck rising from a red coronet. His badges were a white bear with a red

muzzle, and a ragged staff. These were combined to produce the famous badge—

The rampant bear chain'd to the ragged staff.

Warwick's daughter and heir, Anne, married Richard Nevill, son of the Earl of Salisbury of that name, and in due course carried to her husband the Warwick earldom.

FIG. 155. Richard Nevill, Earl of Warwick, and later of Salisbury, "the Kingmaker."

Therefore in 2 *Henry VI* we have two Richard Nevills, father and son, the elder being Earl of Salisbury and the younger Earl of Warwick, each holding his title through marriage with an heiress. Both were Knights of the Garter.

Salisbury was beheaded after the Battle of Wakefield. From the beginning of act ii of 3 *Henry VI*, the Kingmaker is Earl of Salisbury as well as Earl of Warwick, though Shakespeare continues to call him by the latter title.   He is now the mightiest subject, 'proud setter up and puller down of kings,' who declares:

> I'll plant Plantagenet, root him up who dares:

and when Edward fails him, vows to 'replant Henry.'   The lordships and power concentrated in his hands are reflected in his heraldry.   On his shield for battle he used his paternal arms of Nevill with their differencing label, but his banner, horse-bardings and complete achievement of arms (such as might appear on a banner or a tabard) show an assemblage of quarterings significant at a time when an array of coats had no mere genealogical meaning, but indicated that the bearer actually possessed the lordships they stood for.   Three of the quarters of his shield were subdivided.   He bore in the first quarter. *Beauchamp and Neubourg quarterly;* in the second, *Montagu and Monthermer quarterly*, in the third *Nevill;* and in the fourth, *Clare and Despenser quarterly* (155).   (Another version reverses the position of the Clare and Neubourg quarterings.)   His supporters were the muzzled and chained bear of Warwick, and the griffin of Salisbury.   Above his shield he placed two helms each with a crest: the white swan's head and neck rising from a gold coronet, for Warwick; and a demi-griffin issuing from a coronet, for Salisbury.   With the earldom of Warwick he inherited not only the bear, but also the badge of a ragged staff.   To both badges he refers in his advice to York (in 2 *Henry VI*, ii, 2):

> Claim thou the crown, and set thy standard up,
> And in the same advance the milk-white rose,
> And then to guard it will I rouse the bear,
> Inviron'd with ten thousand ragged staves.

Grafton states that Warwick's 'servitures were apparailed in red cotes embraudered with white ragged staves'.   His standard bore, in addition to the customary cross of St George, a muzzled bear supporting a ragged staff, and a number of ragged staves, all white on red (156).

As a Warwickshire man, Shakespeare was, of course, familiar with the bear, but he makes the mistake of associating it not only with Warwick but also with his father, Salisbury; it was never Salisbury's badge, but was derived by Warwick from his father-in-law, the last Beauchamp Earl. In 2 *Henry VI*, v, 1:

> *York:*   Call hither to the stake my two brave bears,
> That with the very shaking of their chains

F

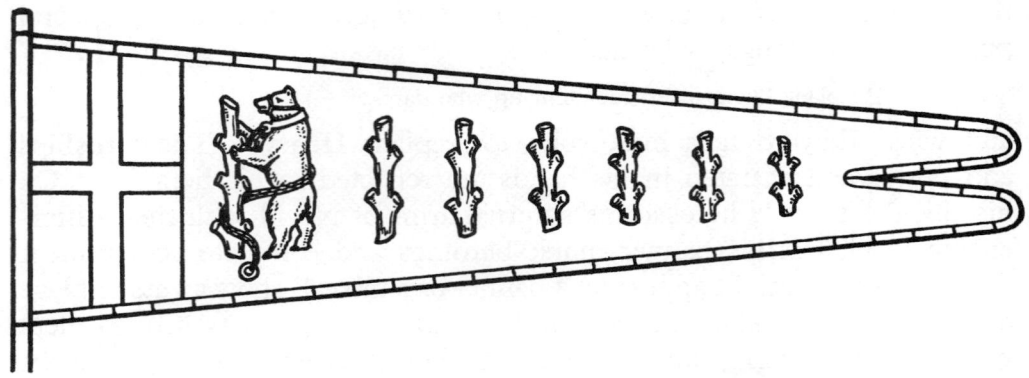

FIG. 156. Standard of Richard Nevill, Earl of Warwick.

> They may astonish these fell-lurking curs:
> Bid Salisbury and Warwick come to me.
> > *Enter the Earls of Warwick and Salisbury.*
> *Clifford:* Are these thy bears? we'll bait thy bears to death,
> And manacle the bear-ward in their chains,
> If thou darest bring them to the baiting place.
>
> *Richard:* Oft have I seen a hot o'erweening cur
> Run back and bite, because he was withheld,
> Who, being suffer'd with the bear's fell paw,
> Hath clapp'd his tail between his legs and cried;
> And such a piece of service will you do,
> If you oppose yourselves to match Lord Warwick.   (*v*, 1)

The erroneous idea that Warwick inherited the bear from his father, Salisbury, clearly appears later in the scene:

> *Clifford:* I am resolv'd to bear a greater storm
> Than any thou canst conjure up to-day;
> And that I'll write upon thy burgonet,
> Might I but know thee by thy household badge.
>
> *Warwick:* Now, by my father's badge, old Nevil's crest,
> The rampant bear chain'd to the ragged staff,
> This day I'll wear aloft my burgonet,
> As on a mountain top the cedar shows
> That keeps his leaves in spite of any storm,
> Even to affright thee with the view thereof.
>
> *Clifford:* And from thy burgonet I'll rend thy bear,
> And tread it under foot with all contempt,
> Despite the bear-ward that protects the bear.

Again, in 3 *Henry VI* Shakespeare associated Warwick's brother, the Marquess of Montague, with the bear badge:

> . . . the two brave bears, Warwick and Montague,
> That in their chains fetter'd the kingly lion,
> And made the forest tremble when they roar'd.   (*v*, 7)

John Nevill, Marquess of Montague, K.G., bore on his shield his paternal saltire with the compony label and a black crescent for difference. His complete arms, such as might be shown on tabard and banner, were: *Montagu and Monthermer quarterly* in the first and fourth quarters, and the above coat of Nevill in the second and third.   For some purposes he placed on the centre of these arms an inescutcheon of the arms of his wife, Isobel Inglethorp.

Two other brothers of the Kingmaker are mentioned in 3 *Henry VI*, though not introduced as characters in the play.   One was Sir Thomas Nevill, whose death at Wakefield is mentioned by Richard of Gloucester (ii, 3):

> Thy brother's blood the thirsty earth hath drunk,
> Broach'd with the steely point of Clifford's lance.

The other was George Nevill, Archbishop of York.   In act iv, sc. 4, Queen Elizabeth says that the captive King Edward:

> Is new committed to the Bishop of York,
> Fell Warwick's brother, and by that our foe.

Talbot

Interpolated into 1 *Henry VI* (perhaps by another hand than Shakespeare's) are the titles of John Talbot, Earl of Shrewsbury, derived from the epitaph stated to have been on his tomb at Rouen:[1]

> *Sir William Lucy:* But where's the great Alcides of the field,
> Valiant Lord Talbot, Earl of Shrewsbury,
> Created, for his rare success in arms,
> Great Earl of Washford, Waterford and Valence,
> Lord Talbot of Goodrig and Urchinfield,
> Lord Strange of Blackmere, Lord Verdun of Alton,
> Lord Cromwell of Wingfield, Lord Furnival of Sheffield,
> The thrice-victorious Lord of Falconbridge;

---

[1] Shrewsbury's body was subsequently brought to England and buried at Whitchurch, Shropshire. The Rouen epitaph is given by Richard Crompton in the *Mansion of Magnanimitie* (1599) and by Ralph Brooke in his *Catalogue and Succession* etc. (1619).   The passage in 1 *Henry VI* appears to have been derived from the former, as the form of place-names in the play corresponds more closely to Crompton's than to Brooke's. For example, Crompton gives Washford, Vrchengfield, and Alton, where Brooke has Weshford, Orchenfield, and Acton.

Knight of the noble order of Saint George,
Worthy Saint Michael and the Golden Fleece;
Great marshal to Henry the Sixth
Of all his wars within the realm of France?
Joan of Arc: Here is a silly stately style indeed!
The Turk, that two and fifty kingdoms hath,
Writes not so tedious a style as this.
Him that thou magnifiest with all these titles
Stinking and fly-blown lies here at our feet.   (*Pt. 1, iv, 7*)

Table VII shows Talbot's descent:

TABLE VII

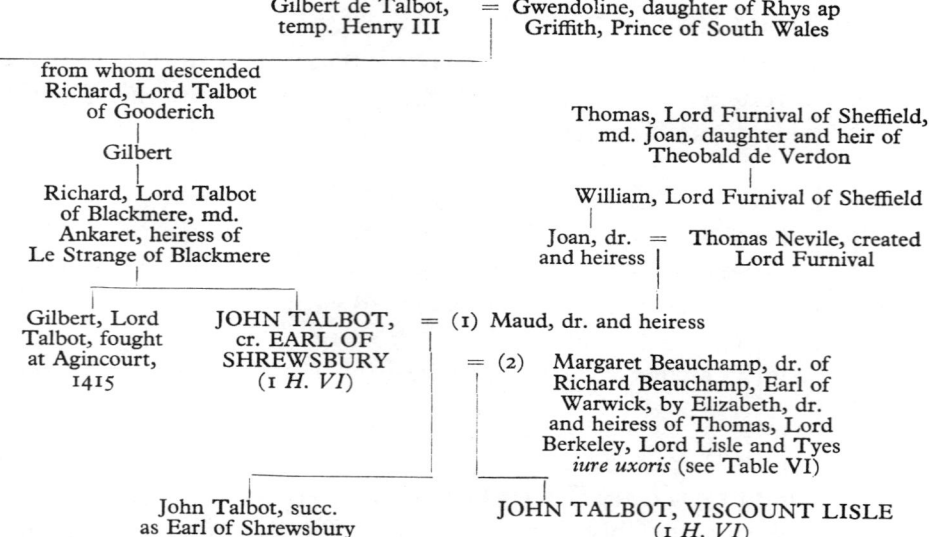

Gilbert de Talbot, temp. Henry III	=	Gwendoline, daughter of Rhys ap Griffith, Prince of South Wales

from whom descended
Richard, Lord Talbot
of Gooderich
|
Gilbert
|
Richard, Lord Talbot
of Blackmere, md.
Ankaret, heiress of
Le Strange of Blackmere
|

Thomas, Lord Furnival of Sheffield,
md. Joan, daughter and heir of
Theobald de Verdon
|
William, Lord Furnival of Sheffield
|
Joan, dr.   =   Thomas Nevile, created
and heiress | Lord Furnival
|

Gilbert, Lord   JOHN TALBOT,   = (1) Maud, dr. and heiress
Talbot, fought   cr. EARL OF
at Agincourt,   SHREWSBURY   = (2) Margaret Beauchamp, dr. of
1415   (1 H. VI)   Richard Beauchamp, Earl of
                                            Warwick, by Elizabeth, dr.
                                            and heiress of Thomas, Lord
                                            Berkeley, Lord Lisle and Tyes
                                            iure uxoris (see Table VI)

John Talbot, succ.   JOHN TALBOT, VISCOUNT LISLE
as Earl of Shrewsbury   (1 H. VI)

As the foregoing table shows, the 'young John Talbot' of 1 *Henry VI* was not the earl's eldest son, but a son by a second marriage, and there was therefore no question of the 'household's name' dying at Bordeaux, as Shakespeare makes Shrewsbury suggest. In fact, the line of Talbot Earls of Shrewsbury continued in Shakespeare's day, and it seems possible that the recitation of the Talbot titles, rather awkwardly dragged into the play, was done out of compliment to the great earl of Elizabeth's time.

Talbot bore arms derived from his remote ancestor, Rhys ap Griffith: *Gules, a gold lion rampant within a gold bordure engrailed.* This he bore quarterly with Furnival: *Silver, a bend gules between six martlets gules* (157). He might be represented bearing the former arms on his shield

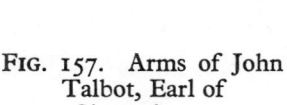

FIG. 157. Arms of John Talbot, Earl of Shrewsbury.

FIG. 158. Banner of Talbot, Earl of Shrewsbury.

FIG. 159. Young John Talbot, Viscount Lisle.

and the quartered coats on his surcoat. His banner included other quarterings. It was parted palewise, the dexter side being: *Quarterly Talbot (as above) and Strange (Silver, two lions passant guardant in pale gules)*, and the sinister: *Quarterly Furnival (as above) and Verdon (Gold, a fret gules.)*. Over all was placed an escutcheon: *Quarterly Lisle and Tyes*, i.e. *Gules, a silver lion passant with a gold crown*, for Lisle, and *Silver, a chevron gules*, for Tyes (158). This inescutcheon represented the lordships derived from his second wife. It sometimes bore the arms of Beauchamp: *Gules, a gold fess between six gold cross-crosslets.*

On Shrewsbury's Garter stall-plate his arms appear as: *Quarterly, 1, Azure, a gold lion within a gold bordure (for the Earldom of Shrewsbury); 2, Talbot; 3, Strange; 4, Furnival.*

Talbot's crest was a lion statant on a chapeau. His livery colours were scarlet and black, and his badge was a talbot dog. The allusion to the name which this badge represents is paralleled in the play by the reference to Shrewsbury's son as 'the young whelp of Talbot's.' The verses of 1449 already quoted include the lines:

> And he is bownden that our dor shuld kepe,
> That is Talbott our good dogge.

His seal as Lord Talbot and Furnival, 1406, shows two talbots in the position of supporters, but holding up the helm, not the shield. On his seal as Earl of Shrewsbury and Marshal of France, 1445, the talbots are replaced by lions.

Shrewsbury's *cri-de-guerre*, 'a Talbot,' occurs several times in the play:

> His soldiers spying his undaunted spirit
> A Talbot! a Talbot! cried out amain
> And rush'd into the bowels of the battle.   (i, 1)

and in act ii, sc. 1:

> *Enter an English soldier, crying ' A Talbot ! a Talbot !' They [the French]*
> *fly, leaving their clothes behind.*
> > *Soldier:* I'll be so bold to take what they have left.
> > The cry of Talbot serves me for a sword,
> > For I have loaden me with many spoils,
> > Using no other weapon than his name.

Shrewsbury's sword, which he lays at the king's feet in 1 *Henry VI*, iii, 4, was inscribed, *Sum Talboti pro vincere inimicos meos*—'I am Talbot's, to conquer my foes.'

'Young John Talbot,' Viscount Lisle, bore the Talbot coat with a silver crescent for difference (159). He did not quarter Furnival, as he was not a son of the marriage which brought in that coat. In his banner he impaled the Talbot arms with: *Quarterly Beauchamp and Neville* i.e. *Gules, a gold fess and six cross-crosslets, with a crescent sable for difference*, for Beauchamp, and *Gules, a silver saltire charged with a rose gules*, for Nevill. In making Shrewsbury liken young Talbot to a hungy lion (iv, 7), Shakespeare was no doubt using only a natural simile for a fierce warrior, but it was also heraldically apt in view of the lion in the Talbot arms.

Stafford

Several members of the great family of Stafford appear in 2 *and* 3 *Henry VI.*

Humphrey Stafford, Duke of Buckingham, K.G., was the son of Edmund, Earl of Stafford, who is mentioned in 1 *Henry IV* as having been slain by Douglas at Shrewsbury while wearing the royal arms. Earl Edmund married Anne, daughter of Thomas of Woodstock, Duke of Gloucester and Earl of Buckingham, son of Edward III. Duke Humphrey accordingly bore Gloucester's arms: *Quarterly France and England within a silver bordure*, quartered with the paternal coat of Stafford: *Gold, a chevron gules*, giving the royal coat the precedence of the first and fourth quarters (160). His badge was a cart-wheel in flames. His crest was a silver swan's head and wings issuing from a gold coronet, and his supporters were two silver antelopes with gold horns. The badge on the livery of his retainers was the Stafford knot.

TABLE VIII

THE LORDS STAFFORD AND DUKES OF BUCKINGHAM

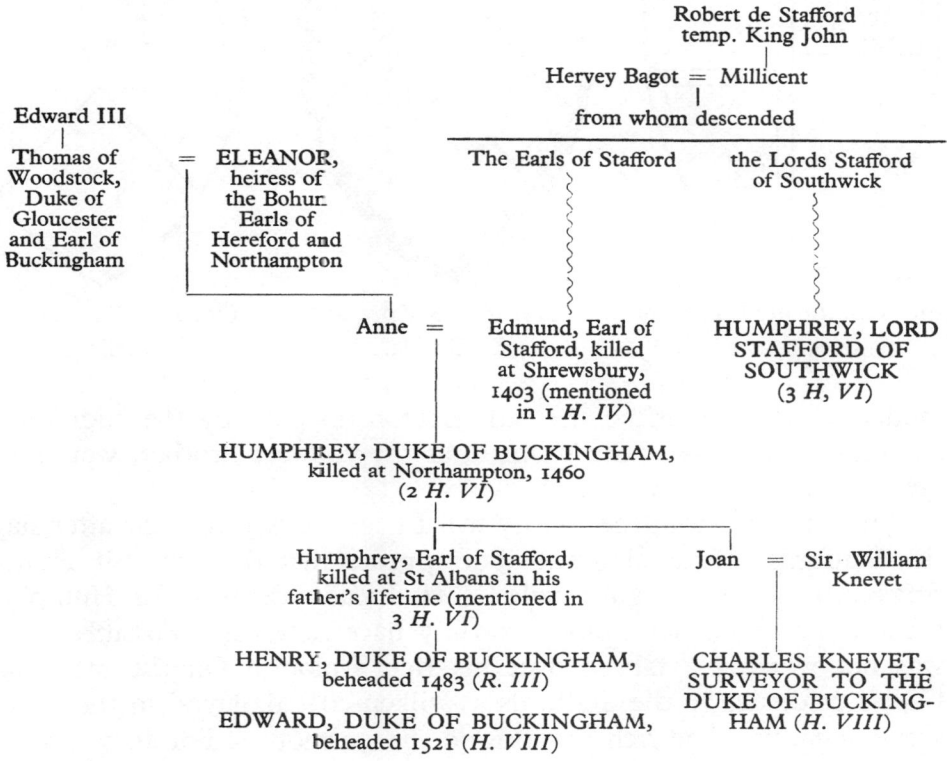

Duke Humphrey was slain at Northampton in 1460. His son the Earl of Stafford, is mentioned in 3 *Henry VI* as having been killed at St Albans. The Duke was succeeded by his grandson, who is Duke of Buckingham in *Richard III*.

The Lord Stafford who makes a brief appearance in 3 *Henry VI* was Humphrey, Lord Stafford of Southwick, created Earl of Devon in 1469. In the play he is mentioned in conjunction with Pembroke as being ordered by Edward IV: 'Go levy men and make prepare for war.' His subsequent desertion of Pembroke led to the Earl's defeat by the Lancastrians. Stafford was seized and beheaded in 1469. His arms were: *Gold, a chevron gules within a bordure engrailed sable* (161).

The two Staffords, Sir Humphrey and Sir William, who were slain by the rebels at Blackheath (2 *Henry V.I*) were members of a branch of the

FIG. 160. Stafford, Duke of   FIG. 161. Stafford of   FIG. 162. Sir Humphrey
         Buckingham.   Southwick.   Stafford.

family which differenced the red chevron on gold by the addition of a
canton ermine (162).   Sir William, as the younger brother, would add a
crescent for difference.

'This monument of the victory will I bear,' says Jack Cade after slaying
the Staffords.   From Holinshed it appears that this was 'sir Humfries
brigandine set full of guilt nailes.'   Had Cade assumed Sir Humphrey's
tabard, the chronicler would probably have noted it.   Possibly Stafford
was not wearing a tabard over his rich armour.   On the other hand,
Cade's reference to the Staffords as 'silken-coated slaves' in the previous
scene suggests some rich covering to their armour.   For stage purposes,
Sir Humphrey may be shown in both brigandine and tabard, and Cade
may take them both.

Widville

Woodvile, Lieutenant of the Tower of London in 1 *Henry VI*, is perhaps
intended for Sir Richard de Widville, K.G., who became Earl Rivers and
Constable of England.   His paternal coat was: *Silver, a fess and a canton
gules* (163).   His complete arms, as shown on his Garter stall-plate, were:
Quarterly, 1 and 4, Widville (as above), *quarterly with Gules, a gold eagle
displayed,* for Prowes; *2 and 3, Vaire,* for Beauchamp of Hache; *over all
an inescutcheon Gules, a gold griffin rampant,* for Rivers.   He married
Jaquetta, daughter of Peter de Luxembourg, Count of St Pol.

Sir Richard's son, Anthony, the Lord Rivers of 3 *Henry VI*, a Knight
of the Garter, married the daughter and heir of Lord Scales, and bore:

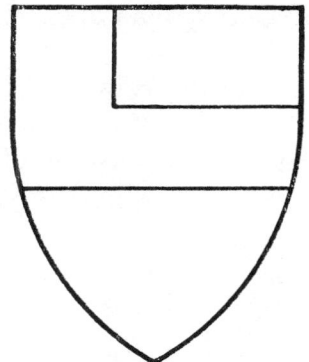
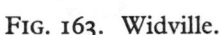

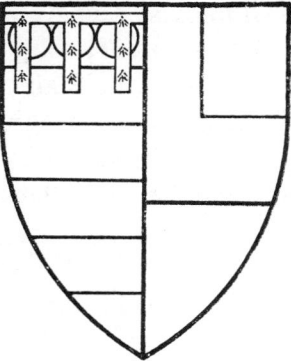

FIG. 163. Widville.　　　　FIG. 164. Widville,　　　　FIG. 165. Grey impaling
　　　　　　　　　　　　　　　　Earl Rivers.　　　　　　　　　Widville.

Quarterly of six, 1 Widville, 2 Scales (Gules, six silver escallops), 3 Luxemburg (Silver, a lion rampant with a forked tail gules with a gold crown), 4 Baux (Gules, a silver star), 5 Rivers, 6 Beauchamp of Hache (164).

Sir Richard's daughter, Elizabeth, as widow of Sir John Grey, Lord Ferrers of Groby, bore Grey (*Barry of six pieces, silver and azure, in chief three roundles gules, a label of three points ermine*), impaling Widville (165). On her marriage to Edward IV she was given arms which stressed her noble descent through her mother: *Quarterly of six, 1 Luxemburg, 2 Baux and France Ancient quarterly, 3 Cyprus (Barry of ten pieces silver and azure, over all a lion rampant gules), 4 Ursius (Gules, three silver bends, on a chief per fess silver and gold a rose gules), 5 St Pol (Gules, three pallets vaire, a gold chief surmounted by a label of five points azure), 6 Widville*. These were impaled with the royal arms (193). Her badge was a pink.

Thomas Grey, Marquess of Dorset, Elizabeth's son by her first marriage, is not introduced in *Henry VI*, but Holinshed says he was present at the murder of Prince Edward after the Battle of Barnet, and he may therefore appear in this scene. He would bear the arms of Grey on shield and tabard. His arms are dealt with under *Richard III*.

Stanley

Two members of the Stanley family appear in *Henry VI*, and another in *Richard III*.

Sir Thomas, first Baron Stanley (grandson of the Sir John Stanley who was granted the Isle of Man by Henry IV), had three sons:

Thomas, second Baron Stanley and first Earl of Derby, who appears in *Richard III*;

Sir William Stanley, who in 3 *Henry VI* assists in freeing Edward IV from captivity at Middleham;

Sir John Stanley, who in 2 *Henry VI* is entrusted with the custody of the Duchess of Gloucester.

FIG. 166. Stanley.

FIG. 167. Stanley, as Lord of Man.

The arms of Stanley were: *Silver, on a bend azure three gold bucks' heads cabossed* (166). Sir William and Sir John would difference this coat, the former with a crescent and the latter with a molet. The Stanley arms were sometimes quartered with those of Man (167).

Other Characters

William de la Pole, Earl (later Marquess and Duke) of Suffolk, K.G., was brother and successor to the Earl who fell at Agincourt. He bore similar arms, but with the introduction of a quarter for Chaucer (his wife being daughter to Sir Thomas Chaucer) i.e. *Quarterly 1 and 4, Pole, 2 Wingfield, 3 Chaucer (Silver, a chief gules, over all a gold lion rampant with a forked tail).*[1] Suffolk's crest was a Saracen's head, and his supporters were an antelope and a lion with a forked tail. His badge was a silver ape-clog with a gold chain. In reference to this, he was derisively nick-

---

[1] These were originally the arms of Burghersh. Sir Thomas Chaucer, son of Geoffrey Chaucer, the poet, took them in place of his paternal coat on his marriage with Margaret, daughter of Sir John Burghersh. The original coat of Chaucer, as borne by the poet, was, *Party per pale silver and gules, a bend counterchanged*. Had Sir Thomas been able to foresee his father's enduring fame, he might not have been so ready to abandon his paternal shield for that of his father-in-law.

named 'Jack-a-napes.' He is alluded to by this badge in the political verses of 1449 already quoted:

> The white lion [the Duke of Norfolk] is leyde to slepe
> Thoroug the envy of the Ape clogge.

And in another contemporary poem we find:

> Jack Napys with his clogge
> Hathe tiede Talbot our gentille dogge.

Threatened with death by the pirates (pt. 2, iv, 1), Suffolk says:

> King Henry's blood,
> The honourable blood of Lancaster,
> Must not be shed by such a jaded groom—

a blunder in genealogy, for Suffolk did not come of the royal house.

John Mowbray, Duke of Norfolk, K.G., great-grandson of the Duke in *Richard II*, bore the arms of Mowbray: *Gules, a silver lion rampant*. His badge was a white lion, and his livery colours were blue and tawny. The last of the Mowbray Dukes of Norfolk, he was succeeded in the dukedom by Edward IV's second son, Richard, Duke of York, who was affianced to Norfolk's only child. After Richard's death, the dukedom passed to the family of Howard (see Table IX).

Henry Holland, K.G., the Duke of Exeter in 3 *Henry VI*, was the son of John Holland, Earl of Huntingdon in *Henry V*, who had the dukedom in succession to Thomas Beaufort, the Exeter of 1 *Henry VI*. He bore: *England with a bordure of France*. His badge as Lord High Admiral (an office which he held in succession to his father) was a blazing cresset, referred to in the 1449 verses:

> The firy Cressett hath lost its lyght,
> Therefore England may make gret mone.

In act v, sc. 7, King Edward, naming the enemies with whose blood the throne was re-purchased, refers to

> . . . two Northumberlands; two braver men
> Ne'er spurred their coursers at the trumpet's sound.

The second Earl of Northumberland, Hotspur's son, was slain at St Albans, and the Northumberland of 3 *Henry VI* is his son, another Henry Percy, the third Earl and a Knight of the Garter. Both bore: *Quarterly Percy and Lucy* as the first earl had done (57). The Percy crest was a lion

FIG. 168. Holland,
Duke of Exeter.

FIG. 169. De Vere,
Earl of Oxford.

FIG. 170. Herbert,
Earl of Pembroke.

statant azure on a chapeau gules turned up ermine; the badges were a silver crescent, and a gold shacklebolt within a silver crescent.

John de Vere, Earl of Oxford, K.G., bore: *Quarterly gules and gold, in the first quarter a silver molet* (169). On his tabard and banner he might quarter this with Howard: *Gules, a silver bend and six cross-crosslets fitchy, also silver*, his mother being the daughter and heir of Sir John Howard. His badge was a boar azure charged with a silver crescent and having gold tusks, hoofs and bristles; he also used this as a crest on a chapeau gules guarded with ermine. Another badge, as Lord High Chamberlain, was a silver bottle with a blue cord. The earl's father and elder brother were attainted by Edward IV and beheaded in 1462. To this Oxford alludes in 3 *Henry VI*, iii, 3:

> Call him my king by whose injurious doom
> My elder brother, the Lord Aubrey Vere,
> Was done to death? and more than so, my father,
> Even in the downfall of his mellow'd years,
> When nature brought him to the door of death?
> No, Warwick, no; while life upholds this arm,
> This arm upholds the house of Lancaster.

William Herbert, Earl of Pembroke, bore: *Per pale azure and gules, three silver lions rampant* (170).

William, Lord Hastings, K.G., was the nephew of the Hastings in *Henry IV*, and bore the same arms, *Silver, a maunch sable* (88). His badge, also used as a crest, was a black bull's head with gold horns and a

  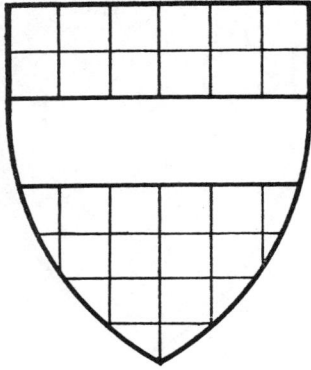

FIG. 171. Sir John Fastolfe.   FIG. 172. Gargrave.   FIG. 173. Clifford.

gold coronet about its neck.   In 3 *Henry VI* he is made to say:

> 'Tis better using France than trusting France:
> Let us be back'd with God, and with the seas,
> Which he hath given for fence impregnable,
> And with their helps only defend ourselves;
> In them, and in ourselves, our safety lies.   (*iv*, 1)

On this Clarence remarks:

> For this one speech Lord Hastings well deserves
> To have the heir of the Lord Hungerford.

However, it was not this Hastings, but his son, who married the Hungerford heiress.

Sir John Fastolfe bore, *Quarterly gold and azure, a bend gules charged with three silver cross-crosslets* (171).   His motto was *Me faunt fare*—'I must be doing.'   He was a Knight of the Garter, and his deprivation of the honour is dealt with later.   His reputation has suffered much at Shakespeare's hands, both by the inaccurate story of his cowardice and degradation, and by the use of his name for the fat knight of *Henry IV* and *The Merry Wives*, and it is due to the historical Sir John to say that neither as Fastolfe nor as Falstaff is he truly characterized.

No arms can be traced for Sir William Glansdale.   Holinshed calls him 'William Glasdale esquire.' He can quite properly appear in plate armour without a tabard.

Sir Thomas Gargrave was presumably akin to, and may be intended for, Sir John Gargrave, Master of the Ordnance to Henry V in France,

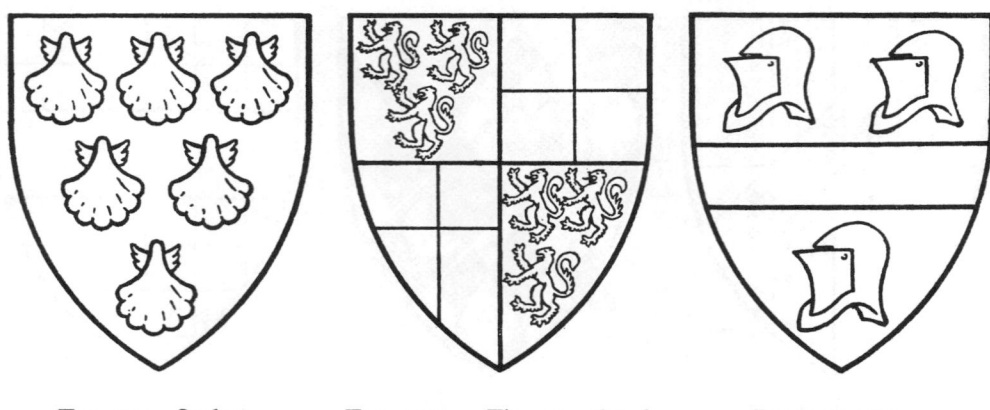

FIG. 174. Scales.   FIG. 175. Fiennes, Lord   FIG. 176. Iden.
                              Say and Sele.

who bore, *Lozengy silver and sable, on a bend sable three silver crescents*
(172).

Sir William Lucy is thought to have been one of the Charlecote family
which bore, *Gules, semé of silver cross-crosslets, three silver luces (pike-fish)
hauriant* (100).

Vernon of the White Rose faction, and Basset of the Red Rose, cannot
be identified. The former has been supposed to be Sir Richard Vernon,
of Haddon, whose arms were, *Argent fretty sable, a canton gules;* and the
latter may have been one of the Bassets of Drayton, who bore *Gold,
three piles meeting in base gules, a canton ermine.* 'Le Sr de Bassett' has
these arms in the Rouen Roll. These characters are only important as
representatives of the incipient factions of York and Lancaster, and need
no personal heraldry. Each should be in the dress of the period, with the
rose of his party embroidered on breast or shoulder.

Thomas, Lord Clifford, bore, *Checky gold and azure, a fess gules* (173).
His son, John differenced these arms with a label. The former was
slain at St Albans, and the son therefore appears as Lord Clifford in
3 *Henry VI*, and should then bear his father's arms without the label.
The Clifford standard (as borne by the next Lord) had the cross of
St George next the staff, the fly being divided down its length into gold
and blue, with a red basilisk and ten rings, five of them blue on the gold
and the others gold on the blue; the standard being crossed with the
motto DESORMAIS.

FIG. 177. Gough.

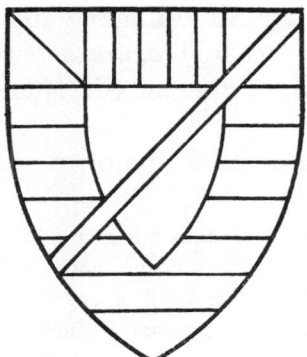

FIG. 178. Mortimer with baston sinister.

FIG. 179. Montgomery.

Thomas, Lord Scales, K.G., bore *Gules, six silver escallops* (174).[1] He used one scallop shell as a badge.

James Fiennes, Lord Say and Sele, bore *Quarterly Fiennes (Azure, three gold lions rampant) and Say (Quarterly gold and gules)*, his grandfather, Sir William Fiennes, having married the daughter and co-heir of Geoffrey, Lord Say (175). Shakespeare, following Holinshed, introduces a Sir James Cromer, son-in-law to Lord Say, also beheaded by the rebels. Historically there was a Sir William Cromer, who was Lord Say's father-in-law. Lord Say's daughter, Elizabeth, married Alexander Iden, Sheriff of Kent, who appears in the play as the slayer of Jack Cade. Iden bore, *Azure, a gold fess between three gold closed helms* (176).

Sir Matthew Gough, slain by the rebels at Smithfield, bore, *Gules, a silver fess between three gold boars' heads couped, and on the fess a lion passant azure* (177).

Sir John Mortimer and Sir Hugh Mortimer, uncles of Richard, Duke of York, and slain with him at Wakefield, are said by Holinshed to have been bastards, and they would therefore bear the Mortimer arms (*Gold, three bars azure, on a gold chief three pallets between two gyrons, all azure*) with a difference for illegitimacy, which might be a baston sinister (178).

Sir John Montgomery: Holinshed names him 'sir Thomas Montgomerie,' who bore, *Gules, a gold chevron and three gold fleurs-de-lys* (179).

Sir John Somerville is presumed to be a member of the Warwickshire family which bore, *Silver, a fess and three annulets gules, with three gold leopards' faces on the fess* (180).

[1] Shown in colour in Plate III.

Vaux may be intended for Sir William Vaux of Harrowden, who bore, *Checky gold and gules, a chevron azure charged with three gold roses.* (254). Sir William was the father of Sir Nicholas Vaux, a character in *Henry VIII.*

Walter Whitmore has not been identified.   He claims to be of gentle birth:

> Never yet did base dishonour blur our name,
> But with our sword we wip'd away the blot;
> Therefore, when merchant-like I sell revenge,
> Broke be my sword, my arms torn and defac'd,
> And I proclaim'd a coward through the world.

He may have been intended as a member of the family whose arms were *Vert, fretty gold.*

Jack Cade claimed to be John Mortimer, a grandson of the Earl of March who married Philippa, daughter of Lionel of Clarence.   Such a person would bear *Quarterly Mortimer and Ulster,* but there is nothing in the play to suggest that Cade appeared in these arms.

The Mayor of London in 1425, the year of the events in which he appears in 1 *Henry VI*, was John Coventry. His arms were, *Silver, a chevron sable between three columbine flowers with their stems, in proper colours, and on the chevron a golden roundle* (181). It does not appear that at this date Mayors impaled their city arms with their own, but the Mayor might be attended by a banner bearing the City arms: *Silver, the cross of St George and in the first quarter the sword of St Paul erect, all gules* (187).

Although the Mayor of St Albans is introduced in Part 2, the town was not incorporated at this date, and the chief townsman would probably be a bailiff acting for the Prior of the Abbey.

At the time of the relevant scenes of 3 *Henry VI*, the Mayor of York was Thomas Beverley, and the Mayor of Coventry was John Brett (French). Rodway attributes to Beverley, *Silver, a chevron sable and a chief sable charged with three silver bulls' heads cabossed.*

The Tutor of the Earl of Rutland was, according to Hall, Sir Robert Aspall, chaplain. He may have been of the family which bore, *Azure, three gold (or silver) chevrons.*

The names of the Lieutenants of the Tower of London at the time of 3 *Henry VI* are not on record.   French suggested that the Governors of the Tower were intended.   These were successively John Tiptoft, Earl of Worcester, and John Sutton, Lord Dudley. Shakespeare would scarcely make Gloucester address so important an officer as 'sirrah,' and it seems more probable that he had no historical person in mind.

The Earl of Wiltshire, whom Montague claims to have wounded at St Albans (Pt. 3, i, 1), was James Butler, K.G., son of the fourth Earl of Ormonde. He bore, *Gold, a chief indented azure* (123).

In the same scene we read,

> Stern Falconbridge commands the narrow seas.

This was William Nevill, Lord Fauconberg or Falconbridge, K.G., a younger son of Ralph, first Earl of Westmoreland. He was created

FIG. 180. Somerville.   FIG. 181. John Coventry, Mayor of London.

Earl of Kent and Admiral of England by Edward IV. He bore his father's arms, *Gules, a silver saltire*, with *a molet sable* on the saltire. His badge was a fish-hook, by which he is referred to in the verses of 1449 already quoted:

> The fischer hath lost his hangulhook,
> Gete theym again when it woll be—

alluding to his captivity in France.

The French

Charles, though styled Dauphin throughout the first part of *Henry VI*, is stated in the first scene to have been crowned king—as in fact he was, in 1423, though at Poictiers and not at Rheims. He should therefore appear in the royal arms of France, *Azure, three gold fleurs-de-lys*, on shield and tabard, rather than the arms of the Dauphin. He was the younger brother of the Dauphin in *Henry V*, who died soon after Agincourt. Louis XI, King of France in 3 *Henry VI*, was the son of Charles VII.

As supporters, Charles VII used the flying stags of his father. Louis XI used first the flying stags, and later two eagles, and finally adopted as supporters, dexter, a gold crowned eagle, and sinister, the figure of St Michael in a tabard charged with three fleurs-de-lys, and bearing a

FIG. 182. Arms, crown and supporters of King Louis XI of France.

lance with a banner of the arms of France (182). Charles had borne the image of this saint in his standard, following the appearance of St Michael defending the bridge of Orleans against an English attack. The French royal *cri*, used as a motto under the arms, was, MONTJOYE, SANCT DENIS.

Reignier (Réné), Duke of Anjou, Lorraine and Bar, and titular King of Naples, Sicily and Jerusalem,

> Yet not so wealthy as an English yeoman,

bore on shield and tabard, *Naples impaling Jerusalem*, i.e. *France Ancient with a label of three points gules*, for Naples, and *Silver, a gold cross potent between four plain crosslets of gold*, for the Crusader Kingdom of Jerusalem (183). (The latter coat was a departure from the heraldic convention that metal should not be laid on metal, probably deliberately made so as to confer distinction on the arms of the Holy City.) Réné's complete achievement was, *Quarterly of six; 1, Hungary (Barry of eight pieces silver and gules); 2, Naples; 3, Jerusalem; 4, Anjou (France Ancient within a bordure gules); 5, Bar (Azure, semé of gold cross-crosslets, two gold barbels hauriant back to back); 6, Lorraine (Gold, a bend gules charged with three silver eaglets displayed.)* These arms were borne by Réné's daughter,

Fig. 183. Reignier, Duke of Anjou.

Fig. 184. Dunois, Bastard of Orleans.

Fig. 185. Joan of Arc.

Margaret, Queen of Henry VI, impaled with the royal arms (191). Margaret's six paternal quarters, placed within a bordure vert, now form the arms of Queens' College, Cambridge, of which she was the first foundress. She bore as a badge, in allusion to her name, the daisy, or marguerite, with the motto, *Humble et loiall*. In compliment to her, the daisy was worn as a favour by people of all classes on her arrival in England, and it would be fitting to make the welcoming lords in the first scene of 2 *Henry VI* wear bunches of daisies.

The arms of Philip, Duke of Burgundy, have been given under *Henry V*.

John, Duke of Alençon, son of the Duke who was slain at Agincourt, bore *France within a bordure gules charged with eight golden roundles* (132).

John, Count of Dunois, the Bastard of Orleans, bore, *France Modern with a silver label and a baton sinister* (184).

The person whom the French King, in Part 3, iii, 3, addresses as

'Lord Bourbon, our high admiral,' was Louis, Count of Roussillon, a natural son of Charles, Duke of Bourbon. He bore the arms of France with a baton raguly gules and a bendlet sinister.

Lady Bona, sister to the French Queen, was the daughter of Louis, Duke of Savoy, who bore, *Gules, a silver cross.*

Joan of Arc is described as having worn a cloak of red velvet embroidered with gold over her armour. Historically, she does not appear to have made any personal use of heraldry. Nevertheless, arms were granted to her (though perhaps posthumously), and for dramatic purposes these

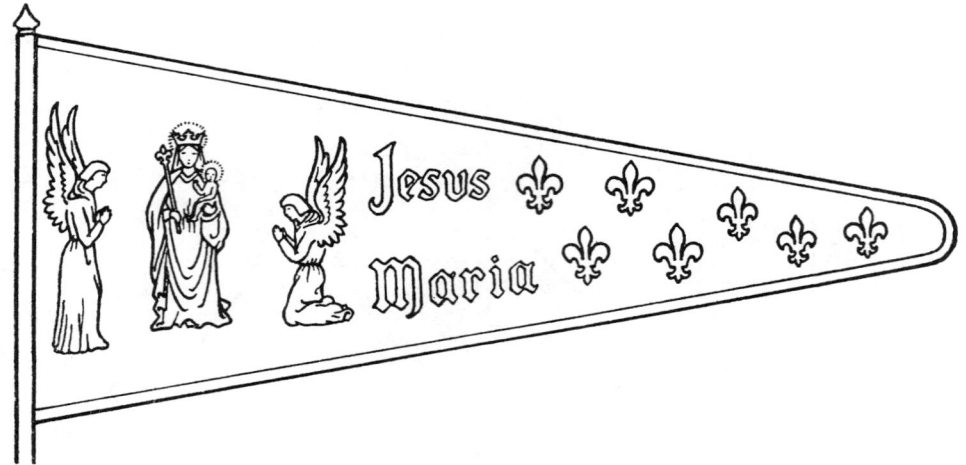

FIG. 186. Standard of Joan of Arc.

may appear on her tabard. They were, *Azure, between two gold fleurs-de-lys a sword erect, point upwards, with a gold pomel and hilt, the blade encircled with a gold crown* (185). She possessed and cherished a standard, said to have been made to her own design, which has been variously described. According to Holinshed, it was white, 'wherein was Iesus Christ painted with a floure delice in his hand.' Another account makes the figure on one side of the standard that of the Almighty holding the world in his hand, and on the other the Madonna and Child between two kneeling angels, with the words JESUS MARIA, and the fly semé of fleurs-de-lys, all gold on white (186). This is the version of the standard suited to the play, in view of Joan's insistence that from 'Heaven and our Lady' she derived her inspiration:

Christ's mother helps me, else I were too weak.

The general of the French forces in Bordeaux is said to have been Potron de Xaintrailles, who bore, *Quarterly, 1 and 4, Silver, a cross couped gules; 2 and 3, Gules, a silver lion rampant* (Rodway).   G. R. French states that the forces which overcame Talbot at Bordeaux were commanded by two Marshals, Andreas de Valle, Lord of Loheauc, and the Sieur de Jalognes.

Cities

Where the Mayor and officers of London appear, a banner of the City arms, *Argent, the cross of St George and in the first quarter the sword of St Paul, both gules,* may be carried (187).

FIG. 187. Banner of London.   FIG. 188. Banner of Paris.

The banner of the City of Paris was of red, with a white ship with one mast, and a white sail with a blue chief and two gold fleurs-de-lys thereon, and a gold fleur-de-lys on each side of the mast (188).

In the scenes which take place under the walls of York and Coventry, the arms of these cities may be displayed over the gates.   These are:

York: *Silver, a cross gules charged with five gold lions passant guardant* (189).

Coventry: *Party per pale gules and vert, an elephant with a castle of three domed towers on its back, all gold* (190).

The townsmen of St Albans, coming to greet their King (Pt. 2, ii, 1) may bear the Abbey banner, *Azure, a gold saltire.*

FIG. 189. City of York.   FIG. 190. City of Coventry.

The Order of the Garter

The insignia of the Order of the Garter are introduced in two scenes of this play, and Shakespeare takes the occasion to refer to the foundation of the Order. In 1 *Henry VI*, iv, 1, Talbot, accusing Sir John Fastolfe of cowardice at Patay, plucks the Garter from his leg—

> Which I have done, because unworthily
> Thou wast installed in that high degree . . .
> When first this order was ordain'd, my lords,
> Knights of the garter were of noble birth,
> Valiant and virtuous, full of haughty courage,
> Such as were grown to credit by the wars;
> Not fearing death, nor shrinking for distress,
> But always resolute in most extremes.
> He then that is not furnish'd in this sort
> Doth but usurp the sacred name of knight,
> Profaning this most honourable order,
> And should, if I were worthy to be judge,
> Be quite degraded, like a hedge-born swain,
> That doth presume to boast of gentle blood.

The incident lacks reality, in that the King, without further inquiry, confirms Talbot's high-handed action and banishes Fastolfe without giving him a chance of speaking in his own defence. It also lacks historical accuracy. It is true that Fastolfe was deprived of the Garter by the Duke of Bedford on an allegation of his cowardly desertion of Talbot at Patay, but it was shown that he only left the field of battle after Talbot's capture, when the position could not be retrieved, and he was reinstated in the Order and again honourably employed.

It is not to be supposed that Fastolfe was alone in wearing his Garter, and we may take it that Shakespeare intended Knights of the Order to wear the insignia in suitable scenes in the play. Although the Garter appears buckled below the left knee on some effigies of men in armour, it would not be worn by men armed for battle, and as a general rule it should be worn by members of the Order only when unarmed and at the King's court.

A contemporary illumination of Talbot presenting a book to Henry VI shows the Earl in the habit of the Order of the Garter, consisting of a scarlet robe diapered with golden Garters. Talbot might suitably appear in such a costume in the scene with Fastolfe, since he stands as the representative of the honour of the Order.

In 2 *Henry VI*, iv, 1, the Duke of Suffolk, captured off the coast of Kent, indicates to Walter Whitmore that he is of a station able to pay a ransom, in the words:

> Look on my George: I am a gentleman.

In this scene Suffolk is in disguise, 'muffled up in rags,' and it would be inconsistent with this for him to be wearing his Garter. What he shows Whitworth is the jewel of the Order, the figure of St George in armour and on horseback in the act of slaying the dragon. This reference to the 'George' slightly antedates its introduction, as it was added to the insignia of the Order by Henry VII. In the source-play it is a ring, presumably engraved with his arms, that Suffolk produces.

Shakespeare's audiences were, of course, familiar with the figure of the national saint in a more popular connection:

> St George, that swing'd the dragon, and e'er since
> Sits on his horseback at mine hostess' door.
> (*King John*)

The Garter was held in such high repute that Shakespeare could associate it with the Crown itself in words given to Richard III:

> *King Richard:* Now, by my George, my garter and my crown—
> *Queen Elizabeth:* Profan'd, dishonour'd, and the third usurp'd.
> *K.R.:* I swear,—
> *Q.E.:*   By nothing; for this is no oath.
> The George, profan'd, hath lost his holy honour;
> The garter, blemish'd, pawn'd his knightly virtue;
> The crown, usurp'd, disgrac'd his kingly dignity.
> (*Richard III, iv*, 4)

In Henry VI's reign, the shield of the Royal Arms was frequently encircled with the Garter, and this became usual in Tudor times. In a passage complimentary to Queen Elizabeth in *The Merry Wives of Windsor*, Shakespeare (by the voice of Mistress Quickly) bids the meadow fairies sing

> Like to the Garter's compass, in a ring:
> Th' expressure that it bears, green let it be,
> More fertile-fresh than all the field to see;
> And 'Honi soit qui mal y pense' write
> In emerald tufts, flowers purple, blue and white,
> Like sapphire, pearl, and rich embroidery
> Buckled below fair knighthood's bending knee.   (*v*, 5)

FIG. 191. Impaled arms
of Henry VI and Queen
Margaret.

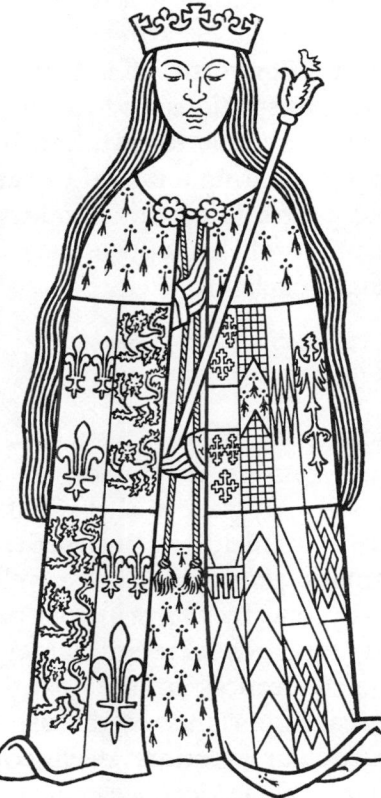

FIG. 193. Impaled arms
of Edward IV and Queen
Elizabeth Widville.

FIG. 192. Queen Anne Nevill in her heraldic mantle of arms of
Richard III and her own.

CHAPTER VIII

KING RICHARD III

DURING THE LATTER part of the fifteenth century, the military
use of heraldry was declining. The knightly shield still bore heraldic
arms and was carried in tournaments, but methods of warfare were
changing and the shield was little used in battle except by heavily armoured
cavalry making or encountering a charge with lances. The heraldic
tabard, worn over plate armour for purposes of display and as a protection
against sun and rain, was probably removed when the knight went into

action, though a leader may sometimes have retained his tabard so as to be recognised.

Holinshed says that at Bosworth, King Richard knew Henry of Richmond 'by certeine demonstrations and tokens, which he had learned and knowen of others that were able to give him full information.' This suggests that Henry was not wearing a tabard or carrying a shield of arms, since the King would of course know his heraldry, and would not need to depend on a description of his appearance. On the other hand, Shakespeare makes Richard exclaim,

> I think there be six Richmonds in the field;
> Five have I slain to-day instead of him.

This suggests that Richmond, in the play, had adopted Henry IV's expedient at Shrewsbury, causing several of his followers to appear in heraldic array like himself. It seems that Shakespeare envisaged the use of heraldic garments and shields at Bosworth; and the licence which must be allowed in dramatic production may well extend to the use of tabards and shields, at any rate by the principal persons.

Armorial banners and standards were still largely used, and are needed on the stage in view of references in the text. They appear to have become of greater practical importance as the use of shields and coats of arms to distinguish particular warriors declined, because the colours rather than the person of the leader became the rallying point of his followers.

Before Bosworth, Blunt, questioned as to the whereabouts of Lord Stanley, says:

> Unless I have mista'en his colours much
> (Which I am well assur'd I have not done),
> His regiment lies half a mile at least
> South from the mighty power of the king.   (v, 3)

Heraldic badges were still commonly worn by the soldiers, and were displayed on the standards of those who led them.

In the imagery of this play, two badges are used with dramatic effect: the sun, the emblem common to all the Yorkist kings, and the boar, the personal cognizance of Richard III. The boar and the white rose *en soleil* appear on Richard's standard (195).

The sun, which in *Henry VI* we saw rising as the badge of Edward IV,

is at its zenith at the beginning of *Richard III:* Richard himself, at
this point still Duke of Gloucester, says:

> Now is the winter of our discontent
> Made glorious summer by this sun of York;
> And all the clouds that lour'd upon our house
> In the deep bosom of the ocean buried.

In act ii, with King Edward's death, come sunset and the fall of the year :

> When clouds appear, wise men put on their cloaks;
> When great leaves fall, the winter is at hand;
> When the sun sets, who doth not look for night ?   *(ii, 3)*

Fig. 194. Richard III, from his Great Seal.

The sun of York had set for ever. This was clearly Shakespeare's thought
in the incident[1] on the morning of Bosworth:

> *King Richard:* Who saw the sun to-day ?
> *Ratcliff:*   Not I, my lord.
> *K.R.:* Then he disdains to shine, for by the book
>   He should have brav'd the east an hour ago:
>   A black day will it be to somebody.
>   Ratcliff!
> *Rat.:* My lord ?

[1] This incident appears to have no historical basis. Hall's Chronicle says that at Bosworth, Richmond 'had the sonne at his backe and in the faces of his enemies.'

K.R.:   The sun will not be seen to-day,
The sky doth frown, and lour upon our army;
I would these dewy tears were from the ground.
Not shine to-day! Why, what is that to me
More than to Richmond? for the selfsame heaven
That frowns on me looks sadly upon him.   (*v*, 3)

Though he tries to reassure himself in the last three lines, Richard is clearly uneasy at the ominous darkness.   It was, in truth, more to him than to Richmond, because the sun's image was the badge of his house, and he looked for the sun's rising as a portent that the day would be York's. We may suppose him viewing the sunless dawn on Bosworth field with a superstitious dread which was the deeper for his remembrance of the 'three glorious suns' which had heralded the Yorkist victory at Mortimer's Cross.

Richard is referred to as the boar, or hog, several times in the play.[1] He may have derived this badge from his father, who is said to have used a boar as a device, perhaps in punning allusion to his dukedom of York, *Ebor*. Shakespeare does not explain that the boar was Richard's badge, though he must have known it because the fact is mentioned by Holinshed in a passage on which he drew.   The allusions to Richard as the boar make sense enough without the knowledge that it was his cognizance, but with that knowledge they have added point.   Shakespeare could not expect many playgoers to be well enough versed in heraldry to know Richard's badge, and it is possible that to ensure that the allusions were understood he made his stage Richard appear in the early scenes wearing the badge prominently.   This would give full effect to Queen Margaret's line:

Thou elvish-mark'd, abortive, rooting hog!

and to Lady Anne's contemptuous reference to Richard as 'hedgehog'.

---

[1] That Richard was covertly referred to as the hog in his own time is shown by the rhyme made by William Collingbourn, sometime sheriff of Wiltshire and Dorset, who was executed for it. This appears to have been written before Richard became king, since it refers to his ambition to secure the throne. It is here quoted from the version given in French's *Shakespeareana Genealogica*.

The Cat, the Rat, and Lovel our Dog,
Doe rule all England, under the Hog.
The crooke backt boare the way hath found
To root our roses from our ground;
Both flower and bud will he confound,
Till king of beasts the same be crown'd:
And then the dog, the cat, and rat,
Shall in his trough feed and be fat.

The cat and the rat are Catesby and Ratcliff; these, with Lovel, are dealt with below. The roses are the other members of the royal house whom Richard is alleged to have removed in his measures to secure the crown for himself.

FIG. 195. Standard of Richard III.

Drawing on Holinshed, Shakespeare makes Stanley send word to Hastings that he dreamed ' the boar had raz'd his helm,' and counselled flight; but Hastings replies:

> To fly the boar, before the boar pursues us,
> Were to incense the boar to follow us,
> And make pursuit where he did mean no chase.
> Go, bid thy master rise and come to me,
> And we will both together to the Tower,
> Where he shall see the boar will use us kindly.

And when Stanley appears, Hastings greets him,

> What, my lord? where is your boar-spear, man?
> Fear you the boar, and go so unprovided?   (*iii*, 2)

In act v, Richmond, addressing his followers, says:

> The wretched, bloody, and usurping boar,
> That spoil'd your summer fields and fruitful vines,
> Swills your warm blood like wash, and makes his trough
> In your embowell'd bosoms, this foul swine
> Lies now even in the centre of this isle,
> Near to the town of Leicester.   (*v*, 2)

For the end of the white boar, we must turn from Shakespeare to Hall, who states that after Bosworth, Richard's naked corpse was 'trussed behynde a persivaunt of armes called *Blaunche Senglier* or whyte bore, lyke a hogge or calfe, the hed and armes hangynge on the one syde of the horse, and the legges on the other syde, and all bysprynckled with myre and bloude . . . When his death was knowen, the proude braggyng whyte bore (whiche was his badge) was violently rased and plucked doune, from every signe and place where it myght be espied, so yll was his lyfe, that men wished the memorie of hym to be buried with his carren corps.'

There was a grim fitness, characteristic of the times, about entrusting Richard's body to the pursuivant named after his personal cognizance. Though Shakespeare did not make dramatic use of it, the closing scenes of a film might include a glimpse of the dead King's body borne behind a man wearing the white boar badge.

FIG. 196. Arms, crown and supporters of Richard III.

Royal Heraldry

The three kings whose reigns are covered by this play—Edward IV, Edward V, and Richard III—all bore the royal arms of *France Modern and England quarterly;* and the same crest as their predecessors, varied in the case of Richard by the addition of an open crown round the chapeau supporting the lion.

During Edward IV's lifetime, his son Edward, as Prince of Wales, differenced the royal arms with a silver label of three points; while his second son, Richard, Duke of York, had a silver label charged on the first point with a canton gules.

Before his accession as Richard III, Gloucester bore the label of three points ermine charged on each point with a canton gules, as in the previous play.

The royal supporters were:

Edward IV: (dexter) a gold lion and (sinister) a black bull; two white lions; a white lion and a white hart.

Edward V: a white lion and a white hart, the latter with a gold coronet about its neck and a gold chain attached thereto.

Richard III: a lion, silver or gold, and a white boar; two white boars.

Edward IV's badges have been given in the chapter on *Henry VI*. Edward V used the white rose, the sun, and a falcon within a fetterlock, all

FIG. 197. Standard of Henry, Earl of Richmond.

associated with the house of York. Richard III, in addition to the boar, the sun, and the white rose, used a falcon with a maiden's head.

The arms of George, Duke of Clarence, have been dealt with in the chapter on *Henry VI*. After the death of his father-in-law, the King-maker, Clarence became also Earl of Warwick and Salisbury. His two children, Edward and Margaret, who appear in *Richard III*, became respectively Earl of Warwick and Countess of Salisbury, and were the last survivors of the Plantagenet house. Edward differenced the royal arms with a label compony silver and azure, from the Nevill arms in token of his mother, and Margaret used an ermine label charged on each point with a canton gules.

FIG. 198. Henry Tudor,   FIG. 199. Jasper Tudor.   FIG. 200. Grey,
Earl of Richmond.   Marquess of Dorset.

Tudor

Henry, Earl of Richmond, son of Edmund Tudor and Margaret Beaufort (see Table V), bore the arms of his father, *Quarterly France Modern and England within a bordure azure charged alternately with gold fleurs-de lys and martlets* (198).   (The ancient arms of Tudor were, *Gules, a silver chevron and three silver helms ;* the sons of Owen Tudor left these for the differenced version of the royal arms, their mother being Katherine of France, widow of Henry V.)

The Tudor livery colours were white and green, and Henry's standard was divided into these colours, charged with a red dragon and red roses, and crossed by the motto, FIDE ET CONSILIO (197).   On entering London after his victory at Bosworth,

> with great pompe and triumphe he roade through the Cytie to the
> cathedral churche of S. Paule, wher he offred his iii standardes. In the
> one was the ymage of S. George, in the second was a red firye dragon
> beaten upon white and grene sarcenet, the third was of yelowe tarterne,
> in the which was peinted a done kowe [dun cow].

Hall's Chronicle.

'Redoubted Pembroke,' mentioned in act iv sc. 5, refers to Jasper Tudor, uncle of Henry of Richmond.   He was created Earl of Pembroke in 1452 by Henry VI, but was deprived of the earldom by Edward IV, who conferred it on William, Lord Herbert, and afterwards on Prince Edward. Not until Henry VII came to the throne was Tudor restored to the earldom of Pembroke (and created Duke of Bedford), so that the reference to him by the title of Pembroke in *Richard III* is not strictly correct; but we may suppose that his Lancastrian friends may still have called him by that name, refusing to recognize his deprivation by the Yorkist king. Pembroke bore the royal arms with a bordure azure charged with gold martlets (199).

Widville and Grey

The arms of Edward IV's Queen, Elizabeth, daughter of Sir Richard Widville, Earl Rivers, and widow of Sir John Grey, Lord Ferrers of Groby, and those of her brother, Anthony, Earl Rivers, are dealt with in the chapter on *Henry VI.*

Queen Elizabeth's two sons by her first marriage were Thomas Grey, Marquess of Dorset, K.G., and Sir Richard Grey, whom Shakespeare styles Lord Grey. The former bore: *Barry of six pieces silver and azure, in chief three roundles gules, and over all a label of three points ermine* (200). The latter would add a crescent as a mark of cadency. Dorset's badge was an ermine unicorn with gold hoofs, horn and mane.

Other Characters

Henry Stafford, Duke of Buckingham, bore the same arms as his grandfather, the Duke in 2 *Henry VI.* His badge was a gold Stafford knot.

Sir John Howard, Duke of Norfolk and Earl Marshal of England, K.G., whose father had married the heiress of the Mowbrays (see Table IX), bore on his shield the arms of Howard: *Gules, a silver bend and six silver cross-crosslets pointed at the foot* (202). Two versions exist of quartered arms such as he would bear on tabard and banner, viz. *Quarterly Howard and Brotherton (England with a silver label)*, and *Quarterly, 1 and 4, Howard; 2 and 3, Quarterly Brotherton and Mowbray (Gules, a silver lion rampant)* (201). His badge was the white lion of Mowbray charged on the shoulder with a crescent azure. He was killed at Bosworth. Thomas, Earl of Surrey, associated with Norfolk in the leadership of Richard's army at Bosworth, was his son, and bore the arms of Howard with a label.

The Earl of Oxford and Lord Hastings are the same as appear in *Henry VI.* The pursuivant whom Hastings greets by his own name appears to have been his own officer and may wear a tabard charged with the Hastings maunch.

G

TABLE IX

THE EARLS AND DUKES OF NORFOLK AND EARL MARSHALS

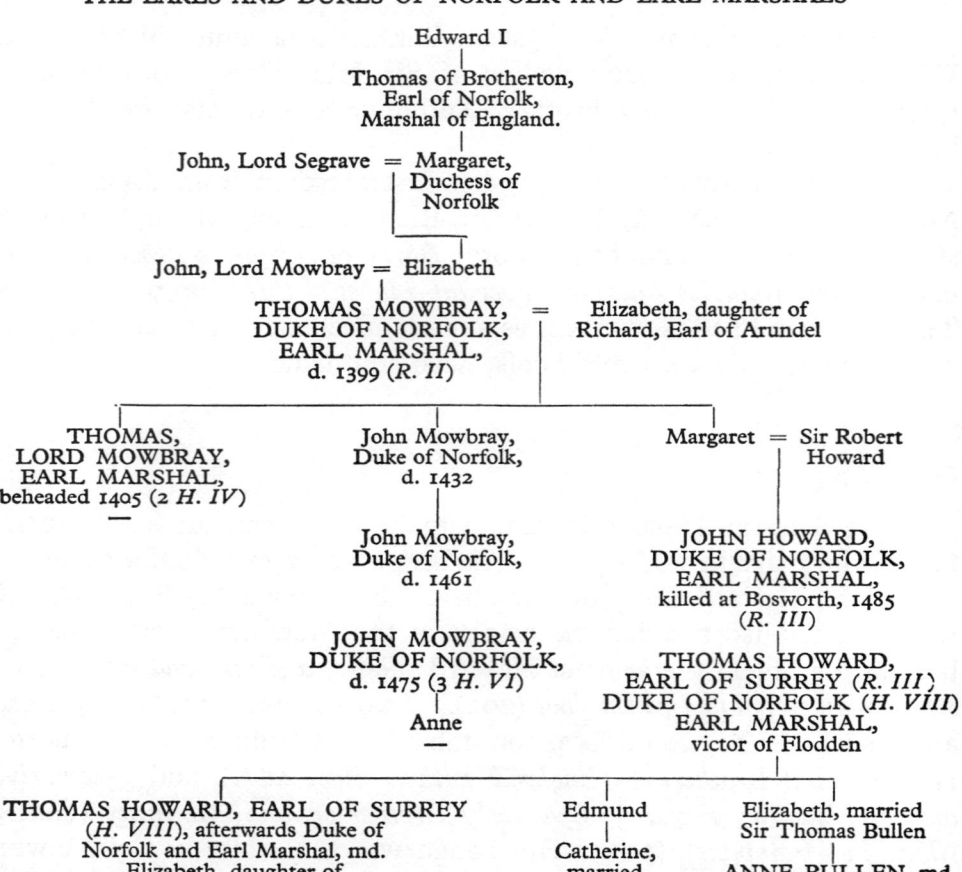

Edward I
|
Thomas of Brotherton,
Earl of Norfolk,
Marshal of England.
|
John, Lord Segrave = Margaret,
Duchess of
Norfolk
|
John, Lord Mowbray = Elizabeth
|
THOMAS MOWBRAY, = Elizabeth, daughter of
DUKE OF NORFOLK,   Richard, Earl of Arundel
EARL MARSHAL,
d. 1399 (*R. II*)

THOMAS,   John Mowbray,   Margaret = Sir Robert
LORD MOWBRAY,   Duke of Norfolk,   Howard
EARL MARSHAL,   d. 1432
beheaded 1405 (2 *H. IV*)

John Mowbray,   JOHN HOWARD,
Duke of Norfolk,   DUKE OF NORFOLK,
d. 1461   EARL MARSHAL,
killed at Bosworth, 1485
(*R. III*)

JOHN MOWBRAY,   THOMAS HOWARD,
DUKE OF NORFOLK,   EARL OF SURREY (*R. III*)
d. 1475 (3 *H. VI*)   DUKE OF NORFOLK (*H. VIII*)
     EARL MARSHAL,
Anne   victor of Flodden

THOMAS HOWARD, EARL OF SURREY   Edmund   Elizabeth, married
(*H. VIII*), afterwards Duke of   Sir Thomas Bullen
Norfolk and Earl Marshal, md.   Catherine,
Elizabeth, daughter of   married   ANNE BULLEN, md.
EDWARD, DUKE OF BUCKINGHAM   HENRY VIII   HENRY VIII
(*H. VIII*)

Thomas, Lord Stanley, K.G., is referred to in the play as Earl of Derby, but was not so created until Henry VII's reign. He bore: *Silver, a bend azure charged with three gold bucks' heads cabossed.* On his banner he quartered this with the arms of Lathom : *Gold, a chief indented azure charged with three gold roundles.* His badge was a gold griffin's claw. His younger brother, Sir William Stanley, bore the Stanley coat with a crescent for difference. At Bosworth, he led the Stanley force of three thousand men who were clad in his livery of red with the badge of a silver buck's head. He is referred to in act iv, sc. 5.

FIG. 201. Banner of
Howard, Duke of Norfolk.

FIG. 202. Howard.

FIG. 203. Banner of
Lord Stanley.

Francis, Lord Lovel, K.G., created Viscount Lovel in 1483, bore: *Barry nebuly of six pieces gold and gules* (204). He held the lordships of Holland, Deincourt, and Grey of Rotherfield, and consequently his full achievement, as shown on his Garter stall-plate, was: *Quarterly, 1, Lovel; 2, Deincourt (Azure, semé of gold billets and a gold fess dancetty); 3, Holland (Azure, semé of silver fleurs-de-lys and a silver lion rampant); 4, Grey of Rotherfield (Barry of six pieces silver and azure, a bend gules); and over all an inescutcheon, Silver, a lion rampant crowned sable holding an acorn between the paws.* His crest was a silver wolf-dog (*lupellus*, allusive to his name), with a gold coronet round its neck, and his badge was a square padlock.

Sir William Catesby bore: *Silver, two lions passant sable, each with a gold crown* (205). His badge was a white cat spotted with black and wearing a gold collar. He was beheaded after Bosworth.

FIG. 204. Lovel.

FIG. 205. Catesby.

FIG. 206. Ratcliff.

Sir Richard Ratcliff, second son of Sir Thomas Ratcliff of Derwent-water, bore: *Silver, a bend engrailed sable, with a crescent for difference* (206). He was slain at Bosworth.

Sir Thomas Vaughan appears to have come illegitimately of the family of Vaughan which bore: *Sable, three silver children's heads couped at the shoulders, each entwined about the neck with a serpent proper.* Apparently on the authority of a shield on Vaughan's tomb in Westminster Abbey, Planché (*Richard III*) attributes to him, *Quarterly, 1 and 4, Gold, a saltire azure; 2 and 3, Gules, a bend engrailed between three gold fleurs-de-lys* (207).

Sir James Tyrell is supposed to have been of the family which bore: *Silver, two chevrons azure within a bordure engrailed gules* (208).

FIG. 207. Vaughan.

FIG. 208. Tyrell.

FIG. 209. Brackenbury.

Sir Walter Herbert, second son of Sir William Herbert, the Earl of Pembroke in *Henry VI*, bore his father's arms with a crescent for difference.

Sir Robert Brackenbury, Lieutenant of the Tower, came of the family which bore: *Silver, three chevrons interlaced sable* (209), to which he added a crescent as a second son. He was slain at Bosworth.

Sir William Brandon, standard bearer to Henry of Richmond at Bosworth, and there slain, bore: *Barry of ten pieces silver and gules, over all a gold lion rampant with a crown per pale silver and gules* (210).

Captain Blunt is probably intended for Sir James Blunt, whom Richmond knighted on his landing at Milford Haven and who is referred to in act iv, sc. 5. He would bear on his shield and tabard the arms

FIG. 210. Brandon.   FIG. 211. Cheney.   FIG. 212. Guildford.

of Blunt : *Barry nebuly of six pieces gold and sable* (90), and in his full achievement he quartered the coats of Ayala, Castile and Beauchamp.

The following were also knighted on the same occasion, and may appear in the battle scene; only the principal coat is given in each case, quarterings being omitted.

Sir Edward Courtenay, afterwards Earl of Devon: *Gold, three red roundles and a label of three points azure* (121). He is mentioned in act iv, sc. 4 as being in arms against the king, together with

the haughty prelate,
Bishop of Exeter, his brother there.

This was Bishop Peter Courtenay. In fact he was akin but not brother to Sir Edward. The badge and crest of the Courtenays was a dolphin, one of the devices of the Byzantine Empire, in commemoration of the fact that three members of the Courtenay family were Emperors at Constantinople in the thirteenth century.

John, Lord Welles: *Gold, a lion rampant with a double tail sable.* His badge was a bucket with chains, allusive to his name.

Sir John Cheney: *Azure, six silver lions rampant, a canton ermine* (211). He encountered King Richard in combat at Bosworth, and though a man of great strength he was felled to the ground.

Sir Richard Guildford: *Gold, a saltire between four martlets, all sable* (212). 'The Guildfords are in arms.' (iv, 4).

Sir Edward Poynings: *Barry of six pieces gold and vert, a bend gules* (213).

FIG. 213. Poynings.   FIG. 214. Owen.   FIG. 215. Fortescue.

Sir Davy Owen: *Gules, a chevron sable between three silver helms garnished with gold, over all a gold bendlet sinister* (214).

Sir John Fortescue: *Azure, on a silver bend engrailed between two gold cotices a molet pierced sable* (215).

Sir John Reisley: *Barry of ten pieces silver and blue, a gold griffin armed gules, a crescent for difference* (216).

Sir Thomas Milborn: *Gules, a silver chevron and three silver scallop shells* (217).

Sir William Tyler: *Vert, a gold bend and six gold Passion nails* (218).

The following were made knights on the field after Bosworth:

Sir Gilbert Talbot (second son of the Earl of Shrewsbury in *Henry VI*): *Azure, a gold lion rampant within a gold bordure,* for Belesme, quartering

FIG. 216. Reisley.

FIG. 217. Milborn.

FIG. 218. Tyler.

2 Talbot, 3 Strange, and 4 Furnival (see the arms of his father). He is referred to in act iv, sc. 5.

Sir John Mortimer : *Mortimer (82) with the inescutcheon ermine.*

Sir Walter Hungerford: *Sable, two silver bars and in chief three silver roundles (118).*

Sir Robert Pointz: *Quarterly silver and blue, the fess line indented (219).*

Sir William Willoughby: *Sable, a gold cross engrailed (220).*

Sir John Turberville: *Silver, a lion rampant gules with a gold crown.*

Sir Rice ap Thomas: *Silver, a chevron between three ravens, all sable* (221). His badge was a raven, and three or four of these birds appeared in his standard. He is referred to in act iv, sc. 5.

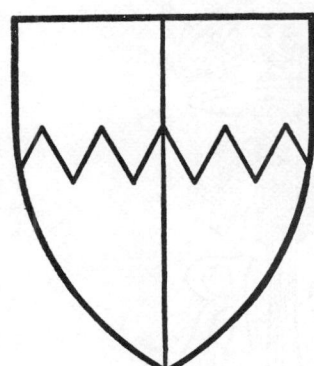
FIG. 219. Pointz.

FIG. 220. Willoughby.

FIG. 221. Ap Thomas.

FIG. 222. Persall.

FIG. 223. Edgecombe.

FIG. 224. Lovell.

Sir Hugh Persall: *Quarterly, 1 and 4, Gold, three bars gules; 2 and 3, Ermine; all within a bordure azure* (222).

Sir Richard Edgecombe: *Gules, on a bend sable between two gold cotices, three silver boars' heads* (223).

Sir Thomas Lovell, stated in act iv, sc. 4, to be in arms, is presumed to be the person of that name who appears in *Henry VIII*. He bore: *Silver, a chevron azure between three squirrels gules, each cracking a nut* (224).

A dramatic incident after Bosworth, omitted by Shakespeare, was the finding of the crown which King Richard had worn on his helm—not the state crown, but probably a circlet of crosses paty and fleurs-de-lys

FIG. 225a. Bray.

FIG. 225b. The crowned hawthorn.

without arches. This was hewn from Richard's helm in the battle, and was found by Sir Reginald Bray in a hawthorn bush, where (it is said) it had been concealed by a soldier. Bray brought the crown to Lord Stanley, who set it on Richmond's head. A crowned hawthorn became a badge of Henry VII (225b). Sir Reginald Bray bore : *Silver, a chevron sable between three eagles' legs erased sable* (225a).

FIG. 226. Archbishop Bourchier.   FIG. 227. Archbishop Rotherham.

Thomas Bourchier, Archbishop of Canterbury and a Cardinal, bore: *Silver, a cross engrailed gules between four water-budgets sable.* He might impale this coat to the sinister with the arms of the See of Canterbury (226).

Thomas Rotherham, Archbishop of York, bore: *Vert, three gold roebucks,* which might be impaled to the sinister with the arms of the See of York, which at this time were the same as those of Canterbury.

John Morton, Bishop of Ely, bore: *Quarterly, gules and ermine, in the first and fourth quarters a silver goat's head erased with gold horns.* These might be impaled to the sinister with the arms of the See: *Gules, three open crowns of gold* (228).

The Mayor of London at the time of Edward V's accession was Edmund Shaa, or Shaw, who bore: *Silver, a chevron between three lozenges sable ermined silver, a bordure gules* (229). Dr. Shaw mentioned in act iii, sc. 5 was his brother.

Tressell and Berkeley, gentlemen attending on the Lady Anne, may wear her scarlet livery with the badge of a silver ragged staff.

FIG. 228. Morton, Bishop of Ely. FIG. 229. Shaa, Mayor of London.

FIG. 230. Arms, crown, supporters and badges of Henry VIII.

CHAPTER IX

KING HENRY VIII

DURING THE thirty-five years from Bosworth to the Field of the Cloth of Gold, described in the first scene of *Henry VIII*, the transformation of heraldry from military uses to the purposes solely of decoration and pageantry was completed. Only Garter King of Arms appears in the play wearing heraldic insignia, which otherwise can be displayed only in the appointments of the various scenes. The royal arms of Henry VIII should be shown behind the King's seat in the council chamber, and his arms and badges may be worked into the decoration of other rooms in the palace. King Henry's arms impaled with those of Queen Katharine may figure in her apartments, while in the closing scenes of the play the royal arms should be impaled with those granted to Queen Anne Bullen. Cardinal Wolsey's achievement should be placed on the 'state' under which his table is set in the hall of York Place. For the trial scene at Blackfriars, the royal arms, and the insignia of Wolsey and Campeius, may be placed

189

behind the seats of the king and the cardinals, as they appear in the famous painting by Mr. Frank Salisbury in the Houses of Parliament.

Royal Heraldry

Henry VIII bore the arms of *France Modern and England quarterly*, as his predecessors had done since Henry IV. In his reign the royal crest underwent a change, the crowned lion being placed on an arched crown (as it remains to-day) instead of on a chapeau encircled by an open crown. Henry's shield was usually surrounded by the Garter, and frequently accompanied by the motto, *Dieu et mon droyt*. It was sometimes supported by a gold lion and a red dragon—English and Welsh emblems (230)—and occasionally the dragon was placed on the dexter side, the sinister supporter being a white greyhound or a white cock.[1] (The greyhound, which was introduced into our royal heraldry by Henry VII, is supposed to be Llewellyn's hound, Gelert; and the cock, *gallus*, may be allusive to Wales, *Galles*.) Henry VIII's badges were the gold portcullis (from the Beauforts), the Tudor rose, the red dragon, the white cock, and a gold fleur-de-lys. He also used a rose cojoined to the pomegranate of Grenada in reference to his marriage with Katharine of Aragon (233).

Queen Katharine bore: *Quarterly, 1 and 4, Castile and Leon quarterly; 2 and 3, Aragon impaling Sicily; and in the point of the shield the badge of Grenada;* i.e., for Castile: *Gules, a gold castle with three towers;* for Leon: *Silver, a lion rampant gules;* for Aragon: *Gold, four pallets gules;* for Sicily: *Per saltire Aragon (as above) and Silver, an eagle displayed sable armed gules;* and for Grenada: *Silver, a pomegranate in proper colours.* These arms were impaled with those of Henry VIII (231). Queen Katharine's badges were a pomegranate, and a sheaf of silver arrows; these badges were sometimes combined.

Anne Bullen, as the daughter of Sir Thomas Bullen, possessed as paternal arms: *Silver, a chevron gules between three bulls' heads couped sable* (234), with certain quarterings ; on her creation as Marchioness of

---

[1] In stage sets for *Henry VIII*, it is perhaps better to use the lion and dragon supporters when displaying the Royal Arms, so as to keep the kingly significance of the lion in mind, to point such a passage as Wolsey's foreboding remark:

> He parted frowning from me, as if ruin
> Leap'd from his eyes. So looks the chafed lion
> Upon the daring huntsman that has gall'd him;
> Then makes him nothing. (*iii*, 2)

Pembroke before her marriage to the king, she was granted arms emphasizing the nobler and suppressing the more plebeian elements in her descent. Sir Thomas's mother was a lady of the great house of Butler, Earls of Ormonde, which was descended indirectly from Edward I by the first earl's marriage with that king's grand-daughter, Eleanor de Bohun. Sir Thomas Bullen's wife was Elizabeth, daughter of Thomas Howard, second Duke of Norfolk of that name, and so a descendant of Thomas of Brotherton, a younger son of Edward I. Wolsey, informed of Henry's

FIG. 231. Arms of Henry VIII and Queen Katharine of Aragon.

FIG. 232. Arms of Henry VIII and Queen Anne Bullen.

intention to make Anne Bullen his queen, exclaimed against the idea of 'the late queen's gentlewoman, a knight's daughter, to be her mistress' mistress—the queen's queen;' but the gentlewoman was doubly if deviously descended from Edward I, and her father, far from being a mere knight, had been raised to the dignity of Viscount Rochford, and Earl of Wiltshire and Ormonde.

Anticipating the criticism, which Shakespeare makes Wolsey voice, Henry thought it advisable to aggrandize Anne Bullen by giving her arms composed of quarterings of the principal houses from which she descended, however distantly, and omitting altogether her paternal coat of Bullen. The arms granted to her were: *Quarterly of six*, 1, *England with a label of France* (for Lancaster); 2, *France Ancient with a label gules* (for Angoulême); 3, *Gules, a gold lion passant guardant* (for Guienne); 4, *Quarterly, Gold, a chief indented azure* (for Butler) *and Silver, a lion rampant sable with a crown gules* (for Rochford); 5, *England with a silver label* (for Brotherton); 6, *Checky gold and azure* (for Warrenne). These were impaled with the royal arms on her marriage (232). By no normal

FIG. 233. Badge of Henry   FIG. 234. Bullen.   FIG. 235. Badge of Queen
          VIII.   Anne Bullen.

method of marshalling arms would Anne Bullen be entitled to include any of these coats in her shield, and it is a sign of the armorial debasement of the period that heraldry should be distorted to support a weak genealogical case.

Anne Bullen's badge was a silver falcon, crowned and bearing a sceptre, sometimes shown standing on a gold tree-stump (235). From this, Queen Elizabeth's falcon badge was derived.

Other Characters

Arms were granted to Cardinal Wolsey in 1516. These were: *Sable, a silver cross engrailed charged with a lion passant gules and four leopards' faces azure; and a gold chief charged with a rose gules and two Cornish choughs in proper colours.* The shield was supported by *two griffins per fess gules and silver with gold wings, beaks and legs.* Wolsey's cardinal's hat was placed above the shield, and behind it, his crosses as legate and archbishop. His motto was *Dominus mihi adiutor.* The emblems in the shield apparently refer to his personal history. His birth at Ipswich is alluded to rather grandiosely by emblems from the arms of the ancient Earls of Suffolk— the engrailed cross of the Uffords, and the leopards' faces of the De la Poles. The lion represents Pope Leo X, from whom Wolsey received

FIG. 236. Cardinal Wolsey.   FIG. 237. Cardinal Campeius.

his cardinalate. The rose stands for his position as a royal minister, and the Cornish choughs, from the arms assigned to St Thomas (Becket) of Canterbury, refer to his Christian name and his patron saint. The arms survive as those of Wolsey's foundation of Christ Church, Oxford. Wolsey might impale his arms with those of the See of York, *Gules, the keys of St Peter in saltire, and in chief a crown with a pointed cap surmounted by a cross, all gold* (236).

Thomas Cromwell appears in the play as servant to Wolsey, and he probably did not obtain arms until later in his career, when he became Earl of Essex and a Knight of the Garter. These consisted of *Azure, a gold fess between three gold lions rampant, and on the fess a rose gules*

and two Cornish choughs sable (238).   This coat was sometimes quartered
with *Party of six gold and gules, three fleurs-de-lys azure and three gold
pelicans.*   The fess in the first coat was clearly derived from the chief
of Wolsey's shield.

Cardinal Campeius (Lorenzo Campeggio) bore: *Silver, an eagle displayed sable, beaked and legged gules,* dimidiating, *Silver, a wolf rampant
sable,* i.e. the coats were each divided vertically, the dexter half of the
former being joined to the sinister half of the latter. As Bishop of Salisbury, 1524-35, he might impale his personal arms with those of the See,
Azure, the Madonna and Child gold (237).   Above his shield he placed a
cardinal's hat.

FIG. 238. Thomas Cromwell.   FIG. 239. Capucius.

In the painting by Mr. Frank Salisbury already referred to, the arms of
Pope Clement VII appear on the wall behind the seats occupied by the
two cardinals.   These consisted of, *Azure, six gold roundles* (the arms of
Medici), the shield being ensigned with the papal tiara and having the
crossed keys of St Peter behind it.

Capucius (Eustachius Chapuys), the Ambassador from the Emperor
Charles V, bore: *Gold, a boar's head proper, a chief gules* (239).

Thomas Cranmer, Archbishop of Canterbury, is believed to have sprung
from a family which bore for arms a chevron between three cranes,
allusive to the name. In his case the cranes were changed to pelicans,
no doubt with religious intent, the pelican feeding its young with blood
from its own breast being the symbol of Corpus Christi.   Cranmer's arms

were: *Silver, a chevron azure between three pelicans sable, with three gold pierced cinquefoils on the chevron.* He might impale these arms to the sinister with those of the See of Canterbury, placing his mitre above the shield (240).

Stephen Gardiner, Bishop of Winchester, appears to have been a member of the Suffolk family which bore: *Party of six, gold and sable, three griffins' heads erased sable.* These might be impaled with the arms of the See of Winchester, a mitre being placed above the shield (241).

FIG. 240. Archbishop
Cranmer.

FIG. 241. Gardiner,
Bishop of Winchester.

FIG. 242. Longland,
Bishop of Lincoln.

John Longland, Bishop of Lincoln, bore: *Silver, a chevron gules between three roundles sable and on the chevron a silver cock; on a chief vert, a gold rose and two silver leopards' faces.* The arms of the See of Lincoln, with which these might be impaled, are : *Gules, two gold lions passant guardant, on a chief azure the Madonna and Child enthroned gold* (242).

The Duke of Norfolk in *Henry VIII* is the Thomas Howard who appears in *Richard III* as Earl of Surrey. After the death at Bosworth of his father, the first Howard Duke, he continued as Earl of Surrey until 1514, when he was restored as second Duke of Norfolk as a reward for his victory over the Scots at Flodden. In commemoration of this victory he was granted an honourable augmentation to the arms of Howard (*Gules, a silver bend between six silver cross-crosslets pointed at the foot*), consisting of an escutcheon, *Gold, a demi-lion rampant pierced through the throat by an arrow, within a double tressure flory counter-flory, all gules* (243), this being placed on the bend in the Howard arms. It will be seen that the augmentation consisted of the royal arms of Scotland with the lion mutilated. Norfolk bore this augmented coat of Howard quarterly

FIG. 243. Howard with the augmentation for Flodden.

FIG. 244. Howard, Duke of Norfolk.

with Brotherton, Warrenne and Mowbray (244). His motto was *Tous jours loyal*. He was made Earl Marshal in 1510 and was also a Knight of the Garter.

Thomas Howard, Earl of Surrey, K.G., eldest son of the second Howard Duke of Norfolk, bore the same arms, with the augmentation and quarterings, differenced by a label. He married, as his second wife, the daughter of the Duke of Buckingham, to whom he accordingly refers in the play as his father-in-law. He succeeded as third Duke of Norfolk on the death of his father in 1524, and it was therefore he who was Earl Marshal at the time of Anne Bullen's coronation in 1533. However, for the purposes of the play, which condenses the events of thirteen years into a stage time of a few months, the second Duke must be presumed to have lived until the christening of Elizabeth in 1533.

Edward Stafford, Duke of Buckingham, K.G., Lord High Constable, was the son of the Duke in *Richard III*. He bore (as his father and great-grandfather had done): *France and England quarterly within a silver bordure,* derived from Thomas of Woodstock. Woodstock's wife was Eleanor, heiress of the Bohun Earls of Hereford and Northampton, and Buckingham held these earldoms, with that of Stafford, as well as his dukedom. Accordingly in his full achievement of arms he bore: *Quarterly, 1, Woodstock* (as above); 2, *Azure, a silver bend with gold cotices between six gold lions rampant,* for Bohun, Earl of Hereford; 3, *as 2, with three molets of six points sable on the bend,* for Bohun, Earl of Northampton; 4, *Gold, a chevron gules,* for Stafford (245). Shakespeare, following Hall, refers to Stafford's

FIG. 245. Stafford,
Duke of Buckingham.

FIG. 246. Brandon,
Duke of Suffolk.

Bohun descent by making him speak of himself as 'poor Edward Bohun' (ii, 1). Buckingham's badges were the Stafford knot, an heraldic antelope sejant with a coronet round its neck, and a white swan with its neck encircled by a coronet, the last two being derived from the Bohuns.

Charles Brandon, Duke of Suffolk, K.G., was the son of Sir William Brandon, Richmond's standard-bearer at Bosworth, whose arms have been given in *Richard III.* Suffolk bore his father's arms quarterly with 2, *Azure, a gold cross moline, and 3, Lozengy ermine and gules* (246). These quarters were derived from his mother, the daughter of Sir Henry Bruyn.

The Lord Chamberlain at the time the play opens was Sir Charles Somerset, K.G., base son of Henry Beaufort, Duke of Somerset, who was the son of the Somerset of 2 *Henry VI* (see Beaufort, Table V). Sir Charles became Lord Herbert of Gower by marriage with the heiress of William Herbert, Earl of Huntingdon (son of the Earl of Pembroke in 3 *Henry VI*), and was made Earl of Worcester in 1513. He bore: *Beaufort with a silver baton sinister, and on an inescutcheon the arms of Herbert* (247).

George Nevill, Lord Abergavenny, was descended from Sir Edward Nevill, a younger son of the first Earl of Westmoreland (see *Henry IV* and *Henry V*). Sir Edward differenced the Nevill arms: *Gules, a silver saltire,* with *a rose gules on the saltire.* From his wife, the only child of Richard Beauchamp, Lord Abergavenny and Earl of Worcester, Sir Edward derived and transmitted to his descendants certain quarterings, and the Lord Abergavenny of *Henry VIII* accordingly bore: *Quarterly, 1, Nevill, differenced as above; 2, Warrenne; 3, Clare and Despencer quarterly; 4, Beauchamp with a crescent sable for difference* (248). His badge consisted

Fig. 247. Somerset,
Earl of Worcester.

Fig. 248. Nevill,
Lord Abergavenny.

of two interlacing staples, one gold and the other silver, and this occurs several times on his standard, with the motto, *Tenir promesse vient de noblesse.*

The Lord Chancellor, as stated in act iii, sc. 2, is Sir Thomas More, whose arms were: *Silver, a chevron engrailed sable between three moorcocks sable crested gules* (249). No doubt it was More that Shakespeare intended to appear, as Lord Chancellor, in the procession at the coronation of Anne Bullen (iv, 1), but actually at this date Sir Thomas Audley had succeeded More in the office. Audley's arms were: *Quarterly, gold and azure, the palewise line indented, on a bend azure between two gold eagles displayed, a gold fret between two gold martlets* (250).

Sir William Sands (or Sandys), K.G., created Lord Sandys by Henry VIII, bore: *Silver, a cross raguly sable* (251).

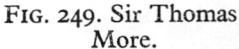

FIG. 249. Sir Thomas
More.

FIG. 250. Sir Thomas
Audley.

FIG. 251. Sir William
Sands.

Sir Henry Guildford, K.G., Master of the Horse and Standard-bearer to
Henry VIII, was a younger son of the Sir Richard Guildford mentioned
under *Richard III* as at Bosworth, and bore the same arms with a gold
molet for difference, quartering, *Silver, a chief sable, over all a bend engrailed gules.* Later he received from King Ferdinand of Spain an augmentation for his services in Grenada. This consisted of an addition to
the Guildford coat of *a silver canton charged with a pomegranate gules with
gold seeds* (252), and on including this in his arms he dropped the differencing molets as being no longer necessary.

Sir Thomas Lovell has been mentioned under *Richard III.*

FIG. 252. Sir Henry
Guildford.

FIG. 253. Sir Anthony
Denny.

FIG. 254. Sir Nicholas
Vaux.

Sir Anthony Denny, Chief Gentleman of the Privy Chamber to Henry VIII, bore: *Quarterly, 1 and 4, Gules, semé of gold crosses formy and a silver saltire,* for Denny; *2, Gold, a fess dancetty gules, in chief three martlets sable,* for More; *3, Azure, three silver trouts fretted in triangle, with a gold molet for difference,* for Troutbeck (253).

Sir Nicholas Vaux, who was created Lord Vaux of Harrowden in 1523, bore: *Checky gold and gules, on a chevron azure three gold roses* (254). He was the the son of the zealous Lancastrian, Sir William Vaux, who is probably the 'Vaux' of 2 *Henry VI*.

FIG. 255. Sir William Buttes.

FIG. 256. Sir Thomas Wriothesley.

FIG. 257. Knevet, Surveyor to the Duke of Buckingham.

Dr Butts, Physician to the King, was Sir William Buttes, who bore: *Azure, a gold chevron between three gold estoiles, and three lozenges gules on the chevron* (255). In Metcalfe's Book of Knights, his crest is given as 'two hands gules, the dexter above the sinister, both grasping a (?) caduceus or.' Possibly what is here doubtfully described as a caduceus was the serpent-twined rod of Æsculapius, emblem of healing, and an early instance of a physician bearing this emblem.

Garter King of Arms at the date of the coronation of Queen Anne Bullen was Sir Thomas Wriothesley. Shakespeare indicates that he is to appear in a tabard of the royal arms, with a gilt copper crown on his head. The crown of a King of Arms is of oakleaves, the rim inscribed, *Miserere mei Deus secundum magnam misericordiam tuam* (262). Wriothesley's personal arms were : *Azure, a gold cross between four silver falcons* (256). These appear to have formed the basis of the arms of the Heralds' College : *Silver, a cross gules between four doves azure, the dexter wings spread and the tips downwards.* Wriothesley's full arms were : *Quarterly, 1 and 4, Wriothesley (as above)* ; *2, Silver, fretty gules within a bordure engrailed sable, on a canton gules a gold lion passant,* for Dunstanville ; *3, Silver, a pale of lozenges gules within a bordure azure charged with golden roundles ;* for Lewsell or Lusteshille. Of the same family was Henry Wriothesely, Earl of Southampton, to whom Shakespeare dedicated *Venus and Adonis* and *Lucrece.*

The Surveyor to the Duke of Buckingham was Charles Knevet, who was akin to the Duke, his mother having been a daughter of the former Duke (see Table VIII). Knevet's arms were: *Silver, a bend sable and a bordure engrailed sable, with a crescent for difference (257).*

FIG. 258.　　　FIG. 259.　　　FIG. 260.
Duke's Coronet.　Marquess's Coronet.　Earl's Coronet.

Insignia of Rank and Office

In the scene at the coronation of Queen Anne Bullen (iv, 1) the Dukes of Suffolk and Norfolk, the Marquess of Dorset and the Earl of Surrey appear wearing their coronets. (We are only concerned with the coronets appropriate to these three ranks in the peerage, because viscounts only became entitled to coronets in the reign of James I, and barons at the coronation of Charles II.)

Coronets were restricted to dukes and marquesses until 1444, when they were conferred upon earls. In the fifteenth century they varied in design and there was no standard type denoting a particular rank. By Shakespeare's time, definite types of coronet had appeared. These are shown in nos. 258-260, based on the illustrations in Ralph Brooke's *Catalogue and Succession of the Kings, Princes, Dukes, Marquesses, Earles* etc. (1619).

From Brooke's drawings, it appears that at this date the coronet of a duke consisted of a circlet heightened with four strawberry-leaves alternating with four trefoils (differing from the present coronet of this rank, which has eight strawberry-leaves without intervening trefoils). The circlet itself was chased as though jewelled, but was probably not actually set with gems.

The marquess's coronet also had a chased circlet set with four straw-berry-leaves, these alternating with points topped with balls. This is similar to the present coronet of a marquess, except that the balls are not now so elevated.

The earl's coronet consisted of a studded circlet heightened with eight lofty rays alternating with eight small trefoils, a large ball being set on the top of each ray. In the present-day coronet of an earl, the circlet is chased to represent jewels (but not set with gems), and small strawberry-leaves take the place of the trefoils between the rays.

Brooke's illustrations do not show any caps to the coronets. It is, how-ever, possible that they were worn over a crimson cap turned up with ermine, as is now the practice.

In Shakespeare's stage directions we read: 'The old Duchess of Norfolk, in a coronal of gold, wrought with flowers . . . Certain Ladies or Count-esses, with plain circlets of gold without flowers.' Here he is so definite that we may take it as an indication of the difference in the types of coronets worn by ladies in his time.

The 'rod of marshalship' borne by the Duke of Norfolk was a gold truncheon tipped with black at each end.

The purse borne before the Lord Chancellor was embroidered with the Royal Arms, with Garter, Crown and supporters (261).

The collar of Esses at this period is shown in Holbein's portrait of Sir Thomas More, from which No. 262 is drawn. It will be noted that the collar terminated in portcullises from which hung a Tudor rose.

FIG. 262. Crown of King of Arms.

FIG. 261. Lord Chancellor's Purse.

FIG. 263. Collar of Esses.

HERALDIC INDEX AND GLOSSARY

(As a rule, only heraldic figures and terms occurring in this book are here included. Consequently this is far from being a complete guide to the terms of heraldry. Numbers in brackets relate to figures; others to pages.)

ABATEMENT: a mark of dishonour. Though referred to by the heraldic writers of Shakespeare's time, it seems never to have existed in practical heraldry, except in the sense of a difference for bastardy, in which case a lowering of the status of the arms, but not dishonour, was implied.

ACHIEVEMENT, or ACHIEVEMENT OF ARMS: a complete heraldic display, including the shield of arms (containing any quarterings accruing to the principal coat), helm with crest and mantling, and (if any) motto, supporters, coronet of rank, and badges.

ANGELS: supporting the arms of Richard II, 19, 64.

ANNULET: a plain ring.

ANTELOPE: in this book the heraldic antelope is understood (the natural animal not being found in ancient heraldry). It was a deer-like creature with tufts, serrated horns, a down-curving horn on the tip of the nose, and the tail of an heraldic lion.

APE-CLOG: a weight with a chain, intended to hamper the activity of a monkey to prevent it escaping; a badge of De la Pole, Duke of Suffolk.

ARGENT: silver or white (here termed silver throughout).

ARMED: when applied to a beast or bird of prey, refers to horns, beak, claws, talons, and other means of offence.

ARMIGER: strictly, an esquire, the rank above that of gentleman; also applied to anyone lawfully possessed of heraldic arms, such a person being termed armigerous.

ARMORIAL BEARINGS: heraldic devices borne on arms, especially on the shield, surcoat and helm; in its widest sense, synonymous with Achievement of Arms (q.v.).

ARMORY: that branch of the herald's lore that deals with armorial bearings.

ARMOUR: styles of, 43, 123, 171, (3), (17), (65), (66), (101).

ARMS (heraldic): strictly, the heraldic devices displayed on shields, surcoats, and banners; but often used to include the other insignia in an achievement.

— right to bear, 22, 121.

ARROWS, sheaf of, badge of Katharine of Aragon, 190.

AUGMENTATIONS: honourable additions to armorial bearings granted by the Sovereign to commemorate some signal service, e.g. the Howard augmentation for Flodden, 196.

AZURE: heraldic blue.

BADGE: an heraldic device associated with but independent of arms and crest, used for personal adornment and as a mark on property, and particularly to denote the retainers and servants of a nobleman's household; also worn by partisans of a cause or faction, e.g. the roses of York and Lancaster, 14 ff.

BANNER: an oblong or square flag bearing a man's arms, i.e. the same as he displayed on shield or surcoat, with or without the addition of any quarterings, but not external ornaments such as crest and supporters. Badges and national and religious emblems were sometimes displayed on banners. (See Flags.)

BARBEL (fish): as a charge, 117.

BARDED, BARDINGS: see Horse-bardings.

BARRY: a field divided by an odd number of horizontal lines into an even number of pieces, usually six or eight. In the case of ten or more the term BARRULY may be used (4).

BARS: horizontal bands extending across the shield, usually in pairs or threes, the field of the shield being seen above, between and below them; thus, two bars have the effect of dividing the shield into five pieces. Bars must be distinguished from a barry field, where the number of pieces is even, (4).

BASCINET: a type of helm originally consisting of a conical cap without face-guard, over which the great helm was placed; and later provided with a beaver, the great helm being dispensed with except for jousting.

BASE: the bottom part of the shield.

BASTON: a narrow diagonal band across the shield from dexter chief to sinister base (a baston on the other diagonal being a baston sinister); usually found as a differencing mark.

BATON: a rod of office; the Earl Marshal's baton is gold tipped with black; see also Warder.

BAYEUX TAPESTRY: shields and flags on, 3.

BEAR AND RAGGED STAFF: badge of the Earl of Warwick, 14, 21, 145 ff.

BEARINGS: as a man bore a shield, so he was said to bear the arms thereon, and these were known as his bearings; see Armorial Bearings.

BEAVER: the moveable face-guard of a helm; also applied to the helm itself.

BEND: a diagonal band across the shield from dexter chief to sinister base (4); a band on the reverse diagonal is a BEND SINISTER.

BENDLET: a narrow bend.

BENDWISE: indicates the position of an object placed diagonally on the shield.

BENDY: a field divided by diagonal lines into an even number of pieces. (Diagonal lines forming an odd number of pieces constitute a number of bends; cf. Bars and Barry.)

BILLET: a small oblong figure set on end, usually found in groups. A field strewn with billets is termed BILLETY.

BISHOP: may impale the arms of his See with his personal coat, and place his mitre above the shield.

BLANCH SANGLIER PURSUIVANT: officer of Richard III, 175.

BLAZON: a verbal description of insignia in heraldic terms. To blazon is to describe arms; to emblazon is to paint them in colours. But poetically, 'blazon' and 'blazonry' are sometimes used as synonymous with heraldry.

BOAR, WHITE: badge of Richard III, 172, 174 ff.

BORDURE: a border to a shield or banner, (4).

BRIZURE: a differencing mark in arms.

BROOM CODS, BROOM PLANT: see *planta genista*.

BULL, BLACK: badge of the honour of Clarence, 129, 130.

BURGONET: a form of helm used in the sixteenth century.

CABOSHED, or CABOSSED: of a bull's or deer's head when set full-faced and cut off so as to show no part of the neck.

CADENCY: the position of junior members or branches of a family in relation to the head, denoted in their arms by differences, or marks of cadency.

CANTING HERALDRY: insignia which form a play on the name, title or office of the bearer.

CANTON: a rectangular division in the dexter chief corner of the shield occupying less than one quarter and at least one ninth of its area, (4).

CARDINAL'S HAT: placed above a shield, 193, 194, (236), (237).

CHAPEAU: a cap, usually crimson turned up with ermine, sometimes forming the basis of a crest (as in fig. 52).

CHAPLET: a garland of flowers and leaves.

CHARGE: any object in an heraldic composition; the shield is said to be charged with the objects upon it, and any charge on which another is laid is itself charged.

CHECKY: divided by vertical and horizontal lines into chequers, forming at least three rows, the alternate squares being differently tinctured, (4). (See also Compony.)

CHEVRON: has its point upwards unless blazoned as reversed, (4).

CHIEF: a horizontal band laid along the top part of the shield, usually a fifth to a third of the shield's depth (4). In chief: the position of a charge in the upper part of the shield.

CINQUEFOIL: a conventional floral form of five petals, (30).

CLARENCEUX KING OF ARMS: has heraldic jurisdiction in the southern parts of England.

COAT OF ARMS: literally, a surcoat or tunic worn over armour and emblazoned with the wearer's heraldic arms; hence it came to be applied to the arms themselves, whether displayed on surcoat or shield. It is sometimes shortened to 'coat.' Shakespeare uses 'coat' for an heraldic shield: 'this coat of worth . . . sometime target to a king; I know it by this mark.' (*Pericles*, ii, 1). In *A Lover's Complaint* we find 'spirits of richest coat,' meaning persons of the highest nobility. Hence coat-armour, a synonym for heraldic arms.

COCK: badge and supporter of Henry VIII, 190.

COJOINED: joined together.

COLLARS: of Lancaster, York, and SS (or Esses), 88, 124, (142), (143, (144), (263).

COLOURS OF HERALDRY: see azure, gules, purpure, sable, and vert; rule against placing colour on colour, 7.

— , LIVERY: colours associated with a royal or noble house, worn (often in conjunction with badges) by servants, retainers, and adherents. The colours of Plantagenet were red and white; of Lancaster, blue and white; of York, murrey and blue; and of Tudor, green and white. Colours were used prominently, and often provocatively, in time of faction; e.g. in 1 *Henry VI*, i, 3, where Gloucester's men set on Winchester's at the cry, "Blue coats to tawny coats."

COLOURS: in Shakespeare's time, the word also had the meaning of military flags, and is often so used in the plays.

COMPONY: a single row of chequers, e.g. the bordure to the shield of Beaufort, (5); where there are two rows, the term COUNTER-COMPONY is used, and three or more rows constitute checky (q.v.).

CORNISH CHOUGH: a black bird of the raven type, often shown with red beak and legs.

CORONETS OF RANK: (as worn in *Henry VIII*), 201, 202.

CORONET, CREST: a decorated circlet, of gold or some other tincture, forming part of some crests. It did not indicate rank.

COTISED: a bend is said to be cotised when it is placed between two narrow bendlets (which may be of a different tincture from the bend), e.g. the arms of Edgecombe (223).

COUNTERCHANGED: an object on a field divided into two tinctures is said to be counterchanged when the part that lies on one tincture is of the other. Thus, the arms of Geoffrey Chaucer consist of a shield divided vertically into silver and gules, and thereon a bend counterchanged, i.e. it is gules on the silver half of the shield, and silver on the gules.

COUPED: cut off (as of the head of an animal), or cut short (as a plain cross whose limbs do not reach the edges of the shield).

CRESCENT: represented with the horns upwards unless otherwise blazoned.

CRESSET: a fire-basket in flames.

CREST: an heraldic ornament worn on the helm; Shakespeare also uses the word in the sense of the skull-piece of the helm itself.

— Royal, 44, 57, 62, 88, 106, 124, 176, 190, (41).

CROSS IN HERALDRY: 6, (4).

— FORMS OF: moline, (59); paty, (35); raguly, (251).

— OF ST GEORGE: a plain red cross on white, (24).

CROSS-CROSSLET: a cross having the limbs crossed; in mediaeval heraldry, often used to powder a field for the purpose of differencing. A field thus semé of cross-crosslets may be described as 'crusily.'

CROWN: 44, 91, 109, 135, 187.

— of John, (12).

— of Richard II, (47).

— of Henry IV, (80). ⟨handwritten note⟩

— of Henry V, (107).

— of Henry VI, (141).

— of Edward IV, (147).

— of Richard III, (196).

— of Henry VIII, (230).

— St Edward's, used at coronations, 91.

— worn on the helm, 44, 106, 187.

DAISY, or MARGEURITE: badge of Margaret of Anjou, 165.

DANCETTY: boldly indented, forming a 'zig-zag' of (say) three points, (4).

DASH (from tache): an abatement (q.v.).

DEXTER: the right-hand side of the shield from the point of view of the man bearing it, and consequently the left to the observer.

DIFFERENCE: a change in or addition to a coat-of-arms or crest made to produce a distinctive design while preserving the main features. A cadet differenced the arms of the head of the family to which he belonged, and some feudal dependants bore a differenced version of the arms of their overlord. DIFFERENCING: effecting a change in the arms for this purpose.

H

PELICAN: in heraldry, usually represented as vulning, or wounding its breast with its bill, to draw blood for the sustenance of its young; hence it is a symbol of Corpus Christi.

In *Hamlet*, Laertes says:

'To his good friends thus wide I'll ope my arms;
And, like the kind life-rendering pelican,
Repast them with my blood.'

PENNON: a small flag, pointed or swallow-tailed, borne on the lance-head and charged with arms or badge. The line in *Henry V*:

'With pennons painted in the blood of Harfleur,'

vividly suggests chivalry whose lances have done grim execution. Long pennons, or pennants, of heraldic colours and bearing badges, were used on ships' masts, and to these Shakespeare refers in his description of Henry V's

'. . . brave fleet,
With silken streamers the young Phoebus fanning.'

PER BEND, PER FESS, PER PALE, etc. (the prefix 'party' being understood): imply a field divided by a bendwise (diagonal), fesswise (horizontal), or palewise (vertical) line, (4).

PIERCED: having a round hole, through which the field is seen.

PILE: a wedge-shaped figure tapering from the chief towards the base of the shield, (4).

PLANTA GENISTA: badge of Plantagenet, 45, 59, 65, (12), (43).

PLUMES: on helms, 90, 106.

POMEGRANATE: badge of Grenada, 190, 199.

POMEI: the ball at the end of the grip of a sword.

PORTCULLIS: badge of Beaufort and Tudor, (152).

POTENT, CROSS: having each arm terminating in a cross-piece, like a crutch-head; an example occurs in the arms of Jerusalem, (183).

'PRINCE OF WALES'S FEATHERS,' see ostrich feathers.

PROPER: in natural or normal colours.

PURPURE: purple.

PURSUIVANT: a junior officer of arms. Like the heralds, pursuivants wore tabards of their master's arms, but in the fifteenth century there was a custom (apparently short-lived) that pursuivants wore the short sleeve-pieces to the front and back, and the long halves of the garment at the sides.

QUARTER: each section of a shield which is divided into four by a vertical and a horizontal line. The dexter chief quarter ranks as the first, the sinister chief as the second, the dexter base as the third, and the sinister base as the fourth. Union of families or lordships (e.g. resulting from the marriage of an heiress) was indicated by quartering the shield, and placing the coats to be combined each in a different quarter. To quarter arms thus means to embody the arms of another family in one's shield by the process of quartering. (See Slender's remark to Shallow: 'I may quarter, coz.'— *Merry Wives of Windsor*.)

QUARTERINGS: each separate coat in a quartered shield is termed a quartering.
— multiplication of, 16.

INDEX OF PERSONS AND PLACES

*The names of characters in Shakespeare's plays are printed in capital letters.
The names of persons mentioned in the plays, and others who may appear
on the stage, are printed in italic.*

BOOKS REFERRED TO IN THE TEXT

It is impracticable to list the many works on Shakespeare and heraldry consulted in compiling this book, but the following are referred to in the text:

Beltz, G. F., *Memorials of the Most Noble Order of the Garter*, 1841.

Boutell, Charles, *Heraldry, Historical and Popular*, (first published as *A Manual of Heraldry*)

Brooke, Raphe, York Herald, *A Catalogue and Succession of the Kings, Princes, Dukes, Marquesses, Earles, and Viscounts of this Realme of England*, 1619.

Chambers, Sir E. K., *William Shakespeare*, 1930.

Crompton, Richard, *Mansion of Magnanimitie*, 1599.

Ferne, Sir John, *The Glorie of Generositie*, 1586.

French, G. R., *Shakespeareana Genealogica*, 1869.

Froissart's *Chronicles*.

Hall's *Chronicle*.

Harrison, G. B., *Introducing Shakespeare*, 1939.

Harrison, William, *Description of England*, 1577.

Holinshed's *Chronicles*.

Hotson, Leslie, *Shakespeare versus Shallow*, 1931.

Lee, Sir Sidney, *Life of William Shakespeare*, 1898.

Leigh, Gerard, *Accedence of Armorie*, 1591.

Palliser, Mrs. Bury, *Historic Devices*, 1870.

Speed, John, *History of Great Britaine*, 1611.

Spurgeon, Caroline, *Shakespeare's Imagery*.

Tucker, Stephen, Somerset Herald, article in *Miscellanea Heraldica et Genealogica*, 1886

Wilson, J. Dover, *Works of Shakespeare* (Cambridge) and *The Fortunes of Falstaff*.